Staging Masculinities

Other books by the author:

Christopher Marlowe's Doctor Faustus: *A Critical Study* (1987)
'Threads' and Other Plays (1990) (editor)
A Preface to Shakespeare's Tragedies (1991)
A Preface to Shakespeare's Comedies (1996)
Writers and Their Work: Edward Bond (1998)

Staging Masculinities

History, Gender, Performance

Michael Mangan

palgrave
macmillan

First published 2003 by
PALGRAVE MACMILLAN
Houndmills, Basingstoke, Hampshire RG21 6XS and
175 Fifth Avenue, New York, N.Y. 10010
Companies and representatives throughout the world

PALGRAVE MACMILLAN is the global academic imprint of the Palgrave Macmillan division of St. Martins Press, LLC and of Palgrave Macmillan Ltd. Macmillan® is a registered trademark in the United States, United Kingdom and other countries. Palgrave is a registered trademark in the European Union and other countries.

ISBN 0–333–72018–0 hardback
ISBN 0–333–72019–9 paperback

This book is printed on paper suitable for recycling and made from fully managed and sustained forest sources.

A catalogue record for this book is available from the British Library.

A catalogue record for this book is available from the Library of Congress.

10 9 8 7 6 5 4 3 2 1
12 11 10 09 08 07 06 05 04 03

Printed in China

To my fathers

Contents

Preface

This project started in the Department of English and Drama at Loughborough University, where it grew out of an MA in Theatre and Gender with Elaine Aston, Ian Clarke and Mick Wallis. It was completed in the Department of Theatre, Film and Television Studies at the University of Wales, Aberystwyth. On the way a large number of people have had input of one kind or another into the project, in the way of discussions, criticism, suggestions, help in tracking down resources, technical aid, collaboration on productions and other kinds of support and encouragement, both professional and personal.

An early version of part of Chapter 3 has appeared in *On Page and Stage*, a collection of essays edited by Krystyna Kujawinska-Courtney (Krakow: Universitas, 2000); some of the material in Chapter 7 appears in *The Professions in Contemporary Drama*, edited by Daniel Meyer-Dinkgräfe (Bristol: Intellect Books, 2002). I am grateful to both these editors for their encouragement and their comments. Substantial sections of Chapters 5 and 6 have been delivered as research papers at seminars and conferences in Aberystwyth, Oxford and Cambridge, where a number of people, but in particular Mike Pearson, Richard Gough, Hazel Walford Davies, Martin Barker, Stephen Gregg and Robert Hume, have provided helpful and stimulating feedback, criticism and conversation.

Thanks are due, too, to Roland Clare and his sixth-form students, for the debate with which the book begins; to Neil Fraistat for asking whether I was including *Peter Pan* – and if not, why not?; to Dennis Flannery for an early conversation about teaching literary masculinities; to David Ian Rabey for reading and commenting on part of the manuscript at a much later stage; to Mick Tattersall and Datasoc for recent sociological data; to Ayshe Kurkcuoglu for the extended loan of *Men's Lives*; to Viv Gardner for obtaining a copy of *Breaking a Butterfly*; to Nigel Sykes and Nick Strong for helping me recover from a potentially disastrous computer crash; to staff at the National Library of Wales, the Hugh Owen Library and the Pilkington Library for help and advice; to colleagues in Loughborough and Aberystwyth, who provided such a stimulating working environment; and to all my students at Loughborough and Aberystwyth, in particular Louis Brownhill and the casts of productions of *Shakespeare's Joan* (2000) and *The London Merchant* (2001).

A note on references: In plays such as those of the sixteenth, seventeenth and eighteenth centuries, where act, scene and line numbers are the normal referencing convention, I have given them. In more modern plays, and also those of the medieval period where editions and translations differ so markedly, I have given references to the page numbers of the particular editions and/or translations used.

Acknowledgements

The author and publisher wish to thank the following for permission to use the copyright material:

Methuen Publishing Ltd, for the extracts from *Oleanna* by David Mamet. Reproduced by permission of Methuen Publishing Ltd.

Every effort has been made to trace the copyright holders but if any have been inadvertently overlooked the publisher will be pleased to make the necessary arrangement at the first opportunity.

1

Staging Masculinities: Introduction and Orientation

1.1 Dionysos in the classroom

> Masculine subjectivity constructed and sustained by patriarchal culture – infused with patriarchal assumptions about power, privilege, sexual desire, the body – inevitably engenders varying degrees of anxiety in its male members.
>
> Mark Breitenberg, *Anxious Masculinity in Early Modern England*, 1996

> Let not me play a woman. I have a beard coming.
>
> Francis Flute, the bellows-mender, *A Midsummer Night's Dream*, I.ii.44

A few years ago, in the early phases of writing this book, I gave a lecture at a secondary school about some of the issues which it raises. It was a good school – somewhat traditional in its values, grant-aided in its economy, still offering Latin A-level and sending a fair number of students to Oxbridge. In many respects it was very much like the grammar school where I was educated in the 1960s and early 1970s. The audience, though, was different. Comprised mainly of sixth-formers doing an English Literature A-level, it was, unlike my single-sex boys' grammar, two-thirds female, one-third male. At the end there was a question-and-answer session, so, once they had asked some questions of me, I asked them some in return. I was interested in hearing about these students' gender expectations of theatre and drama. In terms of their own institution, the school itself, what kind of activities, I asked the audience, did they see as particularly 'masculine'? Is the curriculum itself gendered? Are there 'boys' subjects and girls' subjects'? And what about extracurricular activities – what gendered meanings do they have within the institution? It was fairly familiar ground to

1

them, and a predictable discussion took place about science-based subjects, computers, sports, music and so on. 'And what about drama?' I asked. Is acting in plays something which is seen more as a girls' thing than as a boys'? They were united and vehement that this was not the case. Singing in the school choir maybe: you could hardly find any boys who were willing to do that. But no, drama – whether curricular or extracurricular – was an equal-access zone. Male and female students alike affirmed that involvement in theatre offered no threat, no problematization to their gender identity.

I found myself both cheered and surprised by their response. Again, the comparison with my own schooldays offered itself. What they said was true for them was certainly not true for me. There was, within that male institution, a clear if unarticulated hierarchy of the degrees of masculinity which were assigned to various activities. It was certainly – in the covert value structure which informed the ideology of the school – more masculine to do chemistry than to do Greek. It was more masculine to play sports than to be in the chess club. And this category of 'sports' was itself subject to a gender hierarchy: rugby was definitely more masculine than badminton, cricket was probably more masculine than tennis – except for one summer when a former pupil of the school shone briefly at Wimbledon, during which period school pride, masculine gender identity and nationalist chauvinism coalesced into a mutually reinforcing matrix projected onto the figure of the male sports star.

This institutional stereotype which the school presented is probably a familiar one: I think I assumed it was universal until I was brought up with a shock by my audience of sixth-formers who told me that drama had no specifically gendered meanings for them. Drama in my school felt rather different from that. Certainly it belonged in the territory of the chess-club rather than the rugby team. Yet the school, like many robust institutions, was not crude in the way its ideologies – including its ideologies of sex and gender – informed its structures. It contained, certainly, the inherent homophobia to which the homosocial institution is particularly and reactively prone. This homophobia was probably exacerbated by the fact that the only two male teachers who were actually known to be homosexual were also (quite separately) sexually abusive of the boys in their charge. The elder of these was an otherwise gentle old classicist, who had been known to be fondling boys for many years and whose discreet paedophilia was habitually tolerated as 'harmless' by the school authorities up until the time he retired. The younger was a raw and inexperienced English teacher who was reported to the headmaster after a single clumsy incident in the changing rooms, and summarily dismissed. Such narratives signal the inconsistencies and contradictions which were inherent in the school's gender system.

Similar contradictions and inconsistencies surrounded questions of theatre, drama, plays and play-acting. Since the school's dramatic calendar included an annual satirical revue, which allowed a carnivalesque licence to lampoon the teaching staff, a boy with enough nerve could earn a certain amount of celebrity – or more importantly, playground credibility – by treading the boards. Nor did we have to endure the stigma of cross-dressing – not at least to the same extent as our predecessors from earlier generations who had had to play all the women's parts (the Dramatic Society scrapbook bears witness to this). This, as I say, was the late 1960s and early 1970s, by which time even the most traditional of single-sex boys' schools had the wit to team up for the school play with the local girls' grammar or convent school in order to cast the female roles. Even so, such teaming took more organization than was often available, or deemed worthwhile: for the funny parts, at least, it was often easier to use a boy in drag, and nobody seemed to find this too hard. Down the road at the girls' school, paradoxically, they were far less keen on allowing boys onto the premises to take part in *their* plays, even though they were happy enough to let selected sixth-form girls out for the afternoon to rehearse at our school. As a result, the girls' school productions were consistently cast against gender; ours only intermittently so. They played men rather well; we played women badly or for laughs. Perhaps this is to be expected: certainly it illustrates the more general point that there are many respects in which male-to-female and female-to-male cross-casting are not directly symmetrical the one to the other.

Overall, then, boys who took part in school drama were not necessarily designated 'cissies'; nonetheless, it was generally accepted that they had chosen a less honourable, a less manly path than their friends in the first XV. And a slight, unmistakable air of sexual suspicion was associated with the school theatre. After all, as 'everybody knew', the theatre – the real theatre – *was* a refuge for the effete, the camp, the queer. (We have not lost that sense yet today: when front-bench MPs and newspapers, both tabloid and broadsheet, refer disparagingly to theatre professionals as 'luvvies' they mobilize, in the name of inauthenticity, that same old-fashioned dread of the emotional and of the tactile.) And in a school environment which – for reasons suggested above – contained no self-declared 'out' gays, there was an unspoken but clear shared belief that those who were covertly so inclined would probably gravitate towards places like the

Dramatic Society. This did not necessarily mean trouble. The school's institutional homophobia was, as I have said, quite complex, and in its workings surprisingly mild; like the present-day Church of England, it saw queers as no problem as long as they didn't practise. It was also intuitively correct: there were (of course) closet gays in the school drama society.

Thus it was in my schooldays *circa* 1970: dressing up, putting on make-up, showing off, displaying the body, pretending to be someone else, ostending emotion, the occasional ironized cross-gendering of performance – it was accepted that all these might be done 'in fun'. Even so, they courted the danger of appearing to disavow the codes of 'masculine authenticity' ('being a real man') which the school in its everyday workings still attempted to reconcile with the liberal-humanist ethos of a broad education and the pursuit of academic excellence.

I do not know what it felt like for an adolescent male who identified himself as gay to take part in drama as a social activity at that school. Perhaps for some it offered a sense of homecoming, a refuge where fantasy and role-play could afford some kind of relief from and resistance to the dominant message of hegemonic masculinity which the school conveyed. Perhaps, on the other hand, it felt like a dangerous step into a state of vulnerability – a kind of coded coming-out in itself. Most probably it contained elements of both. I can speak about my own experience, though – at least in so far as I now remember it. As a straight male I had a vague and unarticulated sense that while joining the Drama Society meant taking part in the pleasurable and liberating activities of pretence and performance, it also involved a bit of a risk, since one was aligning oneself publicly with the ambiguous cultural signifiers of a questionable sexual identity. To put it more plainly: play-acting was fun but I think I was a little scared that my mates would think I was queer. For, of course, I wasn't immune from the institution's low-level homophobia. I had nothing against queers: I just didn't want it to be thought that I was one! Whether or not my concerns went any deeper than this anxiety about reputation, I cannot remember. Perhaps there lurked some-where in my psyche the echoes of a centuries-old Puritan fear that play-acting actually had an effeminizing effect on the adolescent male; that doing all this showing-off on stage was not only a symptom but also a cause of an imperfectly achieved masculinity. I cannot say with certainty.

Whatever the case, various unvoiced assumptions concerning sex and gender underlay this thinking. Most of them were shared with my fellow-students, some of them were doubtless all my own work. They included the following:

- that there was one unitary and (probably) transhistorical gender state called masculinity;
- that one criterion for successfully growing up involved the identifying, achieving and maintenance of this state of masculinity;
- that although this state was 'natural' for males, it was also something which took effort to achieve;
- that the extent to which it *was* achieved depended on a combination of inborn attributes, learned behaviours and choices;
- that certain social activities inherently reinforced the achievement and maintenance of masculinity, while others challenged, hindered or problematized it;
- that theatre and play-acting fell into this latter category;
- that femininity and homosexuality existed on the same axis, and constituted the opposite(s) of masculinity;
- that, consequently, the homosexual male was 'less masculine' than his heterosexual counterpart.

The embarrassing list could go on. Hidden within it are one or two glimpses of truths: the realization even then, for example, that masculinity is not an unproblematic 'given' of male biological identity so much as a cultural construct to which the individual is expected to fit himself. But at this stage I do not want to analyse all the erroneous assumptions about gender which I did or did not make at the age of 17. I simply want to record and explain my position at the time, in all its naïvety, in order to delineate a starting-point: that for me the stage was always a place which disrupted and raised questions both intellectual and experiential about gender, power and ideology in general, and about masculinity in particular.

Some of the roots of this book, then, lie way back in my own past. The rest lie in the broader concerns of late twentieth-century criticism and theory of drama, theatre and performance, in particular as they relate to modern gender studies. At present, the issue of masculinity is being foregrounded in a number of academic fields. A wide range of investigations of contemporary masculinities has been undertaken by sociologists and gender theorists, so much so that an academic sub-field of 'Men's Studies' has become recognized – to the ironic amusement and occasional anger of many of the feminists who established Women's Studies precisely because everything *else* seemed already to be 'Men's Studies'. With acknowledgement then of the immense debt owed to these predecessors, this book sets out to analyse ways in which, over a period of several hundred years, masculinity has been represented on stage – mainly, but not exclusively, on the English stage.

It starts from the assumption that both 'masculinities' and 'representation' are problematic terms. Firstly, there are many 'masculinities'; they are historically contingent, continually changing, continually being redefined and renegotiated, and their meanings are closely tied in with those of other kinds of power relations, such as those concerning class and nationality. This is something which sociologists and gender theorists have recognized for a long time, and which (as I hope to show) many writers, dramatists and performers have been exploring in their own ways for an even longer one.

Secondly, 'representation' in the theatre involves those changing conventions which allow us to read the relation between the worlds of the theatrical and the everyday. Thus, for example, even within the patently 'unreal' dramatic world of the British pantomime there are complex representational questions. Widow Twankey might not 'in herself' look or sound very much like a real-life single mother struggling against poverty to bring up her son (those clothes! that deep voice! those hairy legs!). Even so, in her clumsily authoritarian and fondly bullying relationship to Jack we may discern the distorted outlines of a recognizable, or perhaps a stereotypical, pattern of interaction between a mother and a son. And in this specific instance, the question of representation and the question of gender are particularly closely interlinked: after all, Widow Twankey, as I have just suggested, is conventionally represented by a large and stereotypically un-'feminine' male actor. Jack, on the other hand, is more often than not played by a young but sexually mature woman. What we see is clearly not what we get, and the audience has to negotiate the various meanings inherent in the distance between the two. Like gender itself, stage representation may sometimes appear straightforward, as if Hamlet's 'mirror up to Nature' contained no distortions, no problems of perspective. Equally, however, the very act of representation may set in motion all kinds of questions before ever a word is spoken or an action performed.

Cross-casting can have many different meanings, but sometimes it is simply a matter of necessity. My student audience in 1998 felt that gender preconceptions played little part in their experience of theatre and drama within the educational institution: 'doing drama' was not, they felt, a gender-specific activity. Statistics tell a rather different picture. Post-16 educational programmes in Theatre Studies, Drama,

Performing Arts, in the UK at least, generally contain a significant gender imbalance. In both Higher and Further Education, they attract far more women, and female drama and theatre students on BA programmes typically outnumber males by ratios of 3 : 1 or more – sometimes a lot more. This historical study of staged masculinities is being written within a specific institutional context: that of the British education system at the end of the twentieth and the beginning of the twenty-first centuries. And despite the response which I received from my audience of sixth-formers in 1998, I am struck by the sense in which the subject itself remains gendered – and not in a way which seems to speak predominantly to young men. Ironically, the gender balance of the 'classical' dramatic canon, which traditionally offers a couple of decent female roles and eight or nine male ones, is completely reversed within the student body which now studies, and frequently stages these plays. As a result the cross-cast production is now the norm rather than the exception in university theatre, and even in the modern feminist and postfeminist repertoire, there are only a limited number of plays with a large and predominantly female cast. What was once a liberating and subversive gender practice has become a convention necessitated by expedience. As a cast list went up, one of my students, an excellent actress who happened to be slightly taller than average and who wore her hair short, groaned. 'Oh no,' she said, 'I'm not playing a man again, am I!' The ghost of Francis Flute chortled from the shades.

1.2   Masculinity and gender

'All too often,' says Carla J. McDonough 'the male protagonist has been critically treated as if he were non-gendered' (McDonough 1997: 1) This book is one of a growing number which seek to counteract that tendency and to explore masculinity in theatre in a specifically gendered way: that is to say, in a way which does not assume that the masculine voice or the masculine experience is universal. It focuses on plays which explicitly address questions of gender, and on plays on which new light can be thrown by considering the gender issues which are implicit in them. So much has been written now about 'what gender is' that it is tempting to take the term for granted. However, because the term still means different things when used by different writers in different contexts, it may be useful (even at the risk of repeating what to some may be obvious) to say a few preliminary words about how it is being used in this book.

The modern distinction between sex and gender is, effectively, the difference between describing people according to a paradigm based on the biological sciences and describing them according to a paradigm based on the social sciences. Sex, then, is about belonging to a particular biological category, possessing certain kinds of reproductive organs, having or not having the ability to give birth, lactate, etc. Gender, on the other hand, refers to the typical social roles and behaviours attributed to, or performed by members of both sexes. This sounds so straightforward that it is tempting to leave definitions at this point: masculinity is the sum total of the social performance of biological males, and femininity that of biological females. That simplicity, unfortunately, is deceptive – for three reasons at least.

Firstly, in practice males and females, looked at cross-culturally, share so many roles and behaviours that the words would soon become meaningless. What behaviours, apart from those related directly to biological functions, are in fact universally carried out only by biological females? Or, conversely, by biological males? The best we might be able to do is to talk about the tendency towards certain kinds of behaviour *within specific cultures.*

Secondly, and paradoxically, advances in medical science have now reached such a stage of sophistication that those biological categories which were once regarded as immutable are now seen to be less so. On the one hand, new operating procedures allow males to become females and vice versa; and although such transgendered sexualities are not common, neither are they now regarded as totally freakish (see Bornstein 1993, Halberstam 1998). On the other hand, the history of ambiguously-'gendered' (i.e. androgynous or intersexual) people is also being written. The primacy of biological categories, so central to nineteenth-century constructions of gender, may have had its day.

The third and chief reason, however, is that to talk about gender is also to enter the world of values. As textbooks of psychology insist, 'most cultures elaborate the biological distinction between male and female into a network of beliefs and practices that permeate virtually every domain of human activity' (Atkinson et al. 1993: 109). This network is what we call gender, and different cultures have varying beliefs about how this network operates. This could be divided, effectively, into two types: essentialist and anti-essentialist. The essentialist view holds that differences in social roles and behaviours are largely based on some 'essential' programming which precedes the social, and is thus cross-cultural and transhistorical, applicable to every 'normal' man or woman in every culture. For most earlier cultures – and for some contemporary ones – gender essentialism might refer back to a presocial order that is religious in character, while present-day Western essentialist thinking tends to refer to the natural sciences for its framework of presocial reference. At present, this is particularly influential in popular discourse, where contemporary gender essentialism frames gender differences and notions of masculinity or femininity in terms either of biological development and the hard-wiring of the brain, or of evolutionary psychology, or of a combination of the two. Thus, according to one example of this kind of model, teenage boys don't listen because their ear canals in puberty undergo growth spurts which cause temporary forms of deafness; while girls, on the contrary, are good listeners because evolution has ensured that women are hard-wired with acute hearing to enable them to hear babies cry in the night (Pease and Pease 1999: 34, 36).

The position from which this book is written is, predictably enough, an anti-essentialist one. This is not to deny those observable developmental aspects such as the differences between brain patterns and uses of left- and right-hemisphere activity in men and women. Rather it is to insist that what is important is the way in which that 'biological programming', in so far as it exists, is then imbued with different meanings by different cultures. It is also to react sceptically to models of human behaviour which seek to ground it in a single pre-social explanation, whether that explanation is biological, evolutionary or religious.

As a result, the word 'gender' as used in this book does not refer to a category or even a quality so much as to a relationship. It is a word which sets out to explain relations *between* various categories of men and women. This explanation inevitably intersects with – and competes with – other explanations, such as race, class, age, national identity and sexual orientation, which may themselves be relative. And, of course, none of these explanations are ever ideology-free: they are all implicated in the contested meanings which affect larger social debates and practices surrounding social and subjective being.

Gender, then, is always a relationship – and for that reason, this book will be looking at female characters as well as male, at women playwrights as well as men, and indeed at actresses as well as actors. But the relationship which constitutes the engendering of masculinity need not always *be* a male–female one. 'The masculine', of course, may be characterized as 'that which is not womanly'. It may also, however, be defined in relation to *other* kinds of 'non-masculinity'. For example, Jonathan Walters has demonstrated how, in Greco-Roman culture, the categories of boyhood and male adolescence were differentiated from 'real men' in terms of the quality of 'softness', which they shared with women and eunuchs. A boy or youth was not really a man.

Consequently, he was 'fair game' for the predatory adult male in a sexual encounter, provided he played the part of the 'woman' in bed, in the sense of being sexually passive, while the adult male played the sexually dominant role (Walters 1993: 23). The adult male's participation in this sexual activity with the young boy, it should be noted, casts no doubt upon his own masculinity. In other cultures, by way of contrast, same-sex desire or activity is seen as incompatible with the attainment of a truly masculine identity.

Such markers of non-masculinity, then, vary from one culture to another: elsewhere, the marks of a non-masculine male might include a love of music, having the status of a priest or a slave, being unable to bring down a deer with a bow and arrow, wearing an earring, spending time in the company of women, an inability to drink large volumes of alcohol – and so on. But the more the categories proliferate, the more contingent they become and the more paradoxes they generate. For example, in the gender discourse of the imperialist culture of the Victorian era, the binary opposition between the truly 'manly' Englishman and the somehow 'unmanly' savage loomed large. The 'savage' both is and is not a man. This ambiguity may be figured in various ways. If he is living in a tribal society, the savage 'clearly' lacks those manly values which determine civilized behaviour, and so he cannot, of course, be granted full admittance to the masculinities club. If, on the other hand, he is a member of a conquered (and thus 'civilized') people, he is nonetheless still debarred from full membership – this time because of his subject status and the consequent loss of his independence. Mrinalini Sinha's detailed study (Sinha 1995) of the repeated trope in nineteenth-century English writing which contrasts the 'Manly Englishman' with the 'Effeminate Bengali' gives a range of examples of this. Gender ideology can be very versatile in its defence of privilege, constructing shifting sets of binary oppositions which are guaranteed, one way or another, to construct an 'other' which can be excluded.

However, even within the society which constructs the categories in order to protect the status of its own gender assumptions, other meanings are possible. In this example, the 'unmanly' savage clearly *is* a man in many respects – and the resistant thought arises that in some ways perhaps he is *more* so than the civilized male: thus the nineteenth-century English novelist and social theorist Charles Kingsley praised the ruggedly natural manliness which he saw as an attribute of the frontier tribes, but missing from Victorian industrial society. On a less lofty note, white Americans have traditionally been awed by the mythical 'masculinity' (meaning, euphemistically, the penis size) of their fellow-countrymen of African origins, whose slave status had originally marked them off as less than a man.

Masculinity, then, repeatedly defines itself in terms of its opposites, and the history of gender construction is, as often as not, a matter of marking off the 'other'. Yet with disturbing (or perhaps cheering) regularity, the other comes back to haunt the dominant order which had dispelled it. In the cultural assertion of masculine gender identity, a continual interplay arises between the thing itself and the other against which it is being defined.

1.3 Two maps: the range and scope of the book

The focus of this study is not just the concept of 'masculinities', but the way in which different notions of masculinity have been staged over the last six or seven hundred years. To this end, the book conflates two separate historical 'maps'. One is a fairly familiar one: it is a conventional map of Western theatrical and dramatic history, with a strong bias towards my own English cultural tradition. Typically this map shows the following contours:

* Western theatre's supposed ritual origins in ancient Greece;
* the emergence of a secular theatre from a liturgical one in medieval Europe;
* the development in England of a popular and commercial theatre in the Elizabethan and Jacobean period;
* its re-emergence in a new form following the official closure of the theatres during the Civil War and Commonwealth;
* a transitional eighteenth-century phase, during which the theatre becomes subject to greater political control;
* the rise of a European naturalist theatre in the late nineteenth century;
* the reactions against, and developments of, naturalism and realism in twentieth-century drama both in Europe and in North America.

It is, of course, a map which is subject to continual scrutiny, and it is continually being redrawn, questioned and corrected by theatre historians and scholars, both in its detail and its overall lineaments. For example, the nature of the relationship between ritual and theatre, or of that between traditions of medieval secular and religious dramatic traditions, the extent and vitality of theatrical activity during the 'closed' periods of the English Civil War and Commonwealth – all these are the subject of continuing debates. A more radical critique of the map might ask, '*Which* history does this actually tell?' There is ideology at work in any act of cartography, and this one constructs a dominant tradition of theatre history by privileging certain kinds and definitions of 'theatre' over others. It is, for example, deeply Eurocentric; playwrights and permanent companies are treated with greater seriousness than improvisatory traditions or folk plays; certain *kinds* of playwrights and companies are treated more seriously than others ... the list could go on. It might even be concluded that this traditional map is somewhat masculine in itself: a construction of predominantly male scholars, looking at plays about men, written by male playwrights in an institutional theatrical tradition which is dominated by men.

Such critiques are valid; there are certainly other valid maps that could be drawn, and the one that I am using has its limitations. But these limitations are useful to us precisely because they construct a dominant tradition within which to explore dramatic representations of masculinity. The map is an important one not because it is definitive but because it is a construction. It also has the advantage of familiarity, and of its contours being broadly accepted. In the present context this is important, since it offers a relatively stable structure for this investigation. The chapters in this book will, on the whole, follow the routes which the map suggests – with inevitable implications for the range of masculinities with which we will engage. My own area of knowledge relates primarily to British (and especially to English) theatre, and to drama in the English language. Accordingly, that is where the emphasis will lie: there are no chapters, for example, on Racine, on Kleist or on Calderón, though these would have provided fascinating studies. However, at those points when this theatre history tends to stress cultural continuity between the English stage and the theatres of other countries, I have usually followed that cue. Consequently, there are discussions of European as well as English medieval theatre, and on the relationships between developments on the British stage and both nineteenth-century Scandinavian naturalism and contemporary American and Irish drama.

The second map is less familiar, and more contentious. It is a history of masculinities. Although much work is currently being done about the construction of masculinity in different historical periods, it cannot be said that any generally agreed history of masculinity yet exists. One of the best attempts to provide 'a sketch of a vastly complex history' (Connell 1995: 186) is the short chapter entitled 'The History of

Masculinity' in R. W. Connell's influential work *Masculinities*. Connell's history locates the production of masculinity in 'the formation of the modern gender order as a whole ... in the period from about 1450 to 1650, [when] the modern capitalist economy came into being around the North Atlantic, and the modern gender order also began to take shape in that region' (Connell 1995: 186). It then describes the rise of what we call masculinity in connection with four key social and historical developments: 'the cultural change that produced new understandings of sexuality and personhood in metropolitan Europe ... the creation of overseas empires by the Atlantic seaboard states ... the growth of the cities that were the centres of commercial capitalism ...and the onset of large-scale European Civil War ... [which] disturbed the legitimacy of the gender order' (Connell 1995: 186–9). Connell adopts the term 'gentry masculinity' to characterize the model which was produced and stabilized through these processes, and he goes on to argue that 'the history of European/American masculinity over the last two hundred years can broadly be understood as the splitting of gentry masculinity ... [under pressure from] challenges to the gender order by women, the logic of the gendered accumulation process in industrial capital-ism, and the power relations of empire' (Connell 1995: 191).

This history describes the changing patterns of what is more pre-cisely termed 'hegemonic masculinity'. Hegemonic masculinity is that form or model of masculinity which a culture privileges above others, which implicitly defines what is 'normal' for males in that culture, and which is able to impose that definition of normality upon other kinds of masculinity. Its characteristic tactic is the kind of definition-through-opposition, and the marking off and marginalizing of the 'other', which we noted above. Its essential function is to legitimate not only the dominant position of men generally (and the concomitant subordina-tion of women) but also the dominance of particular social groups of men, along with their values, their beliefs and their power and wealth, over other groups. Broadly speaking, each historical era produces its own version of hegemonic masculinity, which operates both on an external level, in terms of social roles and relations, and on an internal one, in terms of subjectivity, feelings, and definitions of self. Hegemonic masculinity is by nature paradoxical, since it seems to stand still but in fact is always on the move. Its normalizing function means that it repeatedly lays claim to universals and appears to refer to static and enduring values; in reality, however, it is continually in the process of changing. Connell's history indicates the way in which these changes relate to wider social and economic movements. His image of gradual formation and disintegration has been influential – although it is by no means universally accepted (see, for example, MacInnes 1998). On the whole, though, I find Connell's model compelling, and in general the arguments in this book will follow the pattern which it suggests – with three qualifications. Firstly there is the necessary caveat that Connell's diagram should not be taken to imply that the history of masculinity is linear and progressive, or that it moves in clear-cut stages from one phase to another. It is a useful tool which enables us to see some general patterns emerging. Cultural change, however, is always a matter of complex transitional movements, and at various points we will find dynamic interrelationships between different forms of masculinity, and tensions between dominant, emergent, subordinate, progressive, reactionary and marginalized definitions of what it means to be a man.

The second, and related, point is that Connell's broad term 'gentry masculinity' is not altogether a satisfactory one. Connell argues that it was the rise to cultural dominance of gentry masculinity that was the culminating point of gender formation about two hundred years ago. The term denotes accurately one key strand within the emergent and dominant models of masculinity in the seventeenth and eighteenth centuries. However, implying as it does a focus on a comparatively small sector of society, the term foregrounds not only the hereditary landowning classes, but also the largely rural and agricultural ambiance with which they were mainly associated. Theatre, on the other hand, is a predominantly metropolitan phenomenon during most of the period under consideration. An exploration of the staging of masculinities needs to concentrate more directly on the urban context in which this usually takes place. Moreover, since class difference is such a frequent motif in drama, any such exploration will have to take into consideration the variety of social classes which the theatre addresses throughout the period. The term 'gentry masculinity' is being asked to do too much work: we need, too, to consider the staging of mercantile masculinities, bourgeois masculinities, aristocratic masculinities – and occasionally artisan and working-class masculinities. In this study, then, I will be looking at places where Connell's broad concept of gentry masculinity overlaps with, shades into and interacts with other masculine models.

Thirdly, it will be seen that the time-scales covered by my two maps are not entirely congruent. Having to negotiate between a time-scale which starts in the Middle Ages and one which starts in ancient Greece, I have tried to find an acceptable compromise. There is no separate chapter on classical drama, although there are references to it in this chapter. The chapter on the medieval theatre does largely focus on texts from around Connell's initial date of 1450, but makes some reference, too, to the question of how masculinity is staged in earlier medieval culture, before 'the modern gender order ... began to take shape'. For while the formation of the modern gender order has both been shaped by and has helped to shape the modern capitalist economy, it is also clear – as the large volume of recent work on masculinities in the Middle Ages testifies – that questions of gender are on the social, and hence the theatrical, agenda in premodern historical periods as well (see Lees 1994; Beidler 1998; Hadley 1999).

As may be seen, then, the book makes no claims to comprehensiveness. The texts, audiences, writers, performers and performances on which I concentrate are intended as a series of 'snapshots' from certain familiar moments in theatre history. As a result there are plenty of gaps in the book's chronology, since, in the best tradition of snapshots, the subjects are very often clustered together. I have tried, where possible, to make close groupings of my compositions, either by focusing on single authors (Shakespeare, perhaps predictably, gets a chapter to himself) or upon a deliberately compressed time-span *within* a historical period: a few years, a decade or so. Even so, word limits have meant that omissions have had to be made, and there are some which I particularly regret – the middle years of the twentieth century being a particular case in point.

There are gaps, too, in the range of masculinities which the study addresses, gaps which it is important for me to acknowledge at the outset. There are many issues which are of concern to contemporary masculinity studies but which are hardly addressed by this book. Although, as I have suggested above, gender as I am using the word necessarily intersects with other explanations such as age, race, national identity, class etc., the theatrical map which I have chosen will guide us towards some of these intersections at the cost of ignoring or marginalizing others. For example, despite the obvious importance that sexual orientation and race both have in discussions of gender identity, this book has comparatively little to say about homosexual masculinities, and nothing at all about black masculinities. This may be no bad thing: it is towards gay and black scholars that we are more likely to turn for an authoritative and insightful treatment of these questions (see, for example, Tokson 1982; Williams 1985; Barthelemy 1987; de Jongh 1992; Chedgzoy 1995; Clark 2001).

The point about such studies, though, is that, as the old joke has it, they wouldn't want to start from here. A book which explored in depth the staging of black or gay masculinities would be likely to choose a

rather different range of theatrical texts and periods. Over the past six
or seven hundred years – the scope of the 'map' of theatre history
which this book traces – the concerns of Anglo-Western theatre have
been predominantly white and professedly heterosexual. These concerns are reflected in the structure of my own enquiry, which does
'start from here', and which is concerned with the theatre's complex
relationship with dominant gender configurations.

These dominant gender configurations are, as I say, inevitably tied
into class configurations. In this study, these, too, are partially determined by the map of theatre history, for they are inscribed within the
narrative of the English theatre's fluctuating relationship with patterns
of class dominance in English society. These patterns are themselves not
always easy to identify; and the question is complicated by the fact that
the dominant social classes have not always been the predominantly
theatre-going classes. But theatre has always had to respond to questions
of social class, questions of subject matter, and of audience formation
and patterns of play-going. Who is the audience? Who is being talked
to? Who is paying and what do they want to pay to see? Elizabethan and
Jacobean theatre companies, supported by court patrons, commissioned
tragedies about monarchs, aristocrats and generals, and comedies about
gentlemen and ladies, and they played them before target audiences,
which included both the court and an emerging urban cross-section.
Restoration theatres expected to play to an aristocratic coterie but found
that their finances depended on attracting lawyers, merchants, tradesmen and apprentices to the theatre too; they held up a comic mirror to
the 'world' of London's fops, belles, wits and 'cits', but on other nights
spun tragic and tragi-comic yarns in fantasy oriental and classical settings. Nineteenth-century theatre managements tapped into an affluent
bourgeois audience keen to see scenes from their own domestic lives
rendered in all the material solidity of a newly-discovered naturalist dramaturgy and scenography. These are oversimplifications, of course – but
they indicate the main point, which is that the map of theatre history to
which I am referring already privileges a certain history of social classes,
which in turn will impinge on the gender history that emerges from its
study. Once more, it is as well to acknowledge this at the outset.

1.4   The performance of gender/gender as performance

As I have suggested, an attempt to conflate the two maps outlined
above imposes certain limitations. But what about the advantages it

offers? To construct a history of (mainly white, mainly heterosexual) masculinities through the ways in which that history has been 'staged': how is this different from constructing a history of masculinity from, say, letters, or diaries, or institutional records, or legal documents, or criminal statistics, or novels, or poems, or sermons, or religious tracts, or courtesy-books? All of the above could be – and many of them have been – used as exploratory tools in this area. What then, does a focus on plays, theatres and performances offer that is different?

Is there, perhaps, some special relationship between theatrical performance and questions of gender? Is theatrical performance itself effectively 'gendered'? And if so, in what way? Consider the following episode from Euripides' *The Bacchae* (c. 405 BC), in which the god Dionysos appears to Pentheus, King of Thebes. Dressed effeminately and wearing his hair long like a woman's, Dionysos' mask and costume represents him in stark contrast to Pentheus, the political and military leader and a stereotype of rational, controlling masculinity. Pentheus has already refused to acknowledge the god, and now he fails, literally, to recognize him. Jeering at the effeminate dress and hair of the stranger before him, Pentheus taunts him:

> You are no wrestler, I can tell from these long curls
> Cascading most seductively over your cheek.
> Your skin, too, shows a whiteness carefully preserved;
> You keep away from the sun's heat, walk in the shade,
> So hunting Aphrodite with your lovely face.
>
> (Euripides 1972: 206)

Dionysos' response is swift and brutal. Entrancing Pentheus, he tricks the King into dressing up as a woman (the cross-dressing is played for laughs this time), and leads him to the secret grove where the Maenads perform their Bacchic rituals. Spying him, the women, led by Agave, Pentheus' mother, turn on him and tear him to pieces.

Dionysos, of course, is the god of theatre, the god at whose celebrations the Greek drama was born: among those things which the doomed rationalist Pentheus attempts to reject or suppress is the spirit of theatre itself. Pentheus' actions lead to the violent encounter between masculine and feminine which the play stages; and, as Ruth Padel puts it, 'someone always gets torn to pieces' in the myths of Dionysos. In her analysis of the mythology surrounding this androgynous god of the theatre, Padel goes on to suggest that the 'idea of femaleness' is intrinsic to Western theatre:

> Character, mask, persona: all those theatrical concepts were façades, invented by men using an idea of femaleness, its made-upness .... *Persona*, a female word, was Latin for dramatic 'role' because it originally meant 'mask' – which the voice 'sounds' (from *sonare*, 'to sound') through (*per*). Like actors, women are 'made up'. They play a part in order to please. *Mascara* means 'mask'.
>
> (Padel 2000: 229, 329)

On one level, Padel seems to be echoing the folk wisdom of my schooldays and stressing the essentially feminine nature of theatre. But even as she introduces the notion, she problematizes it. If theatre *is* associated with this female principle, it is a female principle which has been invented by men. Throughout the history of gender constructions in Western thought, a repeated manoeuvre takes place whereby certain human characteristics are first ascribed to one gender or the other; these characteristics are then (by an intellectual sleight of hand) assigned the status of eternal and verifiable truths; finally they are then metonymically transferred to other social activities, which themselves consequently become 'gendered'. Thus theatre and acting are repeatedly associated with those attributes which fall on the feminine side of the ideological binary divide: illusion, display, emotion, the body. By this process theatre becomes culturally encoded as feminine or female: not just, as Padel punningly suggests, because of its associations with 'make-up' but because it falls on one side of this larger binary divide – the culturally conditioned structure of oppositions which is itself an instrument of masculine power and control.

The idea, then, of theatre being 'essentially' feminine does not enable us to go very far in itself. Nor does the opposing idea – which can also be drawn from the theatre's origins in classical Greece – that the theatre embodies a kind of masculine principle. There is, it is true, a sense in which the origins of Western theatre can be seen as phallic. In Chapter Four of his *Poetics* Aristotle tells us that

> Tragedy – as also Comedy – was at first mere improvisation. The one originated with the authors of the Dithyramb, the other with those of the phallic songs, which are still used in many of our cities.
>
> (cited in Schechner 1988: 4)

The rural Dionysian festivals of preclassical Greece seem to have included 'processions accompanied by ribaldry which carried models of phalluses in honour of Dionysos' (Taplin 1997: 33), while statuettes and vases found at sites from Athens to Southern Italy and dating from the fourth century BC portray comic performers costumed in grotesque masks, tight tunics giving an appearance of nudity, and, for the main male characters, the inevitable *phallos*. If comedy derives from phallic rites, could it be that masculinity itself – or at least its most common cultural signifier, the *phallos* – somehow lies at the deepest core of theatre, and that some deep masculine ritual underlies the birth of theatre?

The idea might well appeal to some tendencies within the modern men's movement. Since the publication of Robert Bly's *Iron John*, the search for masculine rituals which will enable the 'recovery of some initiation [into manhood]' (Bly 1990: 350) has been high on the agenda of what has become called the 'mythopoetic' branch of that movement. The notion that in the past some such masculine ritual might have lain at the roots of tragedy is an attractive one. It is highly unlikely, however, that such a genealogy could ever be firmly established. Aristotle's authority as an ethnologist, or a genealogist of culture, is questionable (see Schechner 1988) and modern anthropological paradigms for understanding relationships between ritual and performance would suggest that any attempt to find the 'origins' of theatre in the male celebrations embodied in the pre-comedic ritual forms of early Greek civilization is unrealistic. In any case, anthropologically speaking, the *phallos* is an unstable signifier. Although the word is often used as if it were more or less synonymous with 'penis', the symbolic *phallos* has a very different meaning. Its roots are in Egyptian mythology: after the dismemberment of the god Osiris, his sister Isis searched the world for her brother's remains, all of which she managed to reassemble with the exception of his penis. The *phallos* is the symbolic replacement which both heals the wound and also marks the loss.

As for the later evidence about theatrical staging, the presence of a *phallos* in comedic costume is not proof of the ritual origins of comedy, and the *phalloi* portrayed on the vases and statuettes are not proud and erect symbols of masculine potency, but are rather limp and dangling leather accoutrements. Rather than proof, then, of the ritual origins of comedy, the Greek comic actor's *phallos* is probably a conventional signifier of gender within the theatrical sign-system of the all-male Greek theatre.

It is this last point that is of real importance: it is not the representation of a symbolic masculinity so much as the hegemonic power of a very real *maleness* which is the significant characteristic of the classical Greek theatre. The Athenian theatre of the fifth century BC was the product of democracy – the vesting of power in the *demos* dating from about 510 BC. At that time this comprised approximately 40,000 freeborn male citizens, for whom attendance at the Athenian spring festival, the City Dionysia (which had been expanded several years earlier in order to include, as well as religious observances, competitions of song, music, dance and – increasingly – theatre) was a civic duty and a ceremonial statement of civic identity. If masculinity is indeed a central issue in the earliest Western theatrical forms to which we have access, its importance lies not in its ritual origins so much as in the fact that the theatre which produced what we think of as the great age of Greek classical drama emerges, in about 508 BC, at a point at which the spiritual power of the masculine ritual – the phallic rites, in so far as we know anything about them – becomes reinscribed as male political power invested in the city state.

To return, then, to the more general question asked at the start of this section: the distinctiveness of a focus on the theatrical staging of masculinities lies in the specific material social and cultural practices that are characteristic of 'Theatre' generally and of various forms of theatre in all their individuality. The theatre continually functions as a particular kind of social space; the performance space is not merely representational – it is also transactional. It demands and depends upon an imaginative contract between the performers and the audience, a collaboration between the sender and the receiver of the dramatic message, which enables the conventions of theatrical narrative to be understood. These collaborations and conventions change along with history, and are part of history. Frequently, as in the example of Greek democratic theatre above, they contain implicit gender assumptions: in order for stage meanings to exist they need to be tied into the larger meanings of the world in which the stage has its being, and the creative collusion will always be shot through with the larger ideological issues of the society in which that collusion takes place. The creative and meaningful transactions in which the stage and audience can engage are part of the theatre's familiar pleasure; but they can take place only in the context of a wider economy – both a literal economy and an economy of meaning.

These theatrical transactions involve two kinds of dual consciousness on the part of the audience. Firstly, they demand that the audience allow themselves to remain 'in two minds' – aware with one part of their consciousness that in front of them on the stage there are simply costumes, props, actors and scenery, but exhorted at the same time to experience these imaginatively as an alternative reality. Secondly, they demand an interplay on the part of the audience between the self as individual and the self as part of a collective entity. 'You go into a theatre an individual and you emerge an audience', say Richard Eyre and Nicholas Wright (Eyre and Wright 2000: 11). This may be an oversimplification: the process may not be as predictably linear as this. Yet the interplay between individual and audience remains important.

I stress this (doubly) split subject position of the theatrical audience in order to locate my attitude towards theatre and drama as a site for exploring historical masculinities. I want to make three general points about this; two of these concern continuities between theatre and everyday life, while the third concerns that which marks theatre off from everyday life. Firstly, gender ideology, too, works in terms of the subject's dual sense of self as individual, and self as member of a group: 'me' and 'me-as-a-man' (or woman). If the communal nature of the audience experience is an important aspect of the way that theatre mediates and communicates meanings, it may be particularly important in areas relating to gender and identity.

Secondly, there is the question of the performativity of gender itself. During the second half of the twentieth century, 'anthropologists tended to see almost all human transactions as basically performative – as enactments of relationships with specific purposes – involving a number of elements which are also those found in ritual and theatre' (Brockett 1991: 3). Theories of social performativity have been developed and applied in a number of contexts – most notably, for our current purposes, in Judith Butler's *Gender Trouble*. Drawing on anthropological sources, such as Victor Turner and Clifford Geertz, who have been so influential in Theatre and Performance Studies, Butler argues that gender attributes are themselves essentially performative, rather than expressive of any prior reality.

> In what senses, then, is gender an act? As in other ritual social dramas, the action of gender requires a performance that is *repeated*. This repetition is at once a re-enactment and re-experiencing of a set of meanings already socially established... Gender ought not to be constructed as a stable identity or locus of agency from which various acts follow; rather gender is an identity tenuously constituted in time, instituted in an exterior space through a *stylized repetition of acts.*
>
> (Butler 1990: 140)

Gender Trouble was felt as empowering and exciting by feminist theatre scholars and practitioners, who found their own gendered theatre practice validated or enriched by its implications, which are couched in terms of resistance to 'masculinist domination and compulsory heterosexuality' (Butler 1990: 141). In fact, later writings by Butler repudiated the model of performativity which these scholars and practitioners attributed to her. Nonetheless, it is that earlier metaphor of gender-as-performance, with its promise of liberation through the realization that gender's *'appearance of substance* is precisely that, a constructed identity, a performative accomplishment which the mundane social audience, including the actors themselves, come to believe...' (Butler 1990: 141), which continues to resonate.

This leads to the third point: if gender (and everything else) is *already* performance, where does this leave a history of staged masculinities? We are taken back to the earlier point that theatre is itself a specific form of social activity. Social performativity and theatrical performance may be congruent, they may be related, and they may resemble each other – but they are not identical. Evidence from past plays and performances has a complex and problematic status. It exists not as raw socio-historical documentation or data, but as the trace of a performed moment which was itself part of the complex dialectic between the real and the imaginary, articulated within a historically specific mode of cultural production that relies on particular kinds of conventions for negotiating relations between the fictional and the real world. Moreover it is usually – as the anthropologists' everyday 'performances' are not – aware of itself *as* performance.

The stage thus operates both as a separate space subject to its own laws, and also as an extension of the everyday. It is a place where the 'performances' of everyday life are themselves re-performed, and in the process changed. It embodies a defined set of cultural practices which are marked off from everyday social reality, while claiming at the same time important forms of continuities between theatrical representation and that everyday reality. To approach the study of masculinities through the medium of the stage will involve us in an engagement with this paradox.

The theme of this book, then, is the way in which the theatre – or, more precisely, *theatres* – have variously articulated, endorsed, undermined, critiqued, analysed or resisted the ideologies of masculinity which have been produced by the dominant gender configurations of successive eras from the Middle Ages onwards. Its subject matter is the theatrical representation of masculinities – and these two problematic terms interact with each other throughout the book. Questions about representation determine some of the findings about the nature of the masculinities explored; the issues about changing and negotiated masculinities impinge upon questions of representation. And, at the same time, theatre holds the paradoxical position of having been, for most of its history, the social domain, either exclusively or dominantly, of men – yet associated with the cultural values relating to 'an idea of femaleness' (Padel 2000: 229). It is because of this uneasy relationship with hegemonic masculinities that the theatre promises to be such an interesting place in which to explore the history of those masculinities.

2

Staging Medieval Masculinities

2.1 Introduction

According to some definitions of the word, 'masculinity' appears not to have existed at all for a large part of the Middle Ages. R. W. Connell makes the point that 'our concept of masculinity seems to be a fairly recent historical product, a few hundred years old at most' (Connell 1995: 68), and in his chapter 'History of Masculinity' he locates its genesis 'in the period from about 1450 to about 1650 ... [when] the modern capitalist economy came into being around the North Atlantic, and the modern gender order also began to take shape in that region' (Connell 1995: 186). This is not to say that nobody before 1450 asked what it means to 'be a man', or what appropriate 'manly' behaviour was, or what were the essential differences between male and female subjectivity. Rather it is to suggest that at some point around the middle of the fifteenth century social, political and economic developments began to provide a certain set of contexts for these questions, and consequently a certain set of answers. These, in turn, produced the gender order that defined masculinity in its modern sense: 'gendered individual character, defined through an opposition with femininity and institutionalized in economy and state' (Connell 1995: 189).

'About 1450' is an interesting starting-point. The date has significance not only in terms of Connell's history and definition of masculinity, but also in terms of a theatre studies perspective, since so much of the theatrical evidence from which we reconstruct the emergence of English drama in the Middle Ages comes from around the middle and late fifteenth century. The folk plays and rituals of Robin Hood appear to have been first performed in the 1420s. As far as the Morality play tradition is concerned, *Mankind* is usually assigned to the period 1465–70, and *Everyman* to the 1490s (Bevington 1975:

901, 939). And while a tradition of performing the Corpus Christi cycles emerged in the late fourteenth century, the versions of these plays that we know today can be traced back only to manuscripts from the middle of the fifteenth: that of the York cycle of Mystery plays dates from approximately 1430–40, the Towneley manuscript from 1450 (Happé 1975: 10–11). Thus the period which Connell locates as the start of the modern gender order seems also to be crucial for the developing English medieval drama. Most of the plays I shall look at in this chapter, then, will come from around that date. First of all, however, I will look at a rather earlier phase of theatre history

2.2   Staging biblical narratives

One of the dominant dramatic narrative types of the Middle Ages is the dramatized Bible story. These biblical adaptations brought together the old and the new: scriptural sources, homiletic and commentarial traditions met with the developing dramatic conventions of the Middle Ages. Setting up and exploiting a tension between apparently diverse discursive modes, this drama was able to present those allegorical meanings which were encoded in its source material of biblical stories and the Christian homiletic tradition in terms of an (often comic) realism, rich in the everyday social detail of medieval life. Thus, whenever a story from the Bible was put on stage, it brought with it a nexus of meanings from its original narrative source, but it also changed those meanings: adaptation necessarily involves interpretation.

   The dramatized biblical narrative appears in a variety of contexts, ranging from the small presentation inserted into the liturgy of a Mass, to the full-length drama, to the cycle play, which appears as a part of a more independent 'theatrical' event such as a Corpus Christi pageant. Theatre history tends to focus on the large-scale civic pageants of the later Middle Ages, but the earlier forms are of interest too. A gradual process of church services incorporating 'dramatic techniques such as dialogue, movement from one symbolic location to another, and the use of props' (Bevington 1975: 21) led to the growth in the tenth and eleventh centuries of dramatic form within the liturgy. The earliest examples of these are the Easter *Quem Quaeritis* tropes, which assign parts in order to dramatize the visit of the three Marys to the sepulchre on Easter Day, and their encounter with the angel who informs them that the one they seek 'is not here, he has risen' (Bevington 1975: 25). If, as traditional theatre history has it, these liturgical questions and responses are the origins of postclassical Western drama, then ironically our drama begins, not with the staging of masculinities at all, but with female impersonation. The *Quem Quaeritis* tropes were a product of the closed religious orders of the Middle Ages; they were performed by and for the all-male community of the monastery. The three Marys are 'brethren' who have secretly costumed themselves in 'copes': that is to say that they are still in clerical garb, though apparently wearing special clothes which set them apart from the rest of the liturgical participants.

This liturgical drama was not merely a 'decoration', but developed into a important part of the devotional life, as a way of articulating essential aspects of the monks' faith. Within, for example, the Benedictine order, it became integrated into the broader disciplines and activities which contributed to the spiritual development of the monastic community (Whitta 1997: n.p.). Dramatic representation in such an environment can be problematic, however, especially where matters of gender are concerned. A single-sex community necessarily negotiates ideas of gender differently from a mixed community. Moreover, in the single-sex community which is dedicated specifically to a path of Christian enlightenment, and in which women are already encoded as 'material', or 'physical' and therefore necessarily threatening to the spiritual project of the male monastic order, there is already considerable anxiety concerning the representation of women by men. The staging of female characters within the liturgical play inevitably brings into the monastery itself the alien other (even if only in representation). And for those actors who play those parts – the cast of male players drawn from the monks of the community itself, and gendered 'feminine' by their casting in the play, and also perhaps by other codes such as dress and gesture – there may then be the further anxiety concerning what might be the threatening 'feminine' within themselves. The potential contradictions of liturgical drama can be seen in the admonitions against the effeminizing effect of theatricality. Aelred of Rievaulx, for example, vigorously warns monastic communities against excessively theatrical 'performances' in their liturgical dramas, and in particular against use of 'lascivious gestures and falsetto voices as imitations of women' (cited in Whitta 1997: note 12). The ritual of the liturgy, after all, is designed to effect a union between the earthly and the divine, a unity which may be disrupted by the theatricality – not to say the sexuality – of the cross-dressed performance that takes too much pleasure in itself. Within the monastic liturgical drama of the early Middle Ages, then, there already dwells a suspicion of theatre itself as an inappropriately erotic incursion into the ritual of the liturgy.

2.2.1 'He created them male and female': gender identity and the Creation myth according to Scripture and stage

It is a commonplace of theatre history that while Latin remained the universal language of Christendom, the vernacular plays based on religious narratives 'continued to be the chief means of religious instruction for a largely illiterate population' (Hartnoll 1998: 35). In fact, this somewhat underestimates the power and importance of the Church's own homiletic tradition and the influence held by the pulpit over the lay medieval mind. Even so, as the religious drama emerged from its liturgical beginnings and found its way (not always easily) into the streets and market-places of medieval Europe, its function as a means of religious instruction was one of the main reasons why – for a while at least – the Church supported and encouraged it. Religious instruction at this time reached into every aspect of men's and women's lives; the medieval stage's role as part of the Church's ideological apparatus inevitably meant that it was implicated in the creation and dissemination of gender ideology.

The Old Testament myth of Creation and Fall, which was one of the Bible narratives most frequently played on the medieval stage, includes one of the primal articulations of gender ideology of Western civilization. In recent years the myth of the Fall has frequently been explored by feminist scholars, looking at the figure of Eve. This is particularly useful for our current purposes, since the bright light they have shone on the myth of Eve/Woman acts as an illumination whereby we can see something of the way in which her shadow, Adam/Man, has been culturally constructed.

Medieval playwrights dramatizing the Creation and Fall had a somewhat contradictory source material to deal with. It is hard to know whether or not it was felt as such, but the Old Testament is tantalizingly ambiguous in its account of sex and gender differentiation. There are actually two separate Creation accounts, one of which (Genesis 1: 26–8) states that on the first day God created a division between daytime and night-time; then, on the second day, he created a sky separate from the firmament; on the third he divided the land from the sea, and created all the plants that grow on the land; days four and five saw the creation of the sun, moon and stars, animals, birds and fish. Then, on the sixth day, having created all these God said:

'And now we will make human beings; they will be like us and resemble us. They will have power over the fish, the birds, and all animals, domestic and wild, large and small.' So God created human beings, making them to be like himself. He created them male and female, blessed them, and said, 'Have many children so that your descendants will live all over the world and bring it under their control. I am putting you in charge of the fish, the birds, and all the wild animals.'

(Good News Bible 1976: 5)

That is one version of the Creation myth that has dominated Western culture for thousands of years. A separate narrative, told in Genesis 2, gives an alternative account, in which God makes the universe first, then makes man out of the soil of the earth, then fills the Garden of Eden with plants and animals. Finally

... the Lord God made the man fall into a deep sleep, and while he was sleeping, he took out one of the man's ribs and closed up the flesh. He formed a woman out of the rib and brought her to him. Then the man said,

'At last, here is one of my own kind –
Bone taken from my bone and flesh from my flesh.
Woman is her name because she was taken out of man.'
   That is why a man leaves his father and mother and is united with his wife, and they become one.

(Good News Bible 1976: 5)

The two accounts contradict themselves in a variety of ways, but it is in the aspect of sexual and gender differentiation that they differ most significantly. In the first Creation myth male and female are created on an apparently equal basis and at the same time. There is no difference in the *way* in which they are created, nor is there any role differentiation between them. There is an unspecified number of them (rather than the very definite 'two' of the Adam and Eve story). Both the males and the females are to have equal dominion over the birds and beasts, and both to benefit equally from the grains and fruits which are there to sustain them. In this account of the birth of humanity, there is at the very least an egalitarianism at work, and some readings of the account would take it further than egalitarianism. The phrase 'He created them male and female' might also be understood to refer to a first creation which is androgynous rather than based on oppositional categories. This interpretation, which dates back in Christian thinking at least to Philo in the first century AD suggests that the humans of the first creation were each both male- and female-sexed (see Brown 1991: 94–5). According

to this exegetical tradition, gender differentiation itself was a consequence of the Fall.

This androgynously gendered version of the Creation myth sits inter-
estingly alongside medieval models of biological sexuality. The work of
historian Thomas Laqueur has brought to light the importance to pre-
Enlightenment culture of a Galenic, one-sex model of human sexual
biology (Laqueur 1990: 1–148). According to this model male and
female sexual organs were seen as, effectively, 'the same', with the
woman's genitalia being nothing more than imperfectly formed male
genitalia, which because of lack of the necessary 'heat' have not fully
developed. Thus, even at the biological level, maleness or femaleness is
not an absolute condition determined by the possession or otherwise of
a particular set of reproductive organs, since those organs were not
identified as different in essence, but as belonging to the different
stages of development of a single form. Moreover, these different stages
of development were to be seen in the light of another ubiquitous
medieval idea – that of a scale of perfection, which ranked men towards
the top and women towards the bottom. In contrast to modern assumptions about male and female being complementary but (because of
biology) essentially different, the underlying medieval belief was that
male and female shared the same form, but that the man embodied the
more perfect manifestation of that form. Consequently, argues
Laqueur, it was *gender* – i.e., the *social* definition applied to being a man
or being a woman – rather than biological sexuality which was the foun-
dational idea in the Middle Ages. Medieval cosmology and biology both
include ways of thinking about the relations of sex and gender which are
very different from modern assumptions.

The tradition of androgynous creation, which stresses the account in
Genesis 1, implies that gender differentiation was a consequence of
the Fall. An opposing model, however, foregrounds the second
Creation account, that told in Genesis 2. According to this, gender
differentiation was inherent in Creation itself from the earliest
moments. Man was the primary, woman the secondary product of the
process. She was an afterthought, created to be a companion (some
translations insist 'helper') to the man, and was created out of him. In
medieval dramatizations of the Creation and Fall we can see elements
of both of these traditions.

The vernacular Anglo-Norman *Ordo Repraesentationis Adae* (*The
Service for Representing Adam*) exists in a thirteenth-century manuscript text, although performances may well date back to the twelfth
century in southern England, where Norman French was still the
official language. This incomplete manuscript actually contains three

narrative sections: it tells the story of Adam and Eve, then that of Cain
and Abel, and these are followed by a prophetic afterpiece in which the
Old Testament prophets foretell the coming of the Messiah. The
players were probably clerics, but there is now a civic audience, and
the play exists as a drama in its own right. Its structure and meaning,
however, are still clearly intertwined with liturgical meanings, and the
presence of church ritual is never far away. Its very title (*Ordo* means
'service') shows the extent to which it is still thought of as part of the
religious ritual, and the church choir sing responsories throughout the
play, as they would in the church service. But the *Ordo* has, literally,
moved out of the church: detailed instructions to actors and stage-
builders show that it was designed to be played on the steps *in front* of
a large church or cathedral. Paradise is located at the top of these
steps, with heaven offstage beyond the church doors, through which
the Figure of God enters and exits. Down below are the world,
represented by a fresh patch of earth, and Hell represented by a
gateway and by a collection of pots, cauldrons and kettles – useful both
for banging and for creating the smoke of hellfire.

The *Ordo Repraesentationis Adae* skips over the Creation story itself:
its action starts with Adam and Eve already created and standing
before a mysterious character whom the stage directions refer to as
'the Figure' – and who is clearly meant to represent God. But when the
Figure refers back to their earlier creation, it is made clear that it is the
Genesis 2 version of the story that is being assumed. The play's action,
however, goes straight to the dramatization of the Fall. It fleshes out
the skeleton of the Genesis story by creating both Adam and Eve as
dramatic characters, and allowing them to engage in 'realistic' conversational exchanges, which contrast sharply with the ritualistic dimensions to be found elsewhere in the play. The following extract is typical
of their relationship:

ADAM:	Tell me, wife, what was that evil Satan
	Asking you about? What did he want from you
EVE:	He talked to me about our advancement
ADAM:	Don't believe the traitor! –
	Yes, he is a traitor
EVE :	I know it perfectly well
ADAM:	How do you know?
EVE:	Because I have tried it out.
	What's wrong with his seeing me?
ADAM:	He'll make you change your mind
EVE:	No he won't, because I will believe nothing
	Until I've tested him.

(Bevington 1975: 94)

As Eric Auerbach put it, 'this first man–woman dialogue of universal
import is turned into a scene of everyday reality' (Auerbach 1953: 151).
But this 'everyday reality' is charged with moral and theological meanings
– not least those relating to the gender assumptions of the Middle Ages.

The process of gender stereotyping starts at the very beginning of
the play. Before a word is spoken, the scene is described, with Adam
and Eve standing before the figure of God: 'Adam somewhat nearer,
with peaceful countenance, Eve on the other hand not quite
sufficiently humble' (Bevington 1975: 80). Eve's pride goes before the
Fall. Much of the early part of the play, indeed, is explicitly concerned
with stating and establishing gender roles. The *Ordo* gives an account
of gender hierarchy which assumes that it is inherent in Creation itself.
The Figure of God, in his first speeches to both Adam and Eve, tells
them several times that she has been made to obey, he to rule. To
Adam the Figure says:

> Let her be subject to your commandment
> And both of you to my wish.
> I formed her from your side;
> I fashioned her from your body;
> From you she issued, not from outside.
> Govern her by reason.
> $\qquad$(Bevington 1975: 82)

And he adds to Eve:

> Love Adam and hold him dear.
> He is your husband and you his wife.
> To him be obedient at all times,
> Do not stray from his discipline.
> Serve and love him with willing spirit
> For that is the law of marriage.
> $\qquad$(Bevington 1975: 82)

The theme of obedience is central to the myth of the Fall.
Humanity's disobedience towards God, the human couple's breaking
of the single commandment not to eat the fruit of the forbidden tree, is
here linked with the vow of obedience which is 'the law of marriage'.
The Figure's speeches to Adam and Eve establish a clear hierarchy:
the divine is at the top, the feminine is at the bottom, and the masculine exists in the middle. The divine principle is that of command, the
feminine principle is that of submission – and the masculine principle
involves a combination of the two. The axis of obedience is the central
determinant of gender in the Creation drama.

How else is masculinity constructed in the *Ordo Repraesentationis Adae*? Firstly, the representation of Adam shows him in both his prelapsarian and his fallen states. The prelapsarian Adam embodies (at first, at least) the qualities of rationality, judgement, and strength of character. Unlike its biblical original, this version of the story shows the Devil first attempting to persuade Adam to eat the fruit. Adam virtuously resists the temptation – and the contrast between himself and Eve is thus stressed. Eve succumbs where Adam triumphed, and the masculine/feminine disparity is established. It is in part at least by appealing to the female vanity, which was established as part of Eve's character in the play's first tableau, that the Devil gets his way, telling her:

> You are a delicate and tender thing,
> And fresher than the rose;
> You are whiter than crystal,
> Than snow that falls on ice in the valley.
> The Creator has made an ill-matched pair:
> You are too tender, and he too hard.
> But notwithstanding you are wiser;
> Your mind has discovered great wisdom
> (Bevington 1975: 91)

The *Ordo* rather brilliantly gets the best of both worlds in staging the Devil, who is represented both by a male humanoid figure, and also by a puppet snake, 'artfully constructed', which rises out of the forbidden tree and whispers to Eve. This devil flatters Eve by inverting the presumed gender order of the Middle Ages, and persuading her that in wisdom she is Adam's superior (of course, as far as the medieval audience is concerned, the fact that she believes the devil reinforces the self-evident truth that the woman is *not* wise: they know how the story will end). When she persuades Adam to eat the fruit, she does so in the following terms:

EVE: I've tasted it. My God, what flavor!
I've never savored such sweetness.
What a taste this apple has!
ADAM: Like what?
EVE: Like no mortal taste.
Now my eyes see so clearly
I am like the allpowerful God.
I know all that has been and is to come;
I am complete master of everything.
Eat, Adam, don't hesitate.
You will take it in a lucky hour.

> *Then Adam will take the apple from Eve's hand, saying:*
> [ADAM]:   I'll trust you in this. You are my partner.
> EVE: Eat. Don't be fearful.
> *Then let Adam eat part of the apple.*
>
> (Bevington 1975: 95–6)

The dominant imagery in this staged discourse of the Fall relates to the distortion of 'proper' gender roles as laid down by the Figure in his commands to Adam and Eve. Eve compares herself to 'the allpowerful God' and even describes herself as 'complete *master* of everything' (in the Norman French, 'maistre': see Bevington 1975: 95). Adam, on the other hand, is abandoning the masculine duty of dominance and authority with which God had entrusted him. Instead of 'governing [Eve] by reason', he obeys her, and then justifies himself by saying, 'I'll trust you in this. You are my partner.' But authority and governance, not partnership, was the ordained relationship between masculine and feminine, and Adam's transgression is a failure of masculinity: he is insufficiently strong to live up to the demands of 'governing' Eve.

Ironically, the gender divide is re-established immediately after the moment of the Fall by the differing ways in which Adam and Eve respond to the eating of the fruit. Eve, as we have seen, luxuriates in a sense of 'mastery' of everything. Adam, on the other hand, responds immediately with a sense of horror and of shame:

> *When he has eaten he will recognise his sin at once and will bend over so that he cannot be seen by the people. And he will strip off his festive garments, and will put on poor clothes sewn together with fig leaves, and, manifesting exceedingly great sorrow he will begin his lamentation:*
>
> Alas, sinful wretch what have I done?
> Now I am dead without escape.
>
> (Bevington 1975: 96)

The stage directions at the beginning of the play had referred to the actors as 'Adam ... robed in a red tunic, Eve in a woman's white garment' (Bevington 1975: 80). Now, this change of clothes enacts the play's symbolic representation of the biblical moment in which Adam and Eve recognize their own nakedness. Thus, in *Ordo Repraesentationis Adae* the Fall is presented as the moment when humanity becomes aware that the hierarchical differences which the Figure of God established between masculine and feminine at the start of the play have a concomitant in the genital and biological differences which they can see between themselves. Like its biblical source material, the Creation play has a double vision of gender and sexual difference. On the one hand, it is something that exists from the very beginning; on the other, it is made dramatically present for Adam and Eve only at the moment of the Fall.

The Creation myth in medieval drama, then, involves, among other things, a statement of the Middle Ages' beliefs about the gender order. The *Ordo Repraesentationis Adae* brings the myth down to earth, recasting what had been the archetypal patterns of 'humanity' and 'life' (which were the original meanings of the Hebrew names of Adam and Eve) as the individual psychology of a man called Adam and a woman called Eve. The dramatic realism of the *Ordo Repraesentationis Adae* offers to its audience a series of stereotyped 'meanings' of both masculinity and femininity. Behind it lies the long line of scriptural commentary on Genesis, from Augustine to Aquinas, which suppresses the contradictions of the scriptural accounts of the Creation and stresses the primacy of the male over the female. Thomas Aquinas, who is described as 'represent(ing) in his writings the culmination of scholastic philosophy, the harmony of faith and reason ... one of the greatest monuments of the medieval intellect' (Harvey 1969: 34) elaborates:

> The image of God, in its principal signification, namely the intellectual nature, is found both in man and in woman. But in a secondary sense the image of God is found in man, and not in woman: for man is the beginning and end of woman; as God is the beginning and the end of every creature.
>   (Aquinas 1921–32: vol. IV, part 1, XCIII, p. 4)

It is from these commentators that the gender orthodoxy arises, which we can see being reiterated in medieval biblical dramas of the Creation and Fall. However, we can also, at times, see some of the debates, differences and contradictions which were inherent in this orthodoxy. Thus, while all the dramatic accounts of the Creation myth affirm man's superiority over women, they do not always agree as to the foundation of that superiority. The *Ordo* describes a divinely-sanctioned hierarchy of the masculine and the feminine which has existed from the very moment of their creation, and then illustrates the 'truth' of this by reference to the role played by Eve in the Fall – the second string to the ideological bow designed to justify masculine spiritual superiority.

If we turn from the thirteenth century to the middle of the fifteenth (Connell's key date for the genesis of 'masculinity' in its modern sense) we see differences of detail and of inflection in the way in which the Creation myth is figured, but the broad pattern remains very similar.

Questions of gender are, perhaps, being asked more urgently within the drama. Certainly, the Drapers' pageant of *The Creation and Adam and Eve* (*c*.1461), from the Chester Corpus Christi cycle, explicitly addresses itself to gender differences, and to the mutual definition of masculine and feminine, at every point in its narrative. Before the Fall, for example, Eve is tempted, not by a male Satan or by the ordinary 'snake' of Genesis, but by a seductive, sphinx-like creature, a monstrous feminine which itself will prey on a weakness in Eve – her love of luxuries – which is already characterized as typically feminine. The devil says

> A manner of adder is in this place
> That wynges like a byrd she hase,
> Feete as an adder, a mayden's face;
> Her kindenes I will take.
> And of that tree of paradice
> She [Eve] shall eate through my coyntice,
> For women are full liccoris...
>   (Happé 1975: 70)

As if to stress woman's responsibility for the Fall, the play portrays not only the tempted, but also the tempter, as female in figure.

In the Chester Creation, as in the *Ordo*, it is the Fall itself that creates the conditions which impose a gender scheme, since it brings about an awareness of sexual difference: Adam eats the fruit and immediately becomes aware of the sexuality of his naked body. The stage direction instructs '*Tunc Adam at Eva cooperiant genitalia sua cum foliis*' ('*Then Adam and Eve cover their genitals with leaves*'; see Happé 1975: 73). But it is the divine punishment for disobedience that really establishes the basic outline of the gender order. After Adam and Eve have eaten the apple, and as they are about to be expelled from Paradise, God tells Eve:

> And woman, I warne thee wytterlie
> Thy mischeife I shall multeply;
> With penaunce, sorrow and great anoye
> Thy children shalt thou beare.
> And for thou hast done to-daye
> The man shall mayster thee alwaye,
> And under his power thou shalt be aye,
> Thee for to drive and deere.
>   (Happé 1975: 74)

The play, then, expresses a clear justification of man's superiority over woman. It is attributed to the divine punishment handed down as a direct consequence of Eve's disobedience: she will be subordinate to man because of what 'thou hast done to-daye'. Far more insistently than the *Ordo* (which simply took for granted a pre-existing gender order) this dramatic text from the middle of the fourteenth century establishes a gender diagram in which masculinity is defined in opposition to femininity, and in which a gender hierarchy is institutionalized through reference to and interpretation of the teachings of the Church.

2.2.2 *Myths of the father and the son*

The mythology of the ancient world abounds in narratives which tell of relationships – and of crises in relationships – between fathers and sons. Sometimes these narratives outlive their own social origins, and are read and reread, told and retold, in circumstances and societies far removed from those which first generated them, so as to offer new meanings for succeeding generations. The story of Oedipus, of course, is one of the most powerful and most enduring of these, and has been culturally appropriated by Freudian and post-Freudian psychoanalytic theory in order to develop and articulate a particularly modern understanding of both gender and subjectivity. In the Oedipus myth, as told by Sophocles, the conflict between father and son is first delayed (by the abandoning of Oedipus on the hillside); it is then apparently resolved by the murder of the father by the son; it then resurfaces in the incestuous aftermath of Oedipus' encounter with Laius at the crossroads and is brought to light with the inevitable tragic results. When Freud used Sophocles' drama as his central emblem for masculine psychic development he focused on that aspect of it which facilitated the central image of his own universalising narrative: the imperative of the son to challenge the potentially castrating father for possession of the mother. Inherent in the Freudian narrative is the nightmare figure of the destroying father, who has to be encountered by the son. It is a figure which Freud might have drawn from a rather different narrative: Genesis 22: 1–13:

> God tested Abraham; he called to him 'Abraham!' And Abraham answered, 'Yes, here I am!'
> 'Take your son,' God said, 'your only son, Isaac, whom you love so much, and go to the land of Moriah. There, on a mountain that I will show you, offer him as a sacrifice to me.'

Early the next morning, Abraham cut some wood for the sacrifice, loaded his donkey, and took Isaac and two servants with him. They started out for the place that God had told him about. On the third day Abraham saw the place in the distance. Then he said to the servants, 'I will go over there and worship and then we will come back to you.'

Abraham made Isaac carry the wood for the sacrifice, and he himself carried the a knife and live coals for starting the fire. As they walked along together, Isaac said, 'Father!'

He answered, 'Yes, my son?'

Isaac asked, 'I see that you have the coals and the wood, but where is the lamb for the sacrifice?'

Abraham answered 'God himself will provide one.' And the two of them walked on together.

When they came to the place which God had told him about, Abraham built an altar and arranged the wood on it. He tied up his son and placed him on the altar, on top of the wood. Then he picked up the knife to kill him. But the angel of the Lord called to him from heaven, 'Abraham, Abraham!'

He answered, 'Yes, here I am.'

'Don't hurt the boy or do anything to him,' he said. 'Now I know that you honour and obey God, because you have not kept back your only son from me.'

Abraham looked round and saw a ram caught in a bush by its horns. He went and got it, and offered it as a burnt-offering instead of his son.

                                                        (*Good News Bible* 1976: 24)

Like the Creation myth, the story of Abraham and Isaac is a vitally important cultural myth – one of the key narratives, in fact, of Western patriarchy. Once more, a complex relationship then develops between the pre-existing myth, the theatrical artefact which a particular society made of it, and the way in which that was appropriated by the culture at large.

It is, in all senses, a dramatic story. The father, in response to a divine authority located beyond himself, is called upon to sacrifice his son, Isaac. He takes him up a hill and prepares to perform the sacrifice. At the last moment there is an interruption: an angel stays his hand, telling him to sacrifice instead a ram which is caught in the nearby briars. Having passed the test of obedience, Abraham and Isaac return home rejoicing. The sparseness of the story in its scriptural form calls out for a theatrical realization. Its overall shape, with its conflict, climax and resolution all closely interwoven, is inherently stageable: it is small wonder that the playwrights of the medieval mystery companies seized upon this as one of the stories to dramatize in their cycles of sacred dramas.

The Brome manuscript of the play *The Sacrifice of Isaac* is the sole surviving text from what was probably a civic cycle of pageants closely related to the Chester cycle. The narrative starts with Abraham and Isaac in prayer. Abraham's prayer of thanks makes a direct reference to how God 'madist Adam, And Eve' – and thus immediately links this play with the story of the Fall and its test of obedience. As with the Tree of Knowledge in the Garden, the Isaac narrative sets in opposition love for God and love for a single prized earthly thing, and then tests one against the other. Abraham is quite explicit:

> I love nothing so myche, iwisse,
> Excepte thine owyn self, dere Fader of blysse
> As Isaac here, my owyn swete son.
>   (Bevington 1975: 308)

Once more the dramatic characterization adds psychological detail which is absent from the biblical account. Where Genesis had simply had God instruct Adam, out of the blue, to 'Take your son ... your only son, Isaac, whom you love so much', the Brome version spends some time establishing Abraham's special love for Isaac – in such a way as to provide a logical cue for God to decide on the 'sacrifice' as an appropriate test of Abraham's obedience. Ironically unaware of the test which awaits him, Abraham continues innocently with his prayers until the Angel delivers God's message. When he receives the message, it provokes a subtle, internal conflict in him: not so much between Abraham and God as between Abraham and himself. His divided loyalties, to the son he loves and to the God whom he worships, conjure up a clear picture of a man pulled in two directions at once. The struggle is short-lived, however, and Abraham and Isaac set off for the mountain: the dramatic irony intensifies as they approach the place of sacrifice, for Isaac does not yet know what this sacrifice will entail. It begins to dawn on him, however, that there is something wrong:

> And also, fader, evermore dred I:
> Where is yowre qweke best that ye schuld kill?
> Both fyer and wood we have redy
> But qweke best have we none on this hill.
> A qwike best, I wot well, must be ded
> Yowre sacrifice for to make.
>   (Bevington 1975: 312)

The boy's insistently repetitive questions about the 'qweke best' – the 'live animal' which is to be used for the sacrifice – add an intensity and a poignancy to the dramatic irony of his situation (it is the equivalent of Isaac's biblical 'Where is the lamb for the sacrifice?'). When finally he learns of his father's intention, he bursts out:

> Now I wold to God my moder were here on this hill!
> Sche woold knele for me on both hir kneys
> To save my liffe.
> And sithyn that my moder is not here,
> I prey yow, fader, schonge yowr chere
> And kill me not with yowyre kniffe.
>   (Bevington 1975: 313)

Isaac's calling upon his mother is another significant addition to the biblical narrative. Genesis 22: 10 simply recounts: 'When they came to the place which God had told him about, Abraham built an altar and arranged the wood on it. He tied up his son and placed him on the altar, on top of the wood. Then he picked up the knife to kill him.' In the play, Isaac's words have the dramatic effect of drawing attention to the absence of the mother. This is a story all of whose protagonists are men: women have no place in it – except to be called upon as the absent principle of a human tenderness and emotion. But if this feminine principle represents compassionate humanity it also, like Eve, represents disobedience to the divine: the absent mother is invoked as one who would *not* obey the divine injunction to kill her own child. We will see at the end of the play what we are supposed to make of this.

Meanwhile the father/son dialogue continues, with Abraham persuading Isaac that if he does not sacrifice him he will be going against God's express command. Isaac responds dutifully:

> Nay, nay, fader, God forbede
> That ever ye schuld greve him for me!
> ... Therefore doo owre Lordys bidding,
> And, whan I am dede, than prey for me.
> But good fader, tell ye my moder nothing.
> Say that I am in another cuntre dwelling.
>   (Bevington 1975: 314)

As Isaac becomes complicit in the act of sacrifice, he moves out of the feminine realm into the masculine, and he and Abraham begin rigorously to exclude the feminine. Now, far from being called upon to intervene, Isaac's mother is not even to be told of the event: Isaac wants her to believe he is alive in another country. The act of sacrifice, the act of obedience, becomes a pact between the father and the son – a pact whose exclusion of the feminine is repeated as Isaac first sends greetings to his mother, and then repeats his injunction of silence to Abraham:

> But fader, I prey yow evermore,
> Tell ye my moder no dell.
> Iffe sche wost it, sche wold wepe full sore,
> For iwisse, fader, sche loveth me full well;
> Goddys blissing mote she have!
> (Bevington 1975: 316)

What is taking place between Abraham and Isaac is a purely masculine ritual – a ritual of fathers and sons, undertaken before the eyes of a God who is also figured as 'Father'. It resembles the male rites of passage which have been of such interest to modern anthropologists. These, too, typical involve a period of sexual segregation, a journey, often the fear or danger of death, and eventually some form of sacred initiation of the adolescent male by the elders of the tribe. And on one level, indeed, it may be that the Old Testament myth of Abraham and Isaac had its roots in some such ritualistic practices.

For the Christian dramatist of the Brome manuscript this myth of the father and the son is a myth which reiterates the theme of obedience: Abraham's obedience to the father-god is mirrored in Isaac's obedience to the tribal patriarch. Both father and son respond to the challenge they are set in ways that are contrasted to the Eden narrative, which had been invoked at the start of the play. Where Adam and Eve had disobeyed, Abraham and Isaac obey, despite the apparent monstrosity of the command, and if Abraham is the focus of attention at the start of the play, it is his son who soon takes centre stage: the pathos of the child facing death is played for all is it worth, and the playwright delays the moment of sacrifice so as to extract maximum dramatic effect from the tension. The happy ending brings about the release of this tension. By obeying in spirit, Abraham is relieved of the necessity of carrying out the consequences of his obedience: the Angel stays his hand, Isaac is sent to fetch the ram, which Abraham offers to God, who proclaims his blessings on Abraham and his tribe. Isaac looks forward to returning home and rejoining his mother:

> Lord God, I thanke thee with all my hart,
> For I am glad that I schall liffe

> And kis onys my dere mother ...
> I had never so good will to gon hom
> And to speke with my dere moder.
>   (Bevington 1975: 319–20)

The masculine segregation is over. However, as the play draws to a conclusion, another figure steps forward: the 'Doctor' – a narrator who will underline the moral, about how 'this story schowith yow here, How we schuld kepe, to owre powere, Goddys commawndmentys without groching'. He challenges the audience as to how they would react under similar situations, and then once more points the gender lesson, pouring scorn on

> ...thise women that wepe so sorowfully
> Whan that hir childryn dey them froo,
> As nater woll, and kind.
> It is but folly, I may well avooe...
>   (Bevington 1975: 321)

Masculine fortitude is being set against feminine weakness, of course. The strength which comes from obedience to God is charac- terized as a specifically masculine quality, to be contrasted with the 'folly' of women who cry for their dead children! This amounts to more than a caricatured male stiff upper lip, however. The Isaac story was used to tell an early version of the sacrificial story which, in its later Christian form, would become the central myth of a civilization.

Christian theology in general, but particularly in the Middle Ages, reads the Old Testament in the light of the New. Many of the stories, events and characters of the Old Testament thus become seen as foreshadowings of those in the New Testament, and their meanings interpreted accordingly. Particularly important are the *antetypes* of Christ: those examples of Christ-like narratives which are to be found in earlier Jewish (and according to some commentators, in Graeco-Roman) mythology. For these could be used to prove Divine purpose, demonstrating that God had planned the ultimate drama of the Crucifixion all along, and had foreshadowed it in events narrated in all innocence by the scribes of the Old Testament. Or, in a more sophisticated version of the same idea, that in the eyes of God for whom all events are immanent, the Crucifixion exists simultaneously in events elsewhere in what we can only dimly perceive through his- torical time. In any case, the story of Isaac is, in this view, an antetype of the sacrifice and the Resurrection of Jesus. It is not only in the overall narrative pattern – the story of a father sacrificing his only son – that the similarity inheres. The details are abundant. The sacrificial place, on a mountain in Moriah, corresponds to the crucifixion hill of Golgotha; Isaac, like Jesus, carries on his back the wood on which he is to be sacrificed; the discourse turns Isaac, in terms which are later to be echoed by New Testament iconography, into the counterpart of the sacrificial lamb, and like both the lamb and the divine sacrificial victim of the New Testament, he is bound for the sacrifice. Even the great age of Abraham (he is, according to the biblical account, well over 100 at this time and seemingly hale and hearty) adds a mythical dimension to the father/son relationship: the father is in some way superhuman, the son all too vulnerably human. And at the climax of this narrative is the miraculous escape, the return to life of the victim. In Isaac's case it happens before the knife falls; in the case of Jesus the miracle is delayed, and eventually located in the resurrection from the tomb. The medieval Christian audience is encouraged to understand these narratives in something like structuralist terms, and to see the staging of the alien Jewish ritual of animal sacrifice as prefiguring the Christian narrative of sacrifice – which is then figured in the familiar Christian ritual of the Mass which metaphorically embodies both. The Brome *Isaac* locates this story in terms of a father/son relationship which elevates everyday filial obedience to a divine principle. In the process it excludes women both in its narrative structure, in the discourse which that narrative structure employs, and in the gender-specific lessons which the Doctor draws from the narrative at the end.

Thus, medieval dramatizations of the Creation myth popularize and to some extent help to create the gendered world-view in which the development of masculinity in its modern sense takes place. The keynote is the sense of duty and obedience. In the plays based on the biblical narrative of Abraham and Isaac, we see a different exploration of masculine identity but with the same underlying theme. And this is the paradox: that the structure of medieval gender relations, drawing on the Eden story, repeatedly insists on the masculine as dominant and the feminine as subservient to masculine authority:

> Love Adam and hold him dear.
> He is your husband and you his wife.
> To him be obedient at all times,
> Do not stray from his discipline.
> Serve and love him with willing spirit
> For that is the law of marriage.
>   (Bevington 1975: 82)

It would be easy to leave it at that and see the masculine as embodying a principle of authority, and the feminine as embodying one of obedience. And, so far as this goes, there is a truth to this. Beyond this, however, there is a level of obedience which is exclusively masculine. It is expected only of men, and it is central to the construction of the masculine: women do not figure in its narrative. It connects the (male) human with the divine, and it is figured in the repeated pattern of the interaction between human and divine which is implicit in the God/Jesus/Abraham/Isaac nexus. Far more explicitly than its scriptural sources, the Brome *Isaac* constructs a masculinity which is based on this principle of sacred obedience.

I have stressed the didactic aspects of the play and the way in which it consciously sets out to address a particular agenda, initially about humanity's relation to the Divine narrative, but also about masculine identity. However, plays work unconsciously as well as consciously, and I want to end this section with an afterthought which is in effect a caveat concerning the relationship between the imagination and ideology. The Doctor's moralising at the end is intended to ensure that nobody in the audience should misunderstand the didactic import of the play. To the men in that audience the play addresses messages about what is expected of them *as* men: as fathers, sons and 'sons' of the Divine father. To women it says something less inspiring: that they are somehow excluded by their very natures from an essential continuum which exists between the obedient masculine human and the divine. However, audiences do not always hear only what they are meant to hear: children in particular are adept at creating meanings of their own. Beneath the narrative, which legitimates patriarchal authority in the name of Divine authority, there lurks the nightmare image of the murdering father, knife raised against his helpless son, carrying out the incomprehensible will of a God whose commands may not be obeyed. The story ends happily and reassuringly. But it is not always the endings of stories which are the most memorable or which have the deepest psychic impacts.

2.3 Gendering moralities

In the English morality plays of the late medieval period, the personified abstractions which are its protagonists, antagonists and supporting characters play out stories which deal with basic questions of personal identity. Although the plays are devised to be acted by an all-male cast, several of these allegorical dramas nonetheless include both male and female characters. Where this happens we can see ways in which the moral absolutes which structure the medieval sense of self have a gendered dimension: it is possible to map 'masculinity' and 'femininity' onto the categories of virtue and vice which make up the individual identity. Given what we have seen earlier in the plays dealing with the creation story, we might almost expect the vices to be gendered feminine, all the virtues masculine. This would fit, too, with how we might expect the Morality plays' typical conflict between heavenly and earthly values to work in relation to the broader medieval gender polarity which can be found in the writings of authorities such as Thomas Aquinas, who abstracted 'the masculine as form, the feminine as matter, with the godlike masculine intellect imposing form on inert, amorphous feminine matter' (Spivack 1988: 137).

However, gender ideology does not always work so predictably. Indeed, in *The Castle of Perseverance*, which is the earliest morality play of which a full text still survives, the diagram is the opposite way round. Of the worldly vices which lead the central character, Humanum Genus (Humankind), towards perdition in the first part of the play, all but one are male. Meanwhile the spiritual virtues who inhabit the Castle itself are 'These ladys of goodnesse', Charity, Humility, Patience, Abstinence, Chastity, Industry, and Generosity (Bevington 1975: 868), who seem to reflect the idealized feminine of the Virgin Mary rather than the fallen feminine of Eve. Thus, in broad terms *The Castle of Perseverance* presents a binary opposition in which the body and its worldly desires are gendered masculine, while the soul's striving towards goodness and eternity are gendered feminine. In fact, it is not quite as straightforward as this, since the one very definitely 'feminine' Vice within the play is Lechery. As Charlotte Spivack argues, 'the concept of the female as the spiritual side of the human being is undermined by its dual and contradictory representation as Chastity and Lechery' (Spivack 1988: 139). The gendering of the virtues and vices in medieval morality plays thus involves various paradoxes. Idealized femininity replaces the fallen Eve, while masculinity represents all the lusts of the flesh, with the exception of the most fleshly of these lusts, lechery itself.

It is in this detail that we can see most clearly the deeper structure of the moral diagram. When Humanum Genus is tempted by Lechery it is in these terms:

> Be a lechour til thou die
> Thy nedys schal be the better sped
> If thou gif thee to fleschly folye ...

> Therefore, Mankind, my leve lemman,
> I[n] my cunte thou schalt crepe
> (Bevington 1975: 832)

The central protagonist is called Humanum Genus, and apparently represents (Hu)Mankind. But, as Lechery's invitation makes clear, Humanum Genus is a man. More powerful, perhaps, than the details of gendering the virtues and vices is the overarching medieval assumption that the default mode of Humankind is masculine.

The title of a later morality play *Mankind* (*c*.1470) performs a similar sleight of hand, eliding the general and the gendered. On one level the play's protagonist seems to be a representative character who stands for all humanity, male and female alike. In fact, though, it is a specifically male figure whose story is told in the play. Mankind, the central figure, is represented as a set of symbolic contradictions which allow him to represent different classes of men: he carries a spade, which marks him as a labourer, and also links him, iconically, to Adam the first gardener, condemned for his disobedience to earn his daily bread by the sweat of his brow. He also, however, carries a scholar's pen and ink, and wears the long gown of the citizen of substance. Mankind represents several classes but only one gender. Unlike *The Castle of Perseverance, Mankind* creates a fictional world which is entirely male. There are no women characters, and women receive few mentions in the dialogue: the Virgin Mary is occasionally invoked in holiness or blasphemy and Nowadays' absent wife becomes the butt of some tired marital jokes. And – in a more sinister key – a passing reference is made to the jailer's wife whom Mischief raped after escaping from prison and murdering her husband.

This all-male play may also originally have been performed in an all-male environment.

> Throughout the play there is no reference to women in the audience. When specific reference is made it is to 'sirs' (331, 474, 696), 'yeomanry' (333), 'master(s)' (468, 609). Only 'sovereigns' – by far the commonest mode of address, however – is not purely masculine. So we are left with an audience of mixed social status, possibly all male, some seated, some standing. The maleness could be the most significant item and point to a male religious house or a Cambridge college or hall, or an all-male civic gathering as the place of performance.
>
> (Meredith 1997: 11)

In medieval drama the relationship between audience and performers is always an intimate one, and the boundaries between the fictional world of the performers and the everyday world of the audience are provisional. The dramaturgy of *Mankind* is sophisticated enough to recognize this and to capitalize on it. In the opening moments of the play the figure of Mercy stands alone on the stage and speaks directly to the audience. He reminds the spectators of the central tenets of the Christian story of salvation in the following terms:

> It may be seyde and verifiede: mankinde was dere bought
> By the pitouse deth of Jhesu he hade his remedye.
> He was purgyde of his defawte, that wrechydly hade wrought,
> By His glorius Passion, that blissyde lavatorye.
> O soverence, I beseche yow yowr condicions to rectifye,
> Ande with humilité and reverence to have a remocion
> To this blissyde prince that owr nature doth glorifye,
> That ye may be participable of his retribucion.
>
> (Bevington 1975: 903)

The shift from the third person to the second in the direct address makes it clear that 'mankind' is the audience itself. Only later (after the appearance of several supporting characters) does a figure called 'Mankind' actually appear on the stage and offer the audience an externalized image of itself. Mankind is both character and audience, and the playwright uses this duality 'to play with the audience's awareness, or lack of awareness of its own identity with the character and consequently of its own involvement in sin' (Meredith 1997: 21). This interplay between the audience and the stage is intensified if the audience, like the play, is indeed an all-male one.

The absence of women in *Mankind* is underscored by the way in which the play represents the figure of Mercy. In medieval iconography Mercy is most commonly represented as a woman. In this play, however, Mercy is represented as a priest or friar: Mankind first addresses him with the greeting 'All heyll, semely father', while Mercy later refers to himself as the 'father ghostly' to Mankind (Bevington 1975: 910, 932). This priestly figure of Mercy is central to the action of the play; he speaks the Prologue and the Epilogue and protects Mankind throughout from the machinations of the Vice-figures, finally bringing him to grace.

In the other well-known morality play from this period, *Everyman* (*c*.1495), the eponymous protagonist (once more male by implication) is not assailed by temptation or vice. Rather, with death impending, he turns to a variety of allegorical figures, both male and female, such as Knowledge, Beauty, Strength, Good-Deeds and others in an attempt to find salvation through them. These personified abstractions represent significant aspects of his identity in his past life; some turn out to be useless to him in the face of approaching death, others offer him good advice or help. *Everyman* shows comparatively little of the humour and playfulness with the audience which characterizes *Mankind*. It is relatively solemn and concentrates intensely on the orthodox teaching of the medieval Christian church regarding the importance of the seven sacraments in the scheme of salvation. At the play's climax Everyman, the protagonist, receives the sacrament of 'Goddes precious flesshe and bloode' (Bevington 1975: 958). The moment in itself could be a theologically as well as a dramatically complicated one, as ritual and theatre confront each other. If a character in a fictional representation enacts the receiving of the sacrament of communion – what does that do to the status of the ritual itself? The medieval playwright evades the question by having the action take place off-stage. To fill the gap in performance, however, a debate takes place between two of the subsidiary characters, Five Wittes and Knowledge. It is Five Wittes who has persuaded Everyman to take the sacrament in the first place, but his argument has led him away from considerations purely of Everyman's own spiritual state towards an encomium on the power and importance of the clergy. Thus, when Everyman announces his intention to go and seek a priest to receive the Mass, Five Wittes replies:

> Everyman, that is the best that ye can do.
> God will you to salvation bringe,
> For preesthode excedeth all other thinge.
> To us holy Scripture they do teche,
> And converteth man from sinne, heven to reche.
> God hath to them more power given
> Than to ony aungell that is in heven.
> With five wordes he may consecrate
> Goddes body in flesshe and blode to make,
> And handeleth his Maker bitwene his hande[s].
> The preest bindeth and unbindeth all bandes,
> Both in erth and heven ...
> No remedy we finde under God
> But all only preesthode.
> Everyman, God gave preest[s] that dignité
> And setteth them in his stede amonge us to be.
> Thus be they above aungells in degree.
>   (Bevington 1975: 958–9)

It is a strange and powerful speech, and it introduces a sequence which (as *Mankind* did in a different way) ensures that it is the priesthood which holds centre stage at the end of the play. While Everyman goes off-stage to receive the sacrament, Knowledge replies somewhat scep-tically to Five Wittes' encomium: he talks of priests who buy and sell the sacraments, and complains that

> Sinfull preestes giveth the sinners example bad:
> Their children sitteth by other mennes fires, I have harde;
> And some haunteth womens company
> With unclene life, as lustes of lechery.
> These be with sinne made blinde
>
> (Bevington 1975: 959)

So at this climactic moment of the play – as the protagonist reaches a spiritual turning-point and receives the sacrament off-stage – the on-stage action involves an argument about the clergy. On the one hand, the priests are 'above aungells in degree'; on the other, many of them are corrupt – and specifically, here, they are sexually corrupt, spawning illegitimate children who sit by other mens' fires like cuckoos in the nest while the priests haunt women's company. It is a debate which had been going on for a few hundred years.

It had its roots in the emergence, during the early Middle Ages, of a male clergy which monopolized many positions of power and influence on both a national and a local scale. Clerical (as opposed to merely monastic) celibacy was an important tenet for this new power elite, who consequently abandoned masculine sexual and marital roles. The medieval cleric also abandoned many of medieval society's traditional visual signifiers of masculinity: in theory at least, he carried no weapons; like a woman he rode a mule rather than a horse; and he wore clothing that was in cut more like a woman's dress than a man's. As a result, the clergy effectively formed a third 'gender' in medieval society, one whose behaviours and values operated outside the established behaviours and values of the non-celibate laity. To describe this 'third gender' the term 'emasculinity' has been coined, referring to the emasculated male, who has chosen quite deliberately to renounce many of the appearances and behaviours of traditional masculinity precisely in order to aspire to the status of being 'above aungells in degree' (Swanson 1999: 161). Emasculation in this sense, however, does not mean powerlessness. On the contrary, the emasculine males of the Christian church monopolized many of the positions of power in the medieval world, to the particular exclusion of women, but to the exclusion also of secular and non-celibate males.

Clerical emasculinity, though, seems to have been treated with some suspicion by the laity, and indeed this assumption of an ambiguous gender identity may well have proved problematic for many monastics and priests themselves. The frequent complaints that priests were often to be found indulging in 'lustes of lechery' show that they were not trusted to have excluded altogether the residual desires of their biological maleness. Another source, however, of the complaints against the priesthood may well have been the threat which emasculinity was seen to pose to the masculine order of medieval secular society:

> In addition to the danger of clerical sexual advances, lay male authority might be challenged in other ways. Clerical idealists who really believed in their emasculinity, and in its benefits, not unnaturally sought adherents and followers. The advancement of emasculinity transformed the threat posed by clerical activity from that of the importation of cuckoo offspring, to the dissolution of lineage and household. Chastity, and the renunciation of family bonds, threatened patriarchy, patrilinearity, and patrimony, especially if male renunciation was encouraged ... Hostility to the mendicant orders found voice in allegations that they enticed young boys to join them, resulting in England in a Statute against the practice.
>
> (Swanson 1999: 171–2)

The power of the emasculate clergy first raised anxieties about gender and masculinity at the time of the Gregorian ecclesiastical reforms of the early medieval period. These anxieties, however, do not seem to have been completely assuaged (in Britain at least) until the time of the Henrician Reformation. In *Everyman*, the complaints against the clergy are acknowledged, but are then brushed aside. Five Wittes' response ends the argument:

> I trust to God no suche may we finde.
> Therefore let us preesthode honour,
> And folowe their doctrine for our soules socoure.
> We be their shepe, and they shepherdes be,
> By whome we all be kepte in suerté.
>
> (Bevington 1975: 959)

The tone and placing of the debate suggests a rhetorical purpose which goes beyond simply restating the commonplace, and which looks more like an urgent defence of a clergy which is already under threat in the years leading up to the Reformation. The central character of the play may be Everyman himself, but its central theme is the importance of the sacraments and of the priesthood. The play seems to be as concerned to stress the power and influence of the 'third gender', the clergy, as it is to depict the spiritual journey of the individual soul. And the debate between Five Wittes and Knowledge suggests that at the end of the fifteenth century the debate about the angelic emasculine and the all-too-earthly masculine was still a pressing one.

2.4 Outlaw and carnival masculinity: the folk plays and games of Robin Hood

> A boy in church, hearing either the Summer Lord with his may-game or Robin Hood with his morris dance going by the church – out goes the boy.
>
> Anon. 1589

Thus the liturgical and cycle plays and the later moralities represented a masculinity which was mediated by the authority of the Church – even if that authority could not always control exactly how they should be understood by their audiences. The masculine figures in the morality plays derive in the first place from the rhetoric of the pulpit, while the original biblical texts which formed the basis for the stories of the liturgical and cycle plays enacted a narrative of masculine authority. The Church and workplace structures, which governed the production of these texts as dramatic performances, reaffirmed and sometimes intensified the authoritative messages of a patriarchal and hierarchical Christian ethical and social scheme. Both as text and as performance, these stories are determined by their relation to a Church-based orthodoxy concerning the truth of masculine personal and societal identity. Alongside these dominant dramatic forms, however, there was another tradition of quasi-theatrical performance in England and Scotland which had a rather different relation to the hegemonic influence of the Church. The folk plays and dramatic games of the period are performative events at which playing, dramatic narrative, ritual and pageant converge. In this section I shall look at the way in which masculinity is represented and problematized in this, rather different, kind of medieval drama.

Inevitably, there are relatively few dramatic texts of these folk plays still in existence which can be confidently attributed to the medieval period. As with much folk art, what there is tends to stem from documentation dating from well after the event. There may be traces of the medieval dramas in the eighteenth- and nineteenth-century local survivals and revivals of Mumming plays and Plough plays, involving various combinations of Hero Combats, Sword Dances and Wooing Ceremonies. Questions of age and authenticity are always complex in such instances; in the case of plays and performances based on the stories of Robin Hood, however, repeated documented references allow us to trace a tradition back to late medieval times.

Robin Hood is a figure who has been used as an icon of heroic masculinity for hundreds of years. He appears repeatedly in plays, poems, novels, films and television programmes, reshaped each time according to the needs of each successive culture. The material for the Robin Hood legend was initially generated and perpetuated in anonymous medieval ballads such as 'Robin Hood and the Potter' and 'Robin Hood and Guy of Gisborne'. Stories of Robin Hood probably first circulated in such rhymed narratives, which seem to have originated during the years just before the Peasants' Revolt. It may be that, on one level at least, this fantasy of the outlaw hero originally represented a political wish-fulfilment narrative. The medieval plays and games based around the figure of Robin Hood probably date from the 1420s, after the ballads were already in circulation, and they may have used the ballads as source material (see Wiles 1981: 2ff.). Medieval spectators almost certainly experienced a sense of continuity between the legendary character whose exploits they had heard depicted in ballads, rhymes and *gests*, and the dramatic-ritualistic figure who paraded and played before them in the Robin Hood plays and games of the fifteenth and sixteenth centuries. Thus these Robin Hood plays not only provide a further example of a dramatized masculinity in the shape of the mythological outlaw; they also become the occasion for a kind of ritualized masculine behaviour which was itself shaped by the framework of the Robin Hood legend.

The performances frequently provided an excuse for rowdy, and even riotous behaviour on the part of the young men of the locality. They offered them licence to roam round, 'proving their manhood' through violent and semi-violent activities in ways which are still recognizable today as the social bonding rites of the adolescent male. The events surrounding the medieval performances of Robin Hood narratives constituted 'play' in both senses of the word – both in the sense of participatory games and in the sense of a dramatic performance. The earliest examples of these seem to have been largely in the form of a procession, in which 'Robin' and his followers would descend upon a local town or community. 'Robin Hood' himself would be an elected figure, and it was not only an honour but also a duty to act if so elected: refusal brought with it a hefty fine. The number of Robin's companions would vary from a dozen to over a hundred. Some of these would be named 'characters' from the legends dressed in full costume; the rest would be bit-part players, clothed in token 'liveries'. Robin's pageant would be secular in principle, though frequently associated with the church in practice, for one essential purpose of the Robin Hood games was the collecting of money for the parish church – sometimes by simply demanding the money, sometimes by selling the 'liveries' of Robin's followers. Little distinction would have been made between spectators and participants, and the celebrations would end in feasting. The Robin Hood game thus took on the character of a rather sophisticated and thematically based 'church-ale', the Tudor community celebration whose purpose was to raise funds which might be used directly for the church itself, or else disbursed for parish activities such as the repair of the roads.

These Robin Hood performances seem mainly to have taken place from Whitsuntide onwards:

> At Paske [Easter] began our morris, and ere Pentecost our May,
> Tho Robin Hood, Li'ell John, Friar Tuck and Marian deftly play.
> (Warner 1589: 108)

wrote the Elizabethan William Warner. It seems probable that, as the Robin Hood play-games developed, they grew more elaborate, and absorbed other forms of entertainment, such as May-games and the Morris. Contests and competitions, in which young men were encouraged to demonstrate their athletic prowess, also became incorporated into the event. In particular, of course, the Robin Hood framework encouraged archery competitions, and this fitted with the Tudor legal requirement that all men under the age of 40 should regularly practise at the longbow – thereby ensuring a skilled reserve force of trained men from which a militia might at short notice be raised. From the late fifteenth century at least, there is also evidence that these celebrations included the formal staging of plays based upon the legendary narratives of the outlaw of Sherwood. The fragmentary texts of a few of these have been preserved. The earliest is a 42-line dramatic fragment, dating from about 1475. It comprises a sparsely written skeleton dialogue around which sequences of physical actions – the chases, fights and escapes which were the main interest of the performance – would be structured, either as improvisation or as rehearsed sequences of dramatic sword-play. From this skeleton it is possible to reconstruct a plot, which appears to involve a scene in which a knight and the sheriff plot to capture Robin Hood. This results in Robin taking on the knight, first of all in a sporting contest and then in a fight to the death; in both of these Robin emerges victorious. Then follows another scene, which is only very loosely connected to the first (see Wiles 1981: 34–5). In this Robin and his outlaws are captured and imprisoned by the Sheriff; they escape, however, and lock the Sheriff and his men in the Sheriff's own prison.

But while a dramatic performance appears to have been an important element of the Robin Hood 'play-games', and in all likelihood an
increasingly frequent and prominent element as time went on, it is the
communal and participatory dimensions of 'playing', the processions
and the money-raising, which are central to these Robin Hood celebrations. Whatever the specific constituents of the celebrations, which
will have varied from place to place, there was always an element of
carnival implicit. At its most extreme, this may have been quite pro-
nounced, in those communities which chose to emphasize Robin's
outlaw status.

This gives rise to a certain degree of ambiguity. Robin, in his identity simultaneously as a figure in a dramatized narrative, and as a
figure of carnivalesque authority in the community which staged the
games, existed somewhere between fiction and reality. This may have
been emphasized by the way in which the events of the holiday itself,
with archery competitions and other such contests, came to mirror
the events of the fictions. Even more significantly, the officially sanctioned money-gathering of Robin and his followers frequently looked
very much like outlaw activity, and could become a fairly boisterous
event. The impersonation of a legendary outlaw occasionally allowed
a genuine lawlessness to assert itself, and the boundaries between
play and riot were not always clear. There are several documented
examples in which the role-playing became reality, and those who
played the part of Robin Hood and his men actually did threaten the
local noblemen, the landowners, and even on occasion effect a rescue
– in the best tradition of later Robins – of a comrade from prison. In
1497 over a hundred men from Wednesbury in the Midlands, led by
Roger (or Robert) Marshall, in the guise of Robin and his band,
assembled in order to rescue two of their fellow-townsmen who had
previously been arrested and imprisoned by the neighbouring Walsall
authorities for assault. Uttering dire threats against any Walsall men
they might meet, 'Robin' and his men descended on Willenhall fair –
with the result that Marshall was accused before the Star Chamber of
riotous assembly. In his defence he claimed that he had simply been
acting out the traditional role of Robin Hood as church fund-raiser,
since

> hit hath byn of olde tymes used and accustumed on the said fere day that
> wyth the inhabitants of Wolverhampton, Wednesbury and Walsall have
> comyn to the said fere the capitanns called the Abot of Marham or Robyn
> Hodys to the intent to gether money with their disportes to the profight of
> the chirches of the seid lordships.

(cited in Holt 1982: 149)

In 1536 we find Sir Richard Morison expressing concern about the effect of the games on secular authority, and warning Henry VIII that:

> In summer commonly upon the holy days in most places of your realm there be plays of Robin Hood, Maid Marian, Friar Tuck: wherein, besides the lewdness and ribaldry that there is opened to the people, disobedience also to your officers is taught whilst these good bloods go about to take from the Sheriff of Nottingham one that for offending the laws should have suffered execution.
>
> (cited in Axton and Williams 1977: 3)

Despite the possible origins of the Robin Hood ballads in the years leading up to the Peasants' Revolt, this early Tudor Robin seldom had much about him of the Saxon guerrilla activist or the populist redistributor of wealth: those were the inventions of later ages. Indeed, Robin's fund-raising activities give rise to the paradox that while from one point of view he could indeed be seen as robbing the rich to give to the poor, from another point of view he looks very much like an unofficial and supplementary local tax-gatherer for the ecclesiastical authorities. There is evidence that in some parishes the part was traditionally played by a churchwarden (see Stokes 1986: 2). Even so, the folk tradition of the Robin Hood plays frequently caused anxiety to those in power, and however unthreatening the plays and games may have been in general, there were certainly those who, like Bishop Latimer, were outraged to find the extent to which the plays appealed to the public imagination. Arriving in a town one Sunday and finding the church deserted, he was angered to hear that 'it is Robin Hoodes day. The parishe are gone abroad to gather for Robyn Hoode' (Latimer 1869: 173–4). The Robin Hood plays, like the May-games in general, became prime targets for the disapproval of Puritan preachers, writers and authorities during the mid- to late sixteenth century, but opposition was not limited to the Puritan faction: it was expressed with equal vehemence by Catholic spokesmen. The games and plays, it seemed, posed a challenge, not to any specific religious position, but to authority as a whole, secular as well as religious.

The masculine role-playing of the Robin Hood celebrations may, perhaps, be seen as a necessary opposite to the exemplary fictions of the liturgical and cycle dramas, the morality interludes and the saints' plays. They embody a very different kind of energy – a carnivalesque masculinity. A flouter of secular and ecclesiastical authority in the ballads and play narratives, Robin's own alternative authority in the celebrations bears some similarities to that of a rustic Lord of Misrule, of the kind whom the Puritan Philip Stubbes famously attacked in his

Anatomy of Abuses (1583). The 'Summer Lord' (or 'Lord of Misrule', or 'Lord of the May', or 'Summer King') was the symbolic ruler of the 'king games' in which 'the wild-heads of the parish, conventing together, choose them a Grand-Captain (of all mischief)', who then presides over a brief period of carnival, in which the participants would march through the town and then 'feast, banquet and dance all that day and peradventure all the night too' (Stubbes (1583) 1877–9: 204). Stubbes saw these celebrations as being essentially ungodly and pagan, and he had plenty of support in this. Most recent studies of the Robin Hood legend see him as inextricably linked with the tradition of the Summer Lord.

There is a tempting argument here which might lead us down a mythopoetic path (see Clatterbaugh 1997: 95–116). The celebrations of the Summer Lord are a well-attested part of rural life in medieval England: borough records and accounts give a clear picture of their existence and nature. But what wider meaning, if any, did Robin as the Summer Lord have? What was he, if anything, apart from a glorified fund-raiser for the parish church? During the 1980s, British television revived the Robin Hood legend once again in a series of programmes which Goldcrest productions made for HTV, for broadcast during peak-time children's viewing hours. Entitled *Robin of Sherwood*, and originally scripted by Richard Carpenter, the series made much of an Anglo-Celtic mythological background with which Robin was associated. Haunting the series, throughout Robin's adventures, was Herne the Hunter, a variant of the Celtic Cernunnos, the Horned God of early Northern European pre-Christian spiritual traditions (Knight 1994: 239). Might kids' TV have instinctively got it right? Did the Robin Hood plays of the late Middle Ages also represent – as some accounts would have it – a vestigial folk memory of a seasonal ritual, a *Sacer Ludus* related to vegetation gods, horned gods and 'Year Spirits'? Is there a spiritual, even a religious, significance to the Robin Hood legend?

If so, then it may be a spirituality which is specifically characterized as 'masculine'. In countless medieval churches and other buildings dating from the fourteenth and fifteenth centuries, the figure of the Green Man appears; there is a significant tradition which has interpreted the Green Man as a kind of vegetation god, a phallic figure representing the male side of nature's fertility (Anderson 1990: 28 and *passim*). Are the Green Man, the Summer Lord and Robin himself perhaps all kinds of vestigial pagan figures, who have been only partially assimilated into a Christian theological and social framework? Robin in particular: if he is indeed a version of the Summer Lord, he is one who stresses the Summer Lord's natural aspects. He is the mythological outlaw in Lincoln (or Kendal) green who emerges from the trees to challenge worldly authority. As an outlaw he represents that which lies outside the agreed boundaries of the community. As a greenwood figure – a 'Green Man' himself in the popular imagination, as the designs on pub signs of that name frequently testify – he represents for the town-dweller a fantasy of the liberty of the forests; he exists at that point where the world of the community and the world of nature meet. He presides over feasting and games; and his celebrations eventually gives rise to a 'drama proper'.

Stephen Knight's analysis of 'Robin Hood in Performance' suggests such a spiritualized dimension to the Robin Hood play-games. In *Robin Hood: A Complete Study of the English Outlaw*, one of the best scholarly accounts of the legend as it is repeatedly reinscribed and modified from medieval times to the present day, he says:

> Whatever performance elements might be fitted into the procession, the basis of the play-game is clearly a public ritual across the border of the natural and the cultural. In the Robin Hood play-game the community celebrates the continued encounter with benign nature, at the season where the renewed promise of summer is clear. This whole process has both social and spiritual aspects.
>
> (Knight 1994: 106–7)

Knight then goes on to cite Glynne Wickham's famous description of early ritual performance:

> At the moment in time deemed to be special, sacred and thus 'holy', the normal routines of life must be suspended; the community, thus released from its mundane preoccupations, must assemble together; the individual recognized to be endowed with special suitability to conduct the ceremony appropriate to the particular occasion must be correctly attired, and perform the agreed rites, aided by other representatives of the community, also correctly dressed, in choric dance and chant. With these incantatory overtures completed, the time is right for the sacrifice to be made (if any be thought to be demanded); the gifts must then be presented; some manifestation of the god must then be consumed; or some other physical action must be executed that is itself indicative of communion with the god.
>
> (Wickham 1981: 9, cited in Knight 1994: 107)

Wickham's account of early English ritual theatre offers an anglicized version of a model of the origins and development of drama that locates its origins in rituals, which eventually develop into tragedy and comedy. The usual setting for this is Ancient Greece. The Cambridge

School of Anthropologists, writing in the early twentieth century, produced a model of the origins and essences of theatre, which traced the drama back to a Primal Ritual of cyclical death and rebirth; this gave rise to various local or regional rites, some linked specifically with Dionysos, and some of which then turned into the *dithyramb* – from which, in turn, Greek tragedy arose. If we put together Wickham's account of ritual in early English stages, with the suggestive mythology of Robin the Green Man, and the ritualistic play-games which are based around him, the Robin Hood plays may offer a British historical narrative which repeats this, several centuries later, in the re-emergence of theatre in England in the late Middle Ages.

Might this, then, be one way in which a gendered approach could help in an understanding of the Robin Hood games: by interpreting Robin, the Green Man, as representing some mythologized phallic power which is analogous with the Frazerian vegetation gods? If we take this line, we have an argument which sees, in England at least, a birth of (popular) drama from the spirit of masculinity, by means of the Green Man's plays and games.

Like the potential link between early phallic rituals and Greek tragedy (see previous chapter), this is a line of thought which might have particular resonance if seen in the light of those recent approaches to masculinities theory that have been based on a renewed exploration of male myths and archetypes. John Rowan, one of the best spokesmen for the mythopoetic men's movement, puts together a powerful and imaginative case, based on a politicised and pro-feminist reading of Wiccan traditions and humanistic psychology, for the importance of the figure of Cernunnos, the Horned God (Rowan 1987). Robert Bly, whose book *Iron John* was seminal to the movement, argues that masculine psychology is influenced by a 'psychic base' of archetypal figures such as the 'Wild Man, the King, the Trickster, the Lover, the Quester and the Warrior' (Bly 1990: 229–30), and explores ways in which such archetypes have manifested themselves culturally both in the present and in the past. For those who find the mythopoetic perspective convincing, the link between the various manifestations of Robin Hood, the Green Man and Cernunnos offers a mythical nature figure, a combination of Trickster and Quester, Wild Man and King, Warrior and Lover, who embodies a benevolent masculine principle within nature.

There are, however, serious doubts about whether these suggestive speculations can be grounded in historical actuality. Just as potential links between early phallic rituals and Greek tragedy cannot be substantiated, so the Robin Hood/Green Man link is one which remains interesting and suggestive, but far from certain. In so far as Robin, whether in the ballads or in the plays of late medieval England, *does* represent a nature spirit, he may well do so precisely as a sentimental projection, as a creation of the very townsmen for whom the greenwood is already becoming (even by the fifteenth century) a locus of fantasy, a pastoral environment of the fairytale sort which Shakespeare dramatized so effectively in *As You Like It* and *A Midsummer Night's Dream.*

Moreover, the whole model of the relationship between ritual and drama which Wickham calls upon now looks suspect. Twentieth-century anthropology has largely undermined the broad Frazerian model upon which the Cambridge School built its argument. The belief of Frazer and his followers that there existed some essential Primal Ritual which underpinned all other rituals has proved unfounded, and with the loss of that keystone much of the edifice has come crashing down. While few theorists have gone so far as to dismiss entirely the relationship between ritual and certain forms of theatre, the originary hypothesis which once seemed almost self-evident must now be regarded with a great deal of caution. For the time being at least, I am inclined not to make too great a claim for that aspect of the Robin Hood plays. Even so, Robin as the ambiguous outlaw masculine, the greenwood figure who can also become either church fund-raiser or the riotous leader of the mob, and who exists both inside and outside his fictional accounts, lays sufficient claim to our attention in a study of the way in which masculinities were imagined in the performances of the Middle Ages – a way very different from that of the liturgical, cycle and morality plays.

3

Sighing like a Furnace and Full of Strange Oaths: Lovers and Soldiers in Shakespeare

3.1 All the world's a typology of masculinity …

> We were raised with a certain script, and if we follow the script, we are told, life will work. What do you do when it's obvious to you that the script is not working? You keep working the script, because that's all you've got till the script just gets torn out of your hands, and you have no choice but to try something else, try a new script. We have plenty of scripts floating around in our heads. You either write a new script, or you realize you don't need a script. The process for me was to write a new script and find out that didn't work, and write a new script until I found a way of acting that brought me some satisfaction.
>
> American Vietnam veteran

> All the world's a stage,
> And all the men and women merely players:
> They have their exits and their entrances;
> And one man in his time plays many parts,
> His acts being seven ages.
> *As You Like It*, II.vii.139–43

A 'part' in Elizabethan theatre practice is also a name for a script. More precisely, it refers to an incomplete script: it is that 'part' of the whole play-text which the actor receives and which has only his own lines, and a few cues and stage directions written upon it so that the actor has to work out for himself how his part fits into the play as whole. In this technical sense, 'part' is perhaps an even better metaphor than 'script' for the way in which an individual relates to gender ideology.

58

But is Jaques' speech anything to do with gender at all? In it the word 'man' undergoes the now familiar slippage between its two meanings: it is sometimes used in a gendered sense, sometimes more generally, to mean 'mankind'. It begins inclusively: the whole world is a stage, and both the men *and women* are players upon that stage. Very quickly, however, and almost subconsciously, Jaques moves into something far more gender specific as he declares 'and one man in his time plays many parts'. As the syntax assumes a masculine subject, so the narrative provides one: the characters in the story Jaques goes on to tell are all male – the schoolboy, the male lover, the soldier, the justice ... While purporting to draw a universal picture of the waxing and waning of human life, it also delineates a sequence of masculine roles in Elizabethan society – and does so in a play in which the performance of masculine roles is a mainspring of the plot. Elsewhere in the forest, the cross-dressed Rosalind is playing the masculine part of Ganymede; later in the narrative, as both director and improviser, she will teach Orlando how to play one of the parts which Jaques identifies – that of the lover.

The speech itself also describes an interesting parabola in gender terms. It works its way through a series of stages in life: infant, schoolboy, lover, soldier, justice, pantaloon and 'second childishness'. The infant 'mewling and puking in the nurse's arms' could in fact be a child of either gender. There are no gendered pronouns, nor any other details, grammatical or descriptive, which allow the audience to assign gender to this infant. Gender begins to enter at the next stage: we are introduced to the school*boy* with *his* satchel (although, as the boy actors of Shakespeare's company knew, to be a boy was to be incompletely masculine). The lover we are shown is another masculine stereotype, 'Sighing like furnace, with a woeful ballad Made to his mistress' eyebrow.' This is one of Shakespeare's favourite figures of fun: it is the role Romeo adopts in the early stages of *Romeo and Juliet* while he is still in love with Rosaline. It is also the role Orlando is about to play in *As You Like It*, as the author of the poems to *his* Rosalind which he hangs on the trees of the forest. The masculine identity becomes even more substantial in the next part which Jaques identifies:

> Then, a soldier,
> Full of strange oaths, and bearded like the pard
> Jealous in honour, sudden, and quick in quarrel,
> Seeking the bubble reputation ...
> (*As You Like It* II.vii.149–52)

Girls may go to school, young women may love, but in Shakespeare's society the role of warrior is an almost exclusively masculine one. Indeed, Jaques' reference to 'the bubble reputation' makes clear an important sense in which social role, reputation and self-definition are interwoven in this masculine social and gender role.

In the soldier and the following 'Age', there is a sense of climax, of apotheosis. Like the soldier, the justice,'In fair round belly with good capon lined ... Full of wise saws and modern instances' (II.vii.154, 156) describes a specifically masculine social function, one which in Shakespeare's day could not usually be undertaken by a woman. Here the fully acquired masculine identity is tied in with concepts of status. The 'bubble reputation' of the soldier gives way to the well-fed *gravitas* (or pomposity?) of the magistrate, whose round belly is a signifier of his social standing.

From this point on, however, the decline begins. The next stage is that of the 'lean and slippered pantaloon' (II.vii.158) – a stereotype from the Italian *commedia dell'arte* stage, still specifically masculine in gender, but now with 'his big manly voice, Turning again towards child-ish treble, pipes and whistles in his sound' (II.vii.161–2). Manliness, it appears, is waning, and the pantaloon's decline continues and becomes a relapse into 'second childishness and mere oblivion...' (II.vii.165). Once more the syntax does much of the work: there are no gendered pronouns and the description of the subject – which as the image develops is seen not only as de-gendered but also effectively 'disem-bodied': 'sans eyes, sans teeth, sans taste, sans everything' (II.vii.166) – could as well apply to the female as to the male. Thus Jaques' actor passes from an unspecified and ungendered infant state, through the liminal phase of childhood to the point where he is playing the fully masculine roles of soldier and justice; this is followed by a decline back through 'second childishness' to the disembodiment of near-death. The structure of Jaques' speech is a strangely modern one, describing a parabola in which masculinity is understood as a construction rather than a biological 'given'. As such it is fragile, unstable and elusive. It is something which the growing male child attains through processes of socialization, and it becomes increasingly defined towards late youth and Middle Age – and then lost.

Contemporary gender theory is concerned with the way in which simultaneous masculine messages are frequently contradictory. Jaques, on the other hand, seems to see a smooth, and almost inevitable transi-tion from one part to another, one which is effected, for better or worse, by the passage of time. In this scheme, biology and socialization are two contending forces, both acting on a man's life, as he first grows towards definition and manhood, but then loses his faculties and relapses, 'sans everything', into a state of chaos. Jaques reiterates the preoccupation with 'Devouring Time' which Shakespeare articulates in his sonnet sequence, and which Spenser addressed in his mutability cantos. The 'Seven Ages' speech gives us a glimpse of masculinity as it might be understood in terms of that cycle of growth and decay which was such a powerful underlying notion of the English Renaissance.

The rest of this chapter will concentrate on two key points in this cycle: the lover and the soldier. I shall be looking at ways in which these two dramatic 'parts' act and interact, at the conflicts and contradictions they engender, and at the various ways in which, in Shakespeare's plays, masculinity is configured in terms of violence.

3.2 Anxiety and dominance: Petruccio, patriarchy, *Patriarcha*

In the previous chapter we considered the way in which Thomas Laqueur draws out the gender implications of the Galenic biological model of human sexual anatomy. Laqueur's analysis gives us some sense of a way of thinking about gender which lies behind Jaques' speech – a single-sex model, in which biological difference is a matter of degree not of kind, and is secondary to socially constructed gender identity. But if Laqueur is right, at the time that Shakespeare was writing a paradigm of human anatomy, as well as of the corresponding sex/gender identity which had prevailed for one and a half millennia, was just beginning to break down. At a time when, in any case, there was an unprecedented period of social and economic changes in England, together with the slow emergence of science and the 'New philosophy [which] puts all in doubt', it is hardly surprising that some murmurs of a general crisis in gender identity might have been heard.

It might appear at first sight that a single-sex model of sexual/gender identity would have encouraged a greater degree of respect and understanding between men and women. A moment's reflection, however, shows how the very opposite could equally be the case. In a society where the demands of a patriarchal sex/gender system are paramount, the sexual/anatomical continuum which it suggests presents itself not as reassurance but as threat. If the boundaries between the masculine and the feminine are not kept separate by biological imperative, then it becomes even more important to the patriarchal state that they should be patrolled and policed by society. Any sign of gender subversion (such as, for example, the late sixteenth- and early seventeenth-century fashion of female transvestism) becomes a potential symptom of wider disorder.

Male gender anxiety in the early modern period was much concerned with the threats which, it was felt, were posed to this still-fragile notion of masculinity – to that gender identity which was defined by the holding of a particular place in society. The Renaissance misogyny was a response to the perceived challenge to masculine identity (itself characterized by control) – anxieties which the Renaissance located in the supposed 'excesses' of femininity: female transvestism; accusations of witchcraft; the supposed excessive sexual potency and/or incontinence of women; women's very talking which threatens disorder; their painting and cosmetics which become signs of vanity or falsity. These in turn are connected to and impinge upon wider political and social concerns of authority and control. Thus during the late sixteenth and early seventeenth centuries there was a ubiquitous anxiety about the gender order, which the historian Anthony Fletcher characterizes as 'Men's dilemmas ... dilemmas of initiative and control which pervade gender relationships from each dawn to each dusk' (Fletcher 1995: 10). More specifically, he asserts, 'What seems undeniable is that there was an acutely felt anxiety in Tudor and early Stuart England about how women could best be governed and controlled' (Fletcher 1995: 27). In the light of this it is perhaps not surprising that Fletcher adds that '*The Taming of the Shrew* is probably the most profound statement about early modern courtship that we have' (Fletcher 1995: 107).

The anxiety can be seen, perhaps, in the tireless way in which Elizabethan and Jacobean conduct-books and books of domestic advice repeat the injunction to the middle classes that good and godly domestic arrangements are all a matter of authority and control. In *A Godly Form of Household Government,* for example, there is the following typical passage:

> The husband and wife are Lords of the house, for unto them the Lord said: 'Be you Lords over the fish of the sea, and over the fowl of the air, and over every beast that moveth upon the earth' (Genesis 1:28). And the selfsame Creator said that 'the woman should be a helper unto the man' (Genesis 2:18). Therefore, the husband, without any exception, is master over all the house, and hath more to do in his house with his own domestical affairs, than the magistrate. The wife is ruler over all other things, but yet under her husband. There are certain things in the house that do only appertain to the authority of the husband, wherewith it were a reproach for the wife, without the consent of her husband, to meddle: as to receive strangers or to marry her daughter.
> (Dod and Cleaver 1621: sig. L6v–L7)

The gender order is, of course, bound in with the social order of class and degree. The Wife 'is ruler over all other things', but still subject to her husband, and the authority of Genesis is cited to legitimate the structure. The arrangements are to be enforced by violence if necessary, since the male head of the house has the undisputed legal right to discipline his subordinates – including, if necessary, his wife. This last is rather ambiguous, it is true, since the wife's own position as one of the 'governors' of the house makes outright wife-beating problematic. Moreover, many prescriptive texts and conduct-books 'urged men *not* to abuse their right to "correct" and discipline their wives [and] worked to separate masculinity from violence. As *A Homily of the State of Matrimony* insists, "And yet a man may be a man, although he doth not use such extremity" ' (cited in Dolan 1996: 218).

Petruccio, arriving in Padua at the start of the main plot of *The Taming of the Shrew* with his express ambition to 'wive it wealthily', may not have read that part of the *Homily of the State of Matrimony*. Moreover, he seems to have misunderstood the details of Jaques' typology of masculinity. In his rough courtship of Katherine he rejects the conventional role of the lover, and uses all the semiotics of the soldier instead. There is evidence (such as Jaques' reference, quoted above, to the 'lean and slippered pantaloon') that Shakespeare knew the stereotypes of the *commedia dell'arte* tradition. Here he refers to that tradition again in a fresh way: Petruccio is the lover *as* braggart soldier – a heady fusion of Inamorato and Capitano. Rather than sighs and ballads, he employs strange oaths and quarrels, and represents a blatant – perhaps even a parodic – example of dominant Elizabethan masculinity. The play dramatizes a male–female conflict which is only resolved through the complete subjection of the female to the male. On the one hand, Petruccio seems to be the representative of a hegemonic masculinity (real or imagined) whose job it is to meet the challenge posed to that hegemony by that rebellious, shrewish woman, Katherine, and to neutralize her challenge. On the other hand, he is the trickster – the improviser who makes the story work, and who drives the narrative. It is no accident that he is a stranger to Padua, for Petruccio stands both within and outside the patriarchal structures of control and dominance which are the norm within Paduan society. It is to his advantage that he is *not* one of the suitors who have regularly taken to haunting Minola's house. He is an outsider – who on his wedding day pretends to be even more of an outsider than he actually is, who virtually acts the role of the outlaw, and whose methods of courtship seem as alien to the men of Padua as they do to Katherine. It is his task in the play to bring these two roles, of eccentric trickster and hegemonic masculine, together – something which he achieves in the 'unexpected' winning of his wager of the final scene.

Petruccio's *other* task, of course, is to re-establish the gender boundaries within the play. Katherine has laid claim to masculine behaviours
and privileges: we see her behaving aggressively, even violently; her
language is strong; she refuses to take a subordinate role towards the
patriarchal authority of her own father; she even dominates other
women (she ties Bianca up!). Most significantly, she refuses the role of
wife. Through a regime of starvation, bullying and mental torture,
Petruccio brings her to the point where she will swear that day is night
to please him, thereby countering her challenge to the hegemony of
male power.

At the end of the play Katherine, finally subdued by Petruccio, has
her big speech about duty. The *gestus* whereby the essence of
Katherine's marriage to Petruccio is represented dramatically is her
speech of submission. It is true that, characteristically, it is a rather
proud speech of submission, in which she rails at other women: but it is
a speech of submission all the same. It contains the famous lines:

> Fie, fie, unknit that threat'ning unkind brow,
> And dart not scornful glances from those eyes
> To wound thy lord, thy king, thy governor … .
> Thy husband is thy lord, thy life, thy keeper,
> Thy head, thy sovereign … .
> Such duty as the subject owes the prince,
> Even such a woman oweth to her husband …
>   (*Shrew* V.ii.141–3, 151–2, 160–1)

The theoretical underpinning, the ideological framework which makes
Katherine's speech possible, is implicit in *A Godly Form of Household
Government*, *A Homily of the State of Matrimony* and other such
prescriptive works. It is most fully articulated, however, nearly 50 years
later, at a time when the very ideas on which it was based were under
threat. Sir Robert Filmer's *Patriarcha*, as its name implies, articulated a
political theory which is explicitly patriarchal in its structure. Its
subtitle 'Or the Natural Power of Kings', indicates the extent to which
the gender order and the political order were intertwined during this
period. Tracing the notion of kingship back to biblical times, and
positing a lineage from the literal patriarchy of the 'law of the father' in
a tribal context, to the surrogate fatherhood of the divinely appointed
leader (Joshua or Moses) to the present political structure of kingship,
he argues that while

> It is true all Kings be not the natural parents of their subjects, yet they all
> either are, or are to be reputed, the next heirs to those first progenitors,

who were at first the natural parents of the whole people, and, in their right, succeed to the exercise of supreme jurisdiction: and such heirs are not only lords of their own children, but also of their brethren and all others that were subject to their fathers ...

(Aughterson 1995: 162)

There is, needless to say, no mention of tribal matriarchs. Filmer's vision insists on a natural order, sanctioned by tradition, and deriving ultimately from divine decree, which identifies the source of earthly authority as the father. Filmer rightly saw that that authority was in crisis, as King Charles came under attack from the Parliamentary faction in the Civil War. One thing which he did *not* feel to be under threat, however, was the gendered nature of that authority: this was taken for granted. 'If we compare the natural rights of a father with those of a king, we find them all one, without any difference at all but only in the latitude or extent of them ...' (Aughterson 1995: 163). Thus God the father delegates authority to the kingly father, who delegates it to the literal father. Filmer summarizes attitudes and assumptions that had been current for generations and which are encoded in sermons and conduct-books, royal proclamations and books of political theory throughout the Renaissance period.

Of course, *The Taming of the Shrew* is one of the most problematic of Shakespeare's plays for a modern audience. Like *The Merchant of Venice*, it contains dark stuff that chokes the comedy. In recent years academic critics, not all of them anti-feminist, have made several attempts to reclaim the play, and to argue that it is more than a simple glorification of male brutality towards women. Stephen Orgel has pointed out that a large proportion of the Elizabethan theatre audience consisted of women, and has argued that the plays and their meanings must 'at the very least represent *cultural* fantasies and women are implicated in them as well as men' (Orgel 1989: 8). Taking a similar point to its logical conclusion, a provocative essay by Nina Taunton, for example, offers an analysis of the Katherine–Petruccio relationship in the context of a loving and consensual sadomasochistic power exchange, in which 'Katherine and Petruccio achieve a kind of "coming out" that ... has to be worked out through mutual private testing and adjusting' (Taunton 1994: 94). However, the more common scholarly view has remained that which Jack J. Jorgens sums up when he describes it as 'a piece of male chauvinist wishful thinking' (Jorgens 1977: 67). In the theatre, meanwhile, several directors throughout the 1980s and 1990s have risen to the challenge of negotiating the play for a present-day audience – either by stressing the harshness of its ending in order to point a feminist moral, or by attempting in various ways to mitigate it. It is not impossible to make the play 'work' for an audience which is not itself steeped in the misogynistic traditions of the Renaissance, but it sails too close to the wind ever to be comfortable. Its humour has too many echoes of domestic abuse to be easily palatable.

In performance the play's effect will depend to a great extent on the way in which the part of Petruccio is played. Again, contemporary productions have played him with various degrees of distaste or sympathy, from the woman-hating thug through to the rather naïve young boy who is attempting to live up to inherited, false ideas about what a man *should* be like. Yet there is always the suspicion that in offering any kind of complexity in a Petruccio, somehow a production is cheating – that it is ignoring or distorting for ideological purposes the 'real' Petruccio which Shakespeare must have written: the simple, sadistic power-fixated bully-boy with whom the heroine is supposed to fall in love, and whom the audience is supposed to adore.

But how true is this? In Shakespeare's own theatre Petruccio seems to have been a comic role, and not one that implied any kind of masculine ideal. According to T. W. Baldwin's analysis of Shakespearean casting (Baldwin 1927), the part was probably originally played by Thomas Pope, while Richard Burbage, the company's natural leading man, was playing Lucentio, the successful wooer of Bianca. The part of Lucentio is, in fact, the more conventional romantic lead, and the wooing of Bianca is the more conventional romantic comedy narrative. The whole Katherine/Petruccio story is a farcical sub-plot whose energy is such that it ends up taking over the whole play.

Baldwin's casting suggestions should be treated with care, it is true: his putative cast lists are the result more of speculation than of evidence. However, his instinct is often good and his findings have been accepted as probable by recent scholars, including Tori Haring-Smith, whose stage history of *The Taming of the Shrew* is the most detailed account that we have (Haring-Smith 1985: 9; see also Shakespeare, ed. Morris 1981: 48–50). If Baldwin *is* right, it is significant, for Thomas Pope, a senior sharer in the Lord Chamberlain's Men, and with a reputation as one of the 'clowns' of the company, was precisely the sort of actor to play the part for a broad and not entirely sympathetic comic effect. Ever since Garrick reinvented the play in 1754 as *Catharine and Petruchio* (*sic*), the part of Petruccio has been played, if not necessarily sympathetically, then at least sexily. But the original effect may have been very different: Pope seems to have been one of the least sexy players in the Lord Chamberlain's Men. Tall, bluff and corpulent, within a couple of years he would be playing Falstaff, the 'old fat man, a tun of a man ... that swollen parcel of dropsies ... that cloak-bag of guts ... that old white-bearded Satan' (*Henry IV Part 1* II.iv.436, 439–40, 450). Much can be done, of course, with a padded costume, a false beard and some imagination, but the Elizabethan companies tended to cast to type where possible, and Haring-Smith's conclusion that Pope's Petruccio 'was probably more braggart than brute' is plausible (Haring-Smith 1985: 9). Quite possibly he was also, as Falstaff says of himself, 'not only witty in [him]self, but the cause that wit is in other men' (*Henry IV Part 2* I.ii.7) – the butt of the jokes as frequently as the instigator of them. His initial function, indeed, might well have been to play the bullying comic straight man to Will Kemp, the company's more famous clown, who was cast as his servant Grumio. The two actors' first entrance sets the tone for their double-act:

PETRUCCIO: Here, sirrah, Grumio, knock, I say.
GRUMIO: Knock, sir? Whom should I knock? Is there any man has abused your worship?
PETRUCCIO: I say, knock me here soundly

(Shrew I.ii.5–8)

The scene of violent slapstick between master and servant is a long-standing dramatic convention in the popular theatre: again, Shakespeare may first have seen it turned into high art by the travelling *commedia dell'arte* companies who occasionally ventured into England. Many of the play's jokes are based on the fact that these knockabout master–servant routines, which we first see played out between Petruccio and Grumio, are then transferred to Katherine. She appears first as master/mistress of her suitors and of Bianca, and then, in a classic example of status inversion, she herself is cast as rebellious servant to Petruccio, whose role as master she first resists and finally accepts. The dramaturgy of the stage gag echoes the structure of Elizabethan domestic patriarchy: the wife is both separate from, and also one of, the household servants.

To see Petruccio as comic braggart rather than romantic lead is not to explain away the essential misogyny of the shrew-taming narrative, nor the baldness of Katherine's final submission speech, as 'just a joke'. It is, however, to suggest that when contemporary productions problematize that narrative, they might not simply be 'cheating', but restoring to it some of the ambiguity that may have surrounded it even for its earliest audiences. The real problem, though, is that however strongly that ambiguity may be played in the early part of the play, Katherine's final speech resists it: the play does seem to collapse back into a raw masculinist supremacy which is impossible to avoid.

In about 1611 Petruccio reappeared on the London stage in a play called *The Woman's Prize, or The Tamer Tamed*, a parodic 'sequel' to *The Shrew*, which takes place after Katherine's death, as Petruccio remarries. The play charts the stratagems by which his new bride ensures that she will not be subject to the same oppressive treatment as her predecessor. She wins hands down, and Petruccio is humbled. The Epilogue sums up the play's message of gender equality:

> The Tamer's Tamed: but so, as nor the men
> Can find one just cause to complain of, when
> They fitly do consider, in their lives
> They should not reign as tyrants o'er their wives:
> Nor can the women, from this precedent,
> Insult, or triumph; it being aptly meant,
> To teach both sexes due equality,
> And, as they stand bound, to love mutually.
> (*The Woman's Prize* Epilogue 1–8)

The Woman's Prize answers, and reverses, the gender politics of Shakespeare's play. The Elizabethan and Jacobean literary scene was used, it is true, to 'battles' between rival poets, parodying and answering each others' poems, plays and ideas. What makes this interesting, however, is the fact that it was written not by an enemy of Shakespeare but by a friend. Its author was John Fletcher, who at that point was about to become not only Shakespeare's successor as the principal playwright of the King's Men, but also a close collaborator with him on at least three new plays. There is no record of Shakespeare's opinion of *The Woman's Prize*, but it is not unreasonable to speculate that the later Shakespeare had no quarrel with this parody of his early work. Certainly this would fit with the way in which Shakespeare himself seems to have rethought gender relationships in his own later comedies, where the conduct-book sermonizing disappears, the witty couples (such as Beatrice and Benedick) come to be more and more equally matched, and the women frequently end up on top. It may well be that what present-day commentators find difficult in the play also troubled its author. *The Shrew* is not a confident statement of patriarchal masculinity, but a play which has its roots in the early modern 'crisis in gender relations', and Petruccio's way of coping with the crisis is offered as humorous not because it is *right* but because it is outrageous. It is true, still, that the play's jokes – like its final moments – depend upon the apparent endorsement of a patriarchal masculinity in which male/female relationships are underscored by violence: the braggart soldier as lover is only funny up to a point. But what in *The Shrew* is offered as a form of resolution, becomes in later plays the problem which is to be explored.

3.3   Hal and Falstaff

Filmer's patriarchy insists on the congruence between the King as head of the nation and the husband as head of the household: it is this that legitimates Petruccio's authority over Katherine. At the end of *Henry V*, we see the same trope from a different angle: another Katherine is being wooed in a rather different kind of courtship scene, in which king and husband are conflated in the figure of Henry himself.

Shakespeare's tetralogy (*Richard II, Henry IV, Parts 1 and 2,* and *Henry V*) is about both masculinity and kingship. The plays raise questions concerning Hal's growth into manhood, military virtues, the Oedipal rebellions and negotiations of the young prince, and father/son relationships, questions which are so clearly foregrounded that it is hard not to talk about the plays in a way which focuses on masculinity. The three Henry plays tell the story of how Hal becomes Henry – the transition from boyhood and adolescence denoted by the diminutive, to the point at which the young man fits himself to the militaristic honour code and thereby attains manhood. On the way he defeats Hotspur, winning his own 'spurs', becoming a man and becoming a fit ruler – and eventually merging the triumph of his masculine identity with the triumph of nationalist and expansionist energy by beating the French. On the way, too, he rejects the 'false father' figure of Falstaff, and having sloughed off the old man, he emerges as the new man. He negotiates a conflict with his father which later generations have seen as blatantly Oedipal, and eventually he 'becomes' his father, the new King Henry who can wear the crown legitimately.

He also takes the time successfully to integrate the role of lover into his narrative, wooing and winning the French Princess Catherine, in a courtship which is represented as both romantic and politically symbolic:

> A good heart, Kate, is the sun and the moon – or rather the sun and not the moon, for it shines bright and never changes, but keeps his course truly. If thou would have such a one, take me; and take me, take a soldier; take a soldier, take a king.
>
> (*Henry V*, V.ii.162–7)

An attentive audience might hear in Henry's imagery of the sun and moon something of Petruccio's phraseology, but in most other respects, Henry's language to *his* 'Kate' is very different from Petruccio's. The offer he makes her is: 'take me ... take a soldier ... take a king'. In Henry's rhetoric, as well as in the narrative, the structure works to bring everything together into harmony. In Henry, Catherine is assured, there exists no conflict, no discrepancy between the lover, the soldier and the king. Petruccio acted the part of the braggart soldier in order to become the lover. King Henry combines the roles in a different way but with mythical success: on the battlefield he is the soldier, in the boudoir he is the lover. And if, in both cases, he is 'conquering' France, that similarity only makes the difference of the rest so much the greater. When Catherine asks, 'Is it possible that I should love de *ennemi* of France?' (V.ii.169–70), King Henry puts all his energy into arguing that he is not the enemy of France, that on the contrary he loves France, that 'Kate, when France is mine, and I am yours, then yours is France, and you are mine' (V.ii.175–6). The consummating image is of their future child – a boy, of course – whose military heroism will transcend national European differences and become a champion of Christendom: 'Shall not thou and I, between Saint Denis and Saint George, compound a boy, half-French half-English, that shall go to Constantinople and take the Turk by the beard?' (V.ii. 204–7). The lover will generate another soldier. The play ends with Henry's speech 'Prepare we for our marriage' – the climax of a successfully negotiated masculinity which is warrior and civil at once. Yet even as he says this the Chorus steps forward and while continuing to hymn the praises of 'this star of England' (Epilogue 6) reminds the audience that the hopes invested in Henry VI were not to be fulfilled. The moment of fruition contains the seeds of its own destruction, as the Chorus reminds the real-life audience of their own historical perspective upon the heroic fantasy, and the extent to which the history play represents it as a form of nostalgia.

This may have had different effects on different audiences. The plays that Shakespeare wrote for the Lord Chamberlain's company were intended for more than one performance context. Quite apart from the need for adaptation for summer touring conditions, in London the plays would have been staged both at Court and in the public theatres. Performances might have very different meanings in such different venues. The specific model of feudal militarism which permeates the tetralogy, and which underlies the model of masculinity that Hal/Harry/Henry enacts, is a thing of the past for all the males of Shakespeare's generation. The two audiences, however, might well feel differently from each other concerning their relationship to that past. For the largely citizen audience of the public playhouses, the masculinity which Hal attains is distanced, in a way similar to that in which the cowboy hero of the Western movie enacted a distanced and romanticized masculinity for office and factory workers in the 1940s and 1950s. The potency of this image was in part at least a function of its being past and unattainable. The stage thus becomes a fantasy area in which this is played out, in which both masculine and nationalist ideals are displayed and largely affirmed.

However, the aristocratic spectators who watched Shakespeare's plays performed at the court of the ageing Elizabeth may have responded with a different sense of their relationship to the play's events. On a very basic level, of course, they would have paid no admission fee. They were not 'buying' access to a specific performance in the way that their citizen contemporaries were: metaphorically speaking they already 'owned' the performance, the company and the writer, by virtue of their wealth and status, and their connection with the patrons who owned the company in a legal and literal sense. The courtly audience knew that according to the cold tally of years they were as distant from the events of the late fourteenth and early fifteenth centuries as their citizen counterparts. However, in a court in which the chivalric codes which permeate the plays still played an immensely important symbolic role, in which theatrical events, tournaments, masques and progresses formed a complex web of performative affirmations of power, authority and status in the English court, the sense of engagement which an audience of this kind would have brought to the theatrical event would have been very different. For the court audience, Hal's model of masculinity might well have been a more immediately relevant phenomenon.

By the end of the sixteenth century, the technology of warfare had advanced considerably. The nobility no longer took to the battlefield as armed knights, and powder and arquebus had replaced the sword and lance as the weapon that would win battles. The ceremonies and mythologies of medieval warfare, however, were kept alive amongst the aristocracy, since Elizabeth's court maintained the practice of mounting elaborate chivalric tournaments. In particular, Elizabeth's Accession Day tilts were magnificent affairs, staged as both celebration of and propaganda for Elizabeth's reign. They were, in many respects, performative counterparts of Spenser's literary tribute to Elizabeth, *The Faerie Queene*, and like *The Faerie Queene* they were redolent with Arthurian imagery validating the Tudor claim to throne and its implied restoration of the Arthurian line, and long-term strategy to effect the unification of Britain. These Accession Day tilts glorified the Order of the Knights of the Garter – another institution

with Arthurian resonances and of which Elizabeth was the head. The
Elizabethan court's enthusiasm for the 'neo-medievalism' of these
events is conjured up in the following description from George Peele's
Polyhymnia:

> In armour bright and sheen fair England's knights
> In honour of their peerless sovereign
> High mistress of their service, thoughts and lives,
> Make to the tilt amain; and trumpets sound,
> And princely coursers neigh and champ the bit:
> When all, addressed for deeds of high devoir,
> Press to the sacred presence of their prince.
>
> (cited in Edelman 1992: 46)

The Accession Day tilts still used rules which had been set down
during the fourteenth century, in the reign of Edward III – and there
was very real danger in taking part in them: in France, similar tilts had
been banned after King Henry II was killed at one. They were also,
however, a complex performance full of pageantry and theatricality, an
unashamedly propagandistic ritual of monarchy. Simultaneously, they
provided a chance for courtiers to assert their manhood and ingratiate
themselves with Elizabeth by performing martial feats. These were both
a trial and a celebration of a chivalric masculinity which was placed at
the service of Gloriana ('in honour of their peerless sovereign').

But if Hal/Henry presents a largely positive side of this nostalgically
chivalric manhood, his companion Falstaff represents its shadow side.
The relationship between Falstaff and Hal, in which Falstaff becomes
'a surrogate father who must eventually be abandoned' (Shakespeare,
ed. Wells and Taylor 1986: 509), has been commented on by many
critics. The two figures also represent different movements in the structure of Elizabethan masculinities. If we think back to Jaques' 'Seven
Ages' speech, with its pattern of rise and fall, we can see that Hal's
story is of the gradual attainment of masculinity, while Falstaff's is of
the disintegration of masculinity. This is implicit in Falstaff's famous
catechism on honour before the battle of Shrewsbury, where he presents a figure who is the very opposite of the archetypal soldier in
Jaques' 'Seven Ages' speech. Far from being 'jealous in honour,
sudden and quick in quarrel, Seeking the bubble reputation Even in
the cannon's mouth', Falstaff contemplates the reality of battle:

> honour pricks me on. Yea, but how if honour prick me off when I come on,
> how then? Can honour set to a leg? No. Or an arm? No. Or take away the
> grief of a wound? No. Honour hath no skill in surgery, then? No. What is

> honour? A word. What is in that word honour? What is that honour? Air. A trim reckoning! Who hath it? He that died a' Wednesday. Doth he feel it? No. Doth he hear it? No.'Tis insensible, then. Yea, to the dead. But will it not live with the living? No. Why? Detraction will not suffer it. Therefore I'll none of it. Honour is a mere scutcheon.
>
> (*Henry IV, Part 1* V.i.129–40)

Falstaff is talking about honour primarily as it relates to the chivalric virtues of martial valour. But the original audiences of *Henry IV, Part 1* would have heard the more complex resonances of that word at the same time and would have known that, in rejecting honour as a 'mere scutcheon', Falstaff is also bidding farewell, in an important sense, to his own sense of self and his own manhood.

For 'honour' is a central component of identity in the construction of early modern masculinities, one which links the individual with the greater scheme of things. 'Take away honour,' said Gervase Markham in 1624, 'where is reverence? Take away reverence, what are our laws? And take away law, and man is nothing but a gross mass of all impiety' (Markham 1624: 4). The honour codes of the sixteenth and seventeenth centuries offer at least a partial articulation of masculine gender ideology of the time, and a response to the 'men's dilemmas' of authority and control, which were noted earlier in this chapter. They comprise a complex set of implicit and explicit rules, assumptions and interpretative conventions which allow meaning about gender identity to be both generated and communicated. Covering topics from ethical precepts to details of dress and deportment, the masculine messages of the Tudor and early Stuart periods are encoded in hundreds of sermons, homilies, character-books, essays, letters and conduct-books, and while they differ one from the other in detail, they share a common theme: that masculinity lies in governance. In the first instance, this means governance of the self; in the second, governance in the sphere of the household and family; in the third, civil governance (see Foyster 1999 *passim*).

'Honour' was gendered during the period in such a way as to demand a double standard from men and women. This doubleness has its roots in social and legal concepts of relationship between the sexes, which amounted to the validation of male ownership of women. For most women, therefore, their most direct experience of the honour code must have been in terms of its prescriptions regarding sexual behaviour. Ruth Kelso put it bluntly but accurately: 'Let a woman have chastity, she has all. Let her lack chastity and she has nothing' (Kelso 1956: 24).

For men the question was slightly more complicated. A man's reputation was not merely sexual, and that aspect of it which *was* to do with sexuality related more to control than to chastity. This could sometimes amount to the same thing: a strict and chaste control of a man's own sexuality may have been recommended in the more sober volumes of conduct-writers and the moralists. However, an equal and opposite tendency is also found: that a man's reputation may (then as now) have been enhanced by a notoriety for sexual conquest. Far more important was a man's control of the sexuality of his wife or intended, since a woman's ruined reputation would also tarnish that of her husband. Cuckoldry, as is demonstrated in the plays of the seventeenth century from Shakespeare to Congreve, is the most mortal affront to the honour of a man. Moreover, the relationship between the sexual dimensions of the honour code and their social and political dimensions was far more complex for men – especially for those of the rank of gentry and above – than it was for women. If the masculine honour code depended upon sexual control within marriage and the household, this was because the household order was a microcosm of the social and political order, which it was up to men to uphold.

Honour in this broader sense was complex and sometimes apparently contradictory. Such honour codes were not fixed and immutable but changed according to the times. The Tudor and Stuart codes drew on medieval chivalric codes of behaviour, which focused upon such martial virtues as courage, fortitude, strength, indomitability, prudence, steadfastness and so on – and then reworked them to apply to times of peace as well as war. Honour was both individualistic and something which transcended the individual. It encompassed the idea of 'self-fashioning' (see Greenblatt 1980) but also related to lineage, ancestry and 'blood'. As the economic basis of society underwent radical changes in the late sixteenth and early seventeenth centuries, so the concept of honour underwent significant changes too. The feudal economy saw land and estates as something that belonged not so much to the individual as to the collective – the family – through time: the individual held these lands in trust for a generation and then passed them on to the next. At the beginning of the sixteenth century the concept of family honour within the gentry had a similarly collective dimension. But just as the rise of the mercantile economy changed attitudes towards land – regarding it not so much as the sacred trust of the lineage, as the negotiable property of the individual – so the concept of honour also changed. It is not that ancestry and lineage ceased to matter to the gentry: on the contrary, the emphasis on the family tree as validation of social status continues to be important. Nonetheless, the developing Elizabethan and Jacobean concept of honour focuses increasingly on that which resides in the individual rather than in his forebears.

The actions which brought honour to the individual 'were those which deployed the manly qualities of strength and reason to worthy ends' (Foyster 1999: 35). Physical skill and courage on the battlefield were particularly important in this respect. This too, however, changed during the sixteenth and seventeenth centuries: as the body politic became characterized not so much by internal feuds between gentry families, as by the growth of an 'ordered' nation state, so military virtue and honour became increasingly characterized by service to that state, rather than by fighting in inter-familial battles (see James 1978) . Linked with this were the rewards of public office – itself, too, another way to win honour for those who would not or could not fight, or who were unlucky enough to be born at a time when no significant wars were being waged. Similarly, in the absence of any literal battles to fight, English youth could assert its manhood and win honour by substituting cognate skills and activities such as horsemanship, hunting, and prowess at other physical sports (and hence, of course, the particular importance of the Accession Day tilts)

Thus, whereas feminine honour codes of the early modern period were stiflingly simple, the corresponding masculine ones were complex, interweaving a variety of different aspects, and encompassing both public and private spheres. They referred both to the public reputation sustained by the individual and also to the individual's private sense of self. The analogies and correspondences between these various spheres are significant: according to the Renaissance commonplace, man was a microcosm, a 'little world', in whom the patterns and structures of the greater world are repeated in miniature. And in so far as the early modern period, and in particular the 60 years before the Civil War, was a time of intense concern about the possible breakdown of the social order, so this was enacted too on the level of the individual psyche. In the years round 1600 there was, as David Underdown puts it, 'a period of strained gender relations in early modern England and … it lay at the heart of the "crisis of order"' (Underdown 1985: 136).

It is fitting, then, that the dishonourable Sir John Falstaff's name contains within it that obvious sexual pun: Fall-staff. Not long after his 'honour' speech on the Shrewsbury battlefield, Falstaff attempts, illicitly, to reclaim his lost military manhood by stealing Hal's glory and claiming the conquest of Hotspur for his own. In a later play, he will be looking to re-establish his sexual manhood by dishonouring the citizens of a provincial English town and their wives.

In 1597 the Lord Chamberlain's Men saw Thomas Pope, their Petruccio of three years earlier, once more playing the braggart soldier as lover, in *The Merry Wives of Windsor*. Critics have often written about the difference between the Falstaff of the Henry plays and the Falstaff of *The Merry Wives*, but any discontinuity may have less to with Falstaff as a character than with his sphere of activity, which is transferred from the battlefield to the bedroom. It is a transition which, according to a tradition dating from eighteenth-century biographies, happened in response to a royal command. Elizabeth had been so taken with Falstaff the soldier in the history plays that she now desired to see him as a lover in a romantic comedy; Shakespeare complied, writing the play in a fort-night. The story is probably untrue; however, it *is* likely that the play was commissioned for a court performance either at Windsor or Whitehall, at a Garter Feast. As such, it too is implicated in the chival-ric pageantry of Elizabeth's court and its Accession Day celebrations. But whereas the Henry plays generate, on the whole, a positive attitude towards chivalric and martial values, *The Merry Wives of Windsor* acts – on a number of levels – as the satyr-play to the sequence. The priapic Falstaff is at the centre of a plot that consistently parodies those chival-ric values which the earlier plays had appeared to endorse. The play is rich in references to details of the Order of the Garter, such as the speech in which Mistress Quickly (brought from Eastcheap to play a parodic fairy queen) instructs her 'elves' to tend to all the trappings and ceremonies of the Garter investiture, all the 'chairs of order' and 'Each fair instalment, coat, and sev'ral crest'

> And *Honi soit qui mal y pense* write
> In em'rald tufts, flowers purple, blue and white
> Like sapphire, pearl, and rich embroidery,
> Buckled below fair knighthood's bending knee.
> (*Merry Wives* V.v.68–71)

The earlier point about Shakespeare's dual audience is important here. Even if the play was written in response to a commission for a specific court occasion, it was also written to be played in the public theatre. In fact the dual audience may be particularly important in *The Merry Wives*, where one of the key narrative dynamics involves the opposition between the citizens and the aristocracy, as Sir John Falstaff descends on the town intending to prey upon its inhabitants. At the Garter Feast, the Knights of the Garter, in a private showing, see one of their own kind disgraced; in the London public theatres the Knight's humiliation at the hands of the citizens is played out before an audience of citizens: chivalric masculinity is doubly humiliated. But for men in either audience, the play must have been an uncomfortable one to watch. If *The Taming of the Shrew* contains, on one level at least, a blatant and unreconstructed hymn to masculine supremacy, *The Merry Wives of Windsor* is a thoroughgoing deconstruction of it. It is not just that the women are witty and successful – in fact a sub-plot sees *them* gulled too. It is more to do with the way in which Falstaff is treated: this paradoxical character, who is both outlaw and part of the hegemonic aristocracy, takes on additional meanings in *The Merry Wives.*

The play's action revolves around Falstaff's increasingly desperate attempts to cuckold Frank Ford and George Page, citizens of Windsor. Ford's concern for *his* sexual honour verges on the pathological, while Page has an easy confidence in his own wife's virtue. In fact, both wives are more than able to hold their own against their would-be seducer. They repeatedly get the better of Falstaff and subject him to a series of humiliations, which appear to parody the rituals whereby disgraced Knights of the Garter were expelled from the Order. Falstaff is first carried out of Ford's house hidden in a buck-basket and dumped in the river. On his next attempt at seducing Mistress Ford, he loses his masculinity symbolically as he is forced to don the disguise of an old woman and is beaten out of the house. Finally, in a scene shot through with complex symbolism, Falstaff disguises himself as Herne the Hunter. Herne is a mythical figure, a local variant of Cernunnos, the horned god of Celtic mythology, and possibly linked with the Green Man and the Robin Hood traditions as a symbol of the masculine principle (Anderson 1990: 140–1). According to local legend Herne haunted Windsor Great Park as half-man, half-deer. Falstaff, then, dressed with horns, waits by the oak-tree. On the one hand, he is a figure of male fertility – and as such he identifies himself with another horned god:

> Now, the hot-blooded gods assist me! Remember, Jove, thou was a bull for thy Europa; love set on thy horns. O powerful love, that in some respects makes a beast a man, in some other a man a beast ... When gods have hot backs, what shall poor men do? For me, I am here a Windsor stag, and the fattest, I think, i'th'forest. Send me a cool rut-time, Jove, or who can blame me to piss my tallow?
>
> (*Merry Wives*, V.v.2–5, 11–14)

On the other hand, Falstaff has himself become that image which has haunted the tale, and Master Ford's fevered imagination, throughout the play: the horn-wearing cuckold, disgraced and taunted in a darkly comic charivari by the citizens, wives and children of Windsor. The play operates on multiple levels: on a narrative and generic level it is a citizen comedy, set (unusually for Shakespeare) in the world of middle-class provincial England and poking fun at the obsession with sexual 'honour' which a townsman like Ford shows. On another level it addresses its court audience directly, using the disgraced knight as a figure who subverts the chivalric values of the Garter Order. More broadly, on an allegorical and symbolic level Falstaff effectively becomes an embodiment of masculine abjection as he is systematically humiliated, degraded, punished, dishonoured and unmanned.

3.4   Elizabeth's performance of masculinity and the Elizabethan crisis in gender relations

> ... when something is about masculinity it isn't always 'about men'
> Eve Kosofsky Sedgwick, 'Gosh, Boy George, You Must Be
> Awfully Secure in Your Masculinity', 1995

The legend that Elizabeth personally commissioned *The Merry Wives of Windsor* may not be true; nonetheless, it is a powerful and suggestive idea that the humiliation of Falstaff should have been staged for the express pleasure of the Queen. For if there was indeed a crisis in gender relations in Elizabethan England, then the figure of the Queen herself was part of that crisis. There are, clearly, some gender confusions and ideological contradictions inherent in the iconic figure of Elizabeth as the female head of state in a social and political system that is so intensely patriarchal. Of course, any ideology worth its salt can cope with contradictions: it is constructed so to do. The question is, what manoeuvres it undertakes in order to negotiate those contradictions.

On one level Elizabeth herself encouraged a kind of gender confusion, frequently asserting, for very pragmatic political reasons, that she had the heart of a man, not of a woman. Her claim is most generally remembered in that version which she was supposed to have delivered to her soldiers at Tilbury in August 1588, as they awaited the possible Spanish invasion. Thomas Heywood, whose theatrical imagination was vivid, reported her as having appeared 'habited like an Amazonian Queene', while the speech she made is one of the most famous of all generals' addresses to their troops. 'I know I have the body of a weak and feeble woman,' she is reported as saying, 'but I have the heart and stomach of a king and of a King of England too' (Fletcher 1995: 80). Again, in the cultural politics of Elizabethan England, legend was paramount, and it was the *idea* of Elizabeth as warrior-queen, inspiring her troops in her steel armour, that was important. The speech was probably not delivered on that occasion at all, but written (perhaps) or approved for publication by Elizabeth as a deliberate exercise in image-creation (see Frye 1992: 95–114). Without doubt Elizabeth was an expert at manipulating the gender scheme to her own political advantage, presenting herself as virgin and mother, male and female, sexed and unsexed, weak and strong, as it suited her. Louis Montrose goes further, arguing that she 'incarnated a contradiction at the very centre of the Elizabethan sex/gender system' (Montrose 1986: 80). Nor did the accession of James I put an end to such contradictions, for he too was an ambiguous figure, who also 'unsettled gender distinctions: he was the powerful patriarch as pacifist and epicene courtier, doting on comely male favorites like Somerset and Buckingham ... James himself readily traversed gender boundaries' (McCandless 1997: 1–2).

Elizabeth (and James after her) may have a symbolic rather than a statistical importance in a study of the sex/gender system of Renaissance England, but that symbolic importance is strong enough to suggest that anxieties about that system were not too far from the surface. In this symbolic mode, Elizabeth's Tilbury speech marks a key moment in the Elizabethan understanding of gender, and hence of masculinity. In it she confronted, and resolved, one of the basic contradictions of her own position as monarch: her biological femaleness. Being a woman did not, of course, disqualify her from succession: kinship patterns were still more powerful among the ruling classes than gender bias, and the laws of primogeniture were sufficiently flexible to allow for *some* deviation from the usual pattern of male supremacy. Yet Elizabeth's position *was* compromised by her sexuality, and the multiple Tudor myths concerning the Virgin Queen were at least partly necessary to nullify the general sense that there was some kind of contradiction in having a woman – even an exceptional woman such as Elizabeth – occupying the throne by herself for any length of time. One tactic which Elizabeth employed effectively was that of appearing to defer to masculine judgement. Many years after her death she was remembered by Lucy Hutchinson for solving the problem of Queenship in just these terms:

[N]ever is [a kingdom] in any place happy where the hands that are made only for distaffs affect the management of sceptres. If any one object the fresh example of Queen Elizabeth, let them remember that the felicity of her reign was the effect of her submission to her masculine and wise counsellors.
(Cited in Keeble 1994: 191)

But the tactic of deferring to 'masculine and wise counsellors' could not work indefinitely. In time of war, of course, public anxiety increased in intensity: it was in response to the felt popular need for an effective male military leader that the Tilbury speech, in which Elizabeth claimed some of the qualities of masculinity for herself, was made and publicized.

Its effect was to articulate, and to give a political meaning to, the crucial distinction between sex and gender. Political theory had long recognized the need for separating out the actual body of the monarch from its ideal symbolic form: the doctrine which historians have dubbed that of the 'King's two bodies' had long stipulated that even though the actual ruler may be, in person, infirm, bad or even mad, his symbolic kingliness is not affected by that. Elizabeth's trick in the Tilbury speech was to transfer this separation to the sphere of sexual and gendered identity. Political expediency made it imperative that she establish that the fact of biological maleness should not be the sole guarantor of the qualities of masculinity. By claiming the 'heart and stomach of a King' rather than that of a Queen, Elizabeth established the possibility of a *female* masculinity. And since that King was a 'King of England too' there was, perhaps, more than a suspicion that such masculinity had an even more positive force when allied with national chauvinism.

The importance of Elizabeth's speech lies in the public and timely nature of its political context rather than in its novelty. After all, the figure of the virago was not itself new: nor was the idea that women may claim manly virtues. Indeed, to do so could be – and often was – seen as a positive attribute. Medieval lives of female saints, or of eminent women such as abbesses, frequently refer to their good qualities in masculine terms; they are praised for having transcended their mere femininity and having achieved something of the more complete humanity which is equated with the male sex. But the Tilbury speech goes beyond this. Elizabeth publicly invests herself with a masculine identity, and does so in a context where she is already publicly enacting a masculine role – that of encouraging the troops before the battle, of 'leading' them into battle, symbolically at least. On a mythic level it is a doubly performative moment. It is supremely theatrical, of course. But it is also performative in the sense that speech-act theory uses the word: it is language that makes something happen.

3.5   Warrior women, warrior men

What happens to heroic masculinity when it comes up against this ambiguous female? We have already seen one answer: in *The Taming of the Shrew* it turns into a fight – one which Petruccio wins by becoming exaggeratedly 'manly' in order to conquer Katherine. Other plays give other answers. In *Henry VI, Part 1,* Joan La Pucelle is a shadow-image of Elizabeth who reduces her enemies to quivering wrecks. Joan dramatizes some of the anxieties below the surface which are generated by the figure of the woman warrior, but she remains a relatively undeveloped character. Her basic function is to embody leadership qualities and a martial prowess which puts the English fighting men to shame – even the English martial hero Talbot, disgusted and ashamed though he is that 'A woman clad in armour chaseth men' (I.vii.3), is unable to best her in single combat. Only towards the end of the play, when Joan's fighting skill is proved to be (as the English had always suspected) demonic in origin, are the English, and traditional heroic masculinity, let off the hook. The ending of *Henry VI, Part 1* re-establishes the gender order by disposing of Joan; her treatment in the play as a whole amounts to an act of containment, a neutralization of the disturbing challenge she poses to that order. Joan, though, has only allies and enemies. More complex are those plays in which the male warrior-hero is the husband or the lover of the warrior-queen. In *Macbeth* and in *Antony and Cleopatra* we see two plays in which this dynamic works itself out in very different ways.

The stereotype of the warrior-hero is one which Shakespeare rarely leaves unchallenged. As Robin Headlam Wells puts it, 'there is in the tragedies and histories a consistently sceptical view of ... heroic masculinity' (Wells 2000: 24). And elsewhere, too: from Titus to Achilles, from Coriolanus to Bertram, from Falstaff to Hamlet, Shakespeare continually explores the contradictions of the role. It is one aspect of the wider concern with sexual stereotyping, which is one of Shakespeare's enduring themes, and which, in *Macbeth*, becomes central to the tragic action. *Macbeth* indeed, has attracted analyses of its representation of 'manliness' for nearly half a century, long before the current vogue for masculinity studies (see, for example, Brooks 1964). A key scene is the confrontation between Macbeth and his wife, in which she persuades him to take Duncan's life.

Lady Macbeth is, perhaps, only metaphorically a warrior-queen. She is not literally a fighter, like Joan, and indeed when the final battle approaches, she is conveniently written out of the play. At the level of the play's imagery, however, this 'unsexed' queen, with her symbolically bloodied hands, becomes a very Elizabethan kind of woman warrior in her own right – one who, like Elizabeth herself, questions the established gender boundaries, and who can claim the 'heart and stomach of a king' by dint of her rhetoric rather than of her martial prowess. Their debate about regicide clearly foregrounds questions of gender construction, and what it means to 'be a man'. As she impugns her husband's manhood, accusing him of cowardice, Macbeth responds:

MACBETH: Prithee peace.
                     I dare do all that may become a man;
                     Who dares do more is none.
LADY MACBETH: What beast was't then
                     That made you break this enterprise to me?
                     When you durst do it, then you were a man;
                     And to be more than what you were, you would
                     Be so much more the man.

(Macbeth I.vii.39–59)

Macbeth gestures rather vaguely towards his own notion of what it might mean to be a man: it involves certain limitations, certain boundaries of decency. It involves taking some physical and moral risks (the audience is reminded of his first appearance as blood-soaked warrior) – but only up to a point: 'Who dares do more is none'. Lady Macbeth disagrees. She offers Macbeth another picture of masculinity – one which is entirely defined by the quality of violent risk-taking; she counters Macbeth's self-image as the man subject to the laws of decency with an image of him as already controlled by the beast of his desire. And then, decisively, she offers him a way to reclaim that lost quality of masculinity: 'When you durst do it, then you were a man'. When she finally persuades him, he confirms that he has accepted the masculine values which she has been struggling to establish, saying to her (in horror? in admiration?):

Bring forth men-children only
For thy undaunted mettle should compose
Nothing but males

(Macbeth I.vii. 72–4)

Lady Macbeth claims the right to define true manliness, and she persuades her husband to accept her vision of it. Other characters in the play offer, briefly, more subtle conceptions of manliness. When Macduff, at Malcolm's court, is brought news of the death of his wife and children, he is griefstricken. 'Dispute it like a man', Malcolm advises him – manliness here being the ability to suppress or conquer his emotions. Macduff is more humane: 'I shall do so,' he replies, 'But I must also feel it as a man' (IV.iii.221–3). To feel emotions such as pity or grief is not, in Macduff's terms, the opposite of manliness, but its very essence. Yet in this scene, too, the ideology of masculinity becomes subsumed into the values of militarism. When Malcolm once more urges Macduff to 'let grief convert to anger', Macduff replies:

> O, I could play the woman with mine eyes
> And braggart with my tongue! But gentle heavens
> Cut short all intermission. Front to front
> Bring thou this fiend of Scotland and myself.
> Within my sword's length set him. If he scape,
> Heaven forgive him too.
>
> (*Macbeth* IV.iii.230–7)

The gender scheme is reinstated as Macduff rejects his tears as 'womanly', while Malcolm, for whom the conversion of Malcolm's grief to anger is a political and military necessity, looks on approvingly and tells him, 'This tune goes manly' (IV.iii. 237).

Coppelia Kahn has given a psychoanalytic reading to the play, arguing persuasively that Macbeth's 'inability to maintain and defend his conceptions of manliness, emanate from his unconscious dependency on [women] as mentors' (Kahn 1981: 173). These mentors, representing the mother from whom the boy-child (like that other bloody warrior Coriolanus) has failed to negotiate a successful separation, include the witches as well as Lady Macbeth. But it is as literal wife as well as metaphorical mother that Lady Macbeth confronts her husband, and the force of the confrontation scene derives in part from the specificity of this relationship. The call to 'be so much more the man' has very different connotations when spoken by the wife from those it would have if it were spoken by, say, a comrade-in-arms. The sexual subtext reverberates powerfully. In order to fulfil the role of husband and lover, his wife instructs him to become more of the soldier, the action hero. He is in a double bind, of course, because on another level to obey these instructions is to accept her authority. With Petruccio and Falstaff Shakespeare plays the relationship between soldier and lover for laughs; with Hal he plays it as *realpolitik*. In *Macbeth* he plays it as the source of tragedy.

The year 1606, when *Macbeth* was first staged, seems to have been a time when Shakespeare was particularly engaged with the contradictions of the dual role of lover and soldier. In the same year he explores the issues again in *Antony and Cleopatra*, a story which, by the time Shakespeare wrote his version, was already shot through with gendered meanings. Tudor accounts of Antony and Cleopatra constructed their narrative in emblematic terms, the nature of which can be seen in the casual reference which Francis Bacon makes to Antony in his Essay 'Of Love':

You may observe, that amongst all the great and worthy persons (whereof
the memory remaineth, either ancient or recent), there is not one that hath
been transported to the mad degree of love; which shows that great spirits
and great business do keep out this weak passion. You must except, never-
theless, Marcus Antonius, the half partner of the empire of Rome, and
Appius Claudius, the decemvir and lawgiver: whereof the former was
indeed a voluptuous man and inordinate ...

(Bacon 1625: 50–1)

Mark Antony exemplifies, for Bacon and his contemporaries, the 'great
and worthy person' brought low by the power of 'this weak passion',
love. This is the moral of the tale as represented in Plutarch, and as it
was mediated for the Elizabethan age by Sir Thomas North's 1579
translation of the *Lives of the Greeks and Romans*:

Antonius being thus inclined, the last and extremest mischief of all other (to
wit, the love of Cleopatra) lighted on him, who did waken and stir up many
vices yet hidden in him, and were never seen to any; and if any spark of
goodness or hope of rising were left in him, Cleopatra quenched it straight
and made it worse than before.

(Plutarch 1964: 199)

Philo, in the opening sequence of the play, presents the 'official'
Roman perspective on Antony. The triumvir has, Philo tells
Demetrius, fallen from his former godlike glory as a soldier and a
leader of men since he met Cleopatra:

PHILO: Those his goodly eyes
            That o'er the files and musters of the war
            Have glowed like plated Mars, now bend, now turn
            The office and devotion of their view
            Upon a tawny front ...
            Take but good note, and you shall see in him
            The triple pillar of the world transformed
            Into a strumpet's fool. Behold and see.

(*Antony* I.i.2–6, 11–13)

Philo, like Plutarch, puts the blame for Antony's decline not on the
abstract 'love' but on Cleopatra herself, the 'tawny front', the 'strum-
pet'. As she and Antony enter together Philo urges both Demetrius
and the audience to 'Behold and see', and as they do so, it appears that
his point of view is at least partially borne out, as Antony loudly and
publicly rejects the Roman messengers, and 'approves the common
liar, who Thus speaks of him at Rome' (I.i.60–1). Demetrius, by the
end of the scene, is convinced that Antony has indeed been corrupted

by Cleopatra – although it is less certain whether the audience in the theatre is asked to subscribe uncritically to the same strait-laced Roman point of view. Even so, it is clear that some important change has taken place in Antony. In another scene, a few minutes later, Caesar characterizes this change in explicitly gendered terms, as a failure of masculinity on Antony's part.

> CAESAR: From Alexandria
> This is the news: he fishes, drinks, and wastes
> The lamps of night in revel; is not more manlike
> Than Cleopatra, nor the queen of Ptolemy
> More womanly than he.
>
> *(Antony* I.iv.3–7)

This is the particular inflection which Shakespeare/Caesar gives to the story of Antony and Cleopatra: not merely that Antony has had his hidden natural vices 'stirred up' by Cleopatra, but that he has been dis-gendered by her. Later in the play Cleopatra will literally attempt to take on the 'manlike' role of warrior, leading her troops (disastrously) into battle, but in these early scenes she mainly represents, for the Romans at least, a destructive feminine principle to which Antony has succumbed.

Nonetheless, like the gender confusions exemplified by Elizabeth and James, the manlike queen and the womanly male ruler have meanings whose implications are both political and personal. For Caesar, of course, it is the political that predominates. Antony has fulfilled the basic fear of the imperialist, and 'gone native'. He has taken on the values and customs of a foreign, and potentially subordinate, culture – and, what is worse, he has done so at a time when there is a significant threat not only to Rome's expansionist programme but to its very existence. Caesar's anger, however, is expressed in a particularly personal register: Antony's implied betrayal of the Roman state is figured in his betrayal of an ideal of soldier-like manliness.

Caesar's speech also establishes a theme which is repeated throughout the play: the fear that Shakespeare's Roman males have of the female. This fear takes various forms, and many of them follow the traditional tropes of Renaissance misogyny: the lasciviousness and inconstancy of women are referred to throughout the play. Underlying this, however, is the deeper fear that the man may himself lose his masculinity, and become 'womanly'. Caesar's despairing description of Antony receives several direct echoes later in the play. For instance, Enobarbus, finding himself and his fellow-soldiers moved to tears by Antony's generosity before the battle at Alexandria, exclaims instinctively, 'For shame, Transform us not to women' (IV.ii.35–6). It is this fear which dictates that in the play's Roman world, women must be kept strictly in their place and subordinated, like Octavia, to the demands of the political world which is the domain of the men. The culture of Egypt, on the other hand (a culture which the bipolar oppositions of the play itself characterize as feminine, in direct contrast to the 'masculinity' of Rome) unsettles the clear gender distinctions by which the Roman male lives.

In response, Roman definitions of properly masculine behaviour become increasingly extreme. Having complained about Antony's current lack of manliness, Caesar goes on to contrast it with the manly heights from which he has fallen:

CAESAR: Antony
Leave thy lascivious wassails. When thou once
Was beaten from Modena, where thou slew'st
Hirtius and Pansa, consuls, at thy heel
Did famine follow, whom thou fought'st against
(Though daintily brought up) with patience more
Than savages could suffer. Thou didst drink
The stale of horses and the gilded puddle
Which beasts would cough at … On the Alps
It is reported thou didst eat strange flesh,
Which some did die to look on. And all this
(It wounds thine honor that I speak it now)
Was borne so like a soldier that thy cheek
So much as lanked not.

(Antony I.iv.55–63, 66–71)

This, in Caesar's eyes, is true manliness: a 'soldier-like' manliness which depends for its definition upon martial values. Yet even as he asserts it, his language slips away from him. The younger Antony's preparedness to 'drink … the gilded puddle Which beasts would cough at' places him, in Caesar's estimation, at a point somewhere near the epitome of manhood. The audience, however, is simultaneously asked to consider – as it was asked in *Macbeth* – whether this 'manliness' makes him more than the beasts with which he is compared, or less.

Because Rome's concept of masculinity is presented as so rigid and narrow, because the Republic's model of relationships between the sexes is so clearly utilitarian, the audience is offered the opportunity to respond more sympathetically to the erotic charge which is apparent between Antony and Cleopatra. But it is important not to underestimate the subversiveness which the relationship represents. Indeed, Caesar's fear and disgust at Antony's 'womanly' nature is given additional power when we remember that it is grounded in a single-sex scheme in which gender boundaries have to be actively maintained rather than taken for granted. Cleopatra's description of their amorous play is more subversive than she knows:

> CLEOPATRA: That time – O times! –
> I laughed him out of patience; and that night
> I laughed him into patience; and next morn,
> Ere the ninth hour, I drunk him to his bed;
> Then put my tires and mantles on him, whilst
> I wore his sword Philippian.
>
> *(Antony* II.v.18–23*)*

This detail of their courtship is not in Plutarch: again, Shakespeare appears to be placing a special emphasis of his own upon the effeminizing influence which Cleopatra has on Antony. He seems, too, to be making the point that Caesar is not wrong. Caesar describes it with disgust, Cleopatra with tenderness, humour and passion; but Cleopatra confirms what Caesar asserts to Lepidus: that in Egypt the gender boundaries become more fluid. Images of dissolution and melting abound in the play, and for Caesar (as for Elizabethan Englishmen), this fluidity is closely tied in with fears concerning the dissolution of other, more directly political, boundaries. When Antony declares 'Let Rome in Tiber melt!' (I.i.33) and Cleopatra echoes later 'Melt Egypt into Nile' (II.v.78), it appears that Caesar might have a point.

To what extent does the play endorse Caesar's point of view? Camille Paglia is one of many critics who read the play as inherently conservative, dramatizing the eventual victory of a reality principle which Caesar personifies:

> Caesar wins in *Antony and Cleopatra* because he represents political order, the dream of the fractured, fractious Renaissance. *Antony and Cleopatra*'s reactionary political premise is borne out by Italian history.
>
> (Paglia 1990: 221–2)

There is certainly room to read the play in this way. To the extent that the Roman analysis of Antony's weakness is eventually supported by the military victory that leads to his downfall, the play appears to stage an action with a conventional moral. Antony, it suggests, allows himself to be led by Cleopatra, and thus himself becomes 'womanly' and unable to act out his 'proper' role of warrior-hero. The scene in which he dismisses his military armour-bearer and allows himself to be dressed – clumsily – for battle by Cleopatra, echoes her earlier description of their transvestite bedroom play, and these echoes serve to emphasize the fact that this is no longer erotic play but the deadly art of war. Antony, it appears, is unable to keep the two spheres separate, and his failures as a military leader are, in the words of his own soldiers, directly related to his failure of masculinity. 'Our leader's led,' laments Canidius, 'And we are women's men' (III.vii.68–9). Again, as the action moves from the bedroom to the battlefield, and as Antony makes tactical blunders by following after the fleeing Cleopatra, Scarus laments 'Experience, manhood, honor, ne'er before did violate so itself.' (III.x.22–3). At the same time, femininity appears to be loaded with negative values. Cleopatra herself displays most of the 'sins' which Renaissance misogyny ascribed to women: inconstancy, sensuality, vanity and so on. The narrative, and the linguistic rhetoric of the play, appear to endorse Caesar's viewpoint.

The performative rhetoric, however, does something different. Take, for example, the famous speech of Cleopatra's before her death, as she contemplates suicide rather than the shameful captivity which she can expect in Rome, where

> CLEOPATRA: the quick comedians
> Extemporally will stage us, and present
> Our Alexandrian revels: Antony
> Shall be brought drunken forth, and I shall see
> Some squeaking Cleopatra boy my greatness
> I' th' posture of a whore.
> *(Antony V.ii.216–21)*

This speech of Cleopatra's is often, rightly, quoted in support of the critical commonplace that the Elizabethan stage was an extremely self-conscious, and self-referential, institution. But we can take this further in the context of the play's concerns with gender issues, since the self-referentiality is clearly gender-related here – and perhaps strangely so. At this intense moment, the stage calls attention to its own artifice, and in particular to the gender of the young male actor who is indeed 'boying' Cleopatra's greatness in front of the London audience. It is easy enough to see it as a kind of proto-Brechtian *Verfremdungseffekt.* Presumably, there is an element of self-congratulation here too: the implication is that the boy actor playing Cleopatra on Shakespeare's stage actually outdid in skill the squeakings and the posturings which he conjures up in his imaginary Roman counterpart. Even so, the moment is one in which the gender play of the Elizabethan theatre is being made, quite deliberately, visible to its audience.

In recent years, the boy players of Shakespeare's theatre have attracted nearly as much attention from Renaissance scholars as they did from the anti-theatrical polemicists of their own day. Now, as then, much of the debate has focused on the erotics of their performances, and much has been written about the extent to which these were addressed primarily to a homoerotic gaze (see, for example, Howard 1988; Orgel 1989 and 1996). Those cultural critics of late sixteenth- and early seventeenth-century England who railed against the theatre seem to have been obsessed with this convention of cross-dressing young male actors. Writers such as Stephen Gosson, William Rankins, John Rainolds, Philip Stubbes and William Prynne pointed repeatedly to the Bible's injunctions against such gender confusion in Deuteronomy 12: 5. In a fairly typical passage from *Th' Overthrow of Stage-Playes*, John Rainolds and his co-authors spend several pages reiterating the point that

> if anie man doe put on Womans raiment, hee is dishonested and defiled, because he transgresseth the boundes of modestie and comelinesse, and weareth that which Gods lawe forbiddeth him to weare, which mans lawe affirmeth hee can not weare without reproofe
>
> (Rainolds 1599: 16)

Their objections went beyond mere biblical proscription. Such cross-dressing, they argued, would have a long-term effeminizing effect on the male. Of course, it is not only the cross-dressing itself, but the whole repertoire by which femininity is represented in gesture and voice which is so disturbing to these antitheatrical polemicists:

> Yet the third reason, wherein playes are charged, not for making young men come foorth in hoores attire, like the lewde woman in the *Proverbs*: but for teaching them to counterfeit her actions, her wanton kisse, her impudent face, her wicked speeches and enticements... [For] *different behaviour becommeth different sexes, and, it beseemeth not men to folow wemens maners.* [Original italics]
>
> (Rainolds 1599: 17)

The italics of the final sentence emphasize the key point. They indicate Rainolds's sense of urgency about maintaining the proper gender boundaries of dress and behaviour. William Prynne, the author of *Histriomastix*, was even more virulent in his description of a popular actor:

> A man enfeebled in all his joynts, resolved into a more than womanish effeminacy, whose part it is to speak with his hands and gestures, comes

forth upon the Stage: and for this one, I know not whom, neither man nor woman, the whole citie flocke together, that so the fabulous lusts of antiq- uity may be acted. Yea, men ... are unmanned on the Stage: all the honour and vigour of their sex is effeminated with the shame, the dishonesty of an unsinued body. He who is most womanish and best resembles the female sex, gives best content.

(Prynne 1633: I, 168)

It is not clear whether Prynne here is talking about a boy playing the part of a woman, or whether, as he seems to suggest, it is *all* men who 'are unmanned on the stage'. The actor, in Prynne's vision, is marginal- ized not only by the indeterminacy of his class position in society, but also by his ambiguous gender status.

Not everybody held these views, of course, but nor was their cur- rency within the culture confined to a lunatic fringe or a bigoted minority of religious extremists. Theatre history traditionally refers to the enemies of the Elizabethan stage as 'Puritans', but the term is an oversimplification: not all of those who spoke out against the stage would have defined themselves as Puritans, and the concerns which the stage raised were shared by people of many different religious alle- giances. The anti-theatrical polemicists articulate an extreme version of concerns about theatrical illusion, which were explored in other ways by other writers – and not least by those who wrote for the theatre itself.

Moreover, this concern about the effeminizing power of the stage has little to do with any generalized cultural homophobia – although occasionally these polemicists do indeed rail against how the stage encourages men 'in their secret conclaves ... [to] play y[e] Sodomites, or worse' (Stubbes 1583: L8v). But as histories of sexuality have repeatedly suggested, it was not until much later that Western culture began to make a categorical distinction between homosexual and heterosexual identities, and to designate the latter as normative, the former as deviant and the two as mutually exclusive (see Trumbach 1977; Foucault 1981; Bray 1982; Winkler 1990). The notion that a man's identity was constituted, to any significant extent, according to his objects of sexual desire was foreign to the Renaissance.

The anti-theatrical concerns about gender were actually related to wider concerns, which have two apparently contradictory dimen- sions. On the one hand, it is a concern about the stage as a place of illusion and falsity, as illustrated by this comment by Stephen Gosson:

> The proof is evident, the consequence is necessary, that in stage plays for a boy to put on the attire, the gesture, the passions of a woman; for a mean person to take upon him the title of a Prince with counterfeit port and train, is by outward signs to show themselves other wise than they are, and so within the compass of a lie.
>
> (Gosson 1582: sig. E5)

Gosson's syntax shows the logic of his position. Gender confusion and class impersonation both come under one encompassing heading: that of the lie. The stage is unreliable because it is false; the world is one way, but the stage represents it as another. The great eternal truths are there to be discovered, but in order that we may do so the theatre's false 'outward signs [which] show themselves other wise than they are' must be stripped away.

This was one dimension of the problem which the stage presents in Elizabethan England: it falsifies eternal truths, creating an illusory new order which rivals Creation. But the social context in which Gosson is speaking is significant here: that of a society in which major religious social and economic upheavals had already taken place and would continue for half a century or more. In late sixteenth-century England, 'Mobility begot confusion over the structure of rank and occupation; confusion over the division of labour, in its turn, bred perplexity over the place of gender in the assignment of tasks, and that in turn, raised questions ... concerning the conditions and future of patriarchal authority' (Agnew 1986: 129). In a world full of such transitions, what price eternal truths? And so, alongside the charge of falsifying reality, there is a more disturbing reason to be suspicious about the theatre. The deeper fear is that the protean nature of theatrical illusion calls into question the stability of meaning itself. In *The School of Abuse,* Gosson calls the stage 'Circe's cup' (Gosson 1579: 10) – the magic catalyst which can change men from one state to another, reducing them to the status of beasts. Like Stubbes, with his concerns about the power of crossdressing in *An Anatomy of Abuses* and his conviction that 'to wear the apparel of another sex is to participate with the same' (Stubbes 1583: sig. F5v), and like Prynne, with his claim that 'men ... are unmanned on the Stage' (Prynne 1633: I, 168), the more extreme forms of anti-theatrical polemic held that theatre itself was literally effeminizing. But as we have already seen, effeminacy, in Elizabethan and Jacobean terms, was the result of too much time spent in the company of women – Antony's problem, as Rome views it. The all-male environment of the Elizabethan theatre company could be seen, paradoxically, as 'effeminizing' because, in Elizabethan cultural terms, the theatre was itself effectively gendered feminine. Its key vices are those which the Renaissance traditionally associated with women: luxury, lechery, falseness and vanity. It was not such a great leap to argue that time spent in theatres as player or spectator led to effeminization.

In *this* argument, an almost magical power is ascribed to the theatre – its ability to effect (on one level at least) actual changes in the real world. These changes may be confined to the moment of illusion on the stage or they may have a more permanent effect; they may take the form of the effeminizing power of the cross-dressed boy who thereby 'participates with' the sex whose clothing he assumes; or of the actor who in playing the part of the vicious tyrant actually becomes, in some measure, that which he performs; or of the audience member, whom the play inspires to lechery or vice. As Stephen Orgel puts it, 'the deepest fear in the anti-theatrical tracts ... is the fear of a universal effeminization' (Orgel 1989: 17).

The irony, then, is that the gender complexities inherent in the story of Antony and Cleopatra are being mediated by an art-form and an institution which itself relies for its meaning on a certain disturbing fluidity in the semiotics of gender. And then, at a key moment in the play the audience is reminded of this by Cleopatra's foregrounding of the boy-player! The resultant effect is that paradoxical one which Judith Butler ascribes to the performance of 'drag' in contemporary culture:

> The performance of drag plays upon the distinction between the anatomy of the performer and the gender that is being performed. But we are actually in the presence of three contingent dimensions of significant corporeality: anatomical sex, gender identity and gender performance ... As much as drag creates a unified picture of 'woman' (what its critics often oppose), it also reveals the distinctness of those aspects of gendered experience which are falsely naturalized as a unity through the regulatory fiction of heterosexual coherence. *In imitating gender, drag implicitly reveals the imitative structure of gender itself.* [original italics]
>
> (Butler 1990: 137)

The theatrical environment itself subverts the fixity of gender schemes which the 'Roman' voice within the play appears to endorse. On stage *Antony and Cleopatra* demonstrates the performativity of gender, and while the subversion of fixed categories which this performativity implies appears to be presented negatively at the level of narrative, it is presented positively at the level of the theatrical performance itself. Of course, to some extent, all plays from the transvestite stage of the English Renaissance have this effect: in *Antony and Cleopatra*, however, the effect is particularly marked because so much of the rest of the play's rhetoric seems to be insisting on the moral and political desirability of some kind of fixity of gender definitions. The play pulls in two directions at once: there is a dialectical tension between form and content which this particular speech highlights.

The speech also draws attention to the play's relationship to its own source material. By invoking the imaginary Roman boy-actor, the 'squeaking Cleopatra' who boys her greatness 'i' th' posture of a whore', Shakespeare's Cleopatra both returns the audience to the actuality of the transgendered speaker who speaks the lines to them – and also simultaneously directs the audience towards *other* potential versions of the Antony and Cleopatra tale. The squeaking boy both is and is not the actor at the Globe, and the characters whose tragedies the audience have witnessed both are and are not the historical figures whose shared emblematic meanings are both referred to and re-evaluated by the play itself. The Antony and the Cleopatra who are represented in this play are sites of contested meanings, and the contest over the meaning of Antony's subverted masculinity is central.

Contemporary popular psychology talks approvingly of the desirability of men 'getting in touch with their feminine side'. The phrase is so well-worn that it has become a cliché, although it would have had little meaning for Shakespeare's audiences. Nor is it a sufficiently subtle tool for thinking about how the play deals with issues of masculinity. The single-sex model of human sexual identity with which pre-Enlightenment audiences are familiar makes better sense, perhaps, both of Macbeth's anxieties and of Antony's lascivious wassails than does the post-Enlightenment model, with its recourse to the evidence of biology and the assumption of an unbridgeable bipolar opposition between the sexes. But it is too overdetermined, too laden with Renaissance assumptions about the relative worth of men and women, to do full justice to the complex gender play which *Antony and Cleopatra* stages. So I would like to finish by quoting a proposition by Eve Kosofsky Sedgwick, and suggesting that it and *Antony and Cleopatra* may illuminate each other. In an article entitled 'Gosh, Boy George, You Must Be Awfully Secure in Your Masculinity' (the quotation is taken from a Long Island disc jockey interviewing the cross-dressed pop star), Sedgwick offers a way of drawing the diagram of the relationship between the sexes which is

different from either of the ones we have looked at so far. She offers
the proposition that

MASCULINITY AND FEMININITY ARE IN MANY RESPECTS
ORTHOGONAL TO EACH OTHER

Orthogonal: that is, instead of being at opposite poles of the same axis, they
are actually in different, perpendicular dimensions, and therefore are independently variable.   [Original typeface]

(Sedgwick 1995: 15)

At first sight this looks rather like a Men-are-from-Mars-Women-
are-from-Venus kind of statement. In fact, it is nothing of the kind.
Sedgwick draws on the research of Sandra Bem, whose work on
psychological androgyny rated people on two separate scales,
measuring stereotypical female-ascribed traits on one scale and
stereotypical male-ascribed traits on the other. Bem found

that many lucky people score high on both, many other people score low on
both, and most importantly, that a high score on either of them does not
predict a low score on the other ... One implication of work like Sandra
Bem's is that not only are some people more masculine or more feminine
than others, but some people are just plain more *gender-y* than others ...

(Sedgwick 1995: 16)

It is a way of thinking about masculinity – and about femininity – which
puts into a whole new light Caesar's contemptuous comment that
Antony 'is not more manlike Than Cleopatra, nor the queen of
Ptolemy More womanly than he' (I.iv.5–6). Shakespeare, of course, did
not have Bem's research to draw upon. Even so, to describe both
Antony and Cleopatra as 'just plain more *gender-y*' (especially in
comparison with the unsexed Macbeths) has a certain satisfying ring.

4

The Spectacle of Masculinity in the Restoration Theatre

4.1 Theatre and Restoration

On his return to England in 1660 Charles II had envisioned the re-establishing of a court theatre of the kind his father had maintained. The finances of the restored royal household, however, were more constrained than those of the pre-War Caroline court, and, consequently, the theatre which actually developed after 1660 was a public and commercial one, largely dependent upon box-office takings for its survival. Whereas Elizabeth, James and Charles I and their courtiers had maintained companies of players as part of their private retinue, and summoned them to court, or to their country houses, for private performances, Charles II doled out licences to favoured courtier-managers, and then went to the public playhouse to watch the resulting performances. In the early years of the Restoration, the dominant presence in these playhouses may have been that of the court and its followers, and it was, perhaps, to this dominant group that the politician-playwrights of Charles's restored theatre first addressed themselves, with a sense of speaking to those who shared their own beliefs, concerns and assumptions about the world. It is clear, however, that before long a broad range of professional and commercial people, citizens and merchants and their households were also attending in significant numbers (see Avery 1966; Holland 1979; Love 1980, and Scouten and Hume 1980). As one of the first Restoration theatre managers, Thomas Killigrew, commented to Samuel Pepys, 'not the King only for State, but all civil people do think they may come as well as any' (Pepys 1970–83: VIII, 56). Nor was this variety necessarily an expression of consensus: the Restoration theatre was, increasingly, both divided and divisive, pulled in different directions by the various class and interest groups which constituted its audiences (Shepherd and Womack 1996: 145).

As the city grew larger, wealthier, better educated, more diverse and socially mobile, an intellectual and cultural milieu grew up that was independent of the court, while at the same time court culture itself was subject to division and fragmentation. The London theatres, caught between these cultures of the court and of the city, began to look more and more towards the city. Companies outgrew their theatres, theatres burned down and were rebuilt, and in the process theatre buildings became larger, enabling (or forcing) managements to target a larger cross-section of the population. The playwrights made fun, in the theatrical language of the day, of the opposition between the 'cits' and the 'wits', but this opposition was symptomatic of deeper societal and political divides, between Whigs and Tories, the moneyed interest and the landed interest. Shifting loyalties, allegiances and alliances within these camps finally led, in 1688, to the flight of the Catholic James II and the 'Glorious Revolution'. This turned out to be a virtually bloodless coup which aligned England with the European Protestant powers against France, and redefined the monarchy – not in the absolutist terms of the Stuart kings, but as a contract between Parliament and the Crown. The Stuart restoration lasted for only 28 years of political and cultural transition. The dramatic representations of masculinity, which we will be looking at in this chapter, come from the middle years of this period, from the 1670s, and they have their roots in the ideological tensions generated by these transitions. The figures of the fop, the rake, the aristocratic libertine and the merchant-citizen all have a political dimension to them, in a theatre and in a society in which masculinity is increasingly being defined in terms of a new sense of national identity and of realigned class interests.

4.2   Actors and actresses: men watching women, women watching men

In the theatres themselves, however, the representation of gender had already been renegotiated, as the first generation of professional English actresses had made their entrance in the early 1660s. While this has rightly been seen as an important chapter in the history of women, it should not be forgotten that it also changes things significantly as far as the representation of masculinity on the stage is concerned. The difference between a theatre in which all parts, male and female, are played by male actors, and one in which the male characters are played by men and the female ones by women, lies in the way in which the balance of the representational equation is changed and made more symmetrical. It creates the stage as a space for a

different kind of erotic interchange, both between the actors themselves and (more importantly in the late seventeenth century) between
the actress and the audience – especially the male playgoer. The
Restoration stage was not slow to exploit such a possibility, and the
representation of masculinities in the Restoration theatre takes place
on this stage, newly charged with this erotic dynamic.

In one sense, the arrival of the actresses can be said to create the
conditions, perhaps for the first time within the theatre, for something
like what Laura Mulvey, writing in 1989, called the 'male gaze' – a heterosexual gaze which is both desiring and controlling. It should not,
however, be assumed that the economics of the look in this period
attributed all the power (as it does in Mulvey's original model, which is
based on classic Hollywood cinema narrative) to the male controller of
the look. In fact, the gendering of the spectator as male and the spectacle as female seems to have taken place rather later, during the course
of the eighteenth century (Straub 1992: 19). In the early modern
period, too, to be the object of the gaze was a token of one's own
power and status – and the Restoration is still, after all, an era when
many attended the theatre not only to see, but also to be seen. One of
the many transitions which took place in the Restoration period
appears to have concerned the politics of the gaze.

The audience gaze in the Restoration theatre is one to which the
stage actress (unlike her screen counterpart) can reply. This ability of
the actress to gaze back at the audience is a crucial aspect of the
implied contract between stage and audience in this theatre. In Samuel
Pepys's account of his relationship with the actress Elizabeth Knepp,
he talks of how she would 'wink and smile on me' (Pepys 1970–83: IX,
326) during her performances – much to the anger of his wife. But, as
the chatty, bantering Prologues and Epilogues of Restoration plays
testify, the compact theatres of the Restoration were designed to
enable this kind of close contact between the actors and the audience,
who got to know each other well – and sometimes intimately. Pepys
again:

> 5 October 1667 ... and so to the King's house. And there, going in, met with
> Knepp and she took us up into the tiring rooms and to the women's shift
> where Nell [Gwynn] was dressing herself and was all unready and is very
> pretty, prettier than I thought ...
>
> (Pepys 1970–83: IX, 326)

Nell Gwynn was only the most famous example of the actress for
whom the stage was effectively a stepping-stone towards a more comfortable life as the wife or (more frequently) the kept mistress of a

rich and powerful man. Living on a decent pension (perhaps £300 per year) and enjoying the luxury of private lodgings and a coach and pair, there are numerous instances of actresses who left the stage in lean times in order to become the prized 'possession' of anyone from a member of the minor gentry up to the King himself. Not surprisingly it was a custom which was not entirely popular with the players, theatre managers and writers, who frequently saw their main attractions lured away for private use, and complained to these would-be keepers that

> our Women who adorn each Play
> Bred at our cost, become at length your Prey
> While green, and sour, like Trees we bear 'em all,
> But when they're mellow straight to you they fall.
> (Nathaniel Lee, *The Rival Queens*, Epilogue
> cited in Wilson 1964: 53)

But if the status of the actress was compromised in one way by the erotics of the Restoration theatre, what about the male actor? Was his position compromised too? Clearly not in such a direct way: there are no records of any comparable custom whereby ladies of 'quality' visited the male actors' dressing-rooms to watch them changing. Yet the status of actors was suspect in other ways. Before the Civil War, actors had faced the Puritan accusation that the theatre was sinful because, among other things, it involved boys dressing up as women, and adult men enacting love scenes with transvestite boys; the actor, according to this line of argument, flirted with the possibility of male same-sex desire and sodomy on the stage and (probably) actually indulged in the act itself off it. And while the disappearance of the boy-players in the Restoration theatre put paid to this specific line of attack from the anti-theatrical faction, the masculinity of male players in the Restoration and eighteenth-century theatre continued to be seen as ambiguous. The actor continually puts himself on display (literally making a spectacle of himself), because he pretends to be what he is not, because his whole lifestyle transgresses, or at least calls into question, conventional social and moral boundaries: all of these posed problems for an age which was trying to rewrite the norms for masculinity in ways which stressed stability. Could an actor ever truly be 'manly'? In the early eighteenth century, as a separate homosexual identity became more and more sharply defined in English society, the male actor's propensity to display led to his sexuality being increasingly constructed as 'deviant' (see Straub 1992). This construction is embryonically present in some Restoration writings about actors as well.

Here, however, while this deviance might on occasion be linked (as it was in a series of satires against the comedian James Nokes) with accusations of sodomy, it is as much to do with an otherness, which includes both class and questions of 'authenticity'. The actor is 'other' because he stands outside – or in opposition to – the stable signifiers of society. Thus his deviance may as well be constructed in terms of an excessive heterosexuality as of a stigmatized homosexuality.

Moreover, the gender identity of the male actor, like that of his female colleagues, was subject to suspicions of commodification. It was not unknown for the career of the male actor to follow a similar trajectory to that of the actresses who left the stage for the ambivalent comforts of being kept by a gentleman or lord. One of the few examples of gender equality which the Restoration period had to offer was that both the aristocracy and the upper gentry of both sexes could increase their prestige by being seen to keep a player as a social and erotic accessory. In a satirical poem on the theatre of his day, Robert Gould exclaimed:

> Now hear a wonder that will well declare,
> How extravagantly lewd some women are,
> For even these men [the actors] base as they are and vain
> Our Punks of highest quality maintain,
> Supply their daily wants (which are not slight)
> But 'tis that they may be supply'd at night.
>
> (Gould 1689: 90)

Even the famously ugly comedian Joseph Haynes boasted, in his Epilogue to John Crowne's *The Ambitious Statesman* (1679), about his own status as a kept man to his audience at the Theatre Royal, making comic capital out of the fact that theatrical stardom bestowed an erotic glamour, even on one of his physical unattractiveness. Perhaps a more significant case, though, is that of Haynes's colleague in the King's Company, the flamboyant Cardell Goodman, whose Cambridge education led him not – as it was supposed to – into a comfortable Church of England living, but to a high-profile career on the London stage. There he made his name in a number of parts, most notably that of Alexander in Nathaniel Lee's *The Rival Queens*, a role in which he was so successful that he became known, affectionately, as 'Alexander the Great', and Thomas Betterton in later years reminisced about the 'Force' and 'agreeable Smoothness' with which Goodman played the part (Wilson 1964: 88). The play is a melodramatic love story, and Alexander is the hero of the overtly erotic narrative. From contemporary accounts and pictorial evidence, Goodman appears to have cut rather a dashing figure. John Harold Wilson, his biographer, describes him as follows:

> He was tall, dark, and graceful, and under the soft candle-light of the stage, dressed in a long-coated silk brocade suit, with Flemish lace cuffs and cravat, embroidered gloves, high-tongued shoes with ribbon bows, a fair periwig, a forest of feathers in his hat, and a regal truncheon in his hand, he was every inch a hero
>
> (Wilson 1964: 2)

This persona of the handsome, powerful, royal lover won Goodman some fame but little fortune – at least, not from the King's Company, whose precarious finances were rarely sufficient to pay him a wage enabling him to live in the style to which he aspired. It did, however, lead him into a range of erotic liaisons worthy of any stage libertine. Eventually it also led him into the arms, the bed and eventually the household of Barbara, Duchess of Cleveland, ten years his senior, but reputedly one of the most beautiful women in England, and formerly mistress to King Charles. She seems to have been satisfied enough to trade the actual monarch for the player-King, 'Alexander the Great'. Goodman left the stage in 1684 at the age of 31 to live with her – officially as her Gentleman of Horse, a high-status member of the household, a 'gentleman', well above the servant class – and enjoyed her support and her open affection for a number of years. Since, as well as being an actor and an aristocrat's paramour, Goodman's career encompassed highway robbery, gambling, accusations of attempted murder, being the associate of counterfeiters, and involvement in political conspiracies, the protection of the Duchess, who succeeded in getting him out of several serious brushes with the law, was invaluable to him.

Predictably, court satirists and lampoonists pilloried 'scum Goodman' for his liaison with the Duchess. This mention in the anonymous poem 'On the Dutchess of Portsmouth's place Expos'd for sale' (c.1686) is fairly typical of the tenor of the satire:

> Cleveland offer'd down a Million
> But was told of her pock-fret Stallion   (Mr. Goodman the Player which
> At the very name she fell a-weeping   she keeps as a Stallion)
> And swore she was undone by keeping ...
>
> (Wilson 1964: 101)

As a kept man Goodman seems to have given up any claim to his traditional masculine position of economic independence and domestic dominance, and it might be thought that he was open to the charge of being less than a man because he was a rich woman's paramour. Surprisingly, though, this was not the main burden of the satires against the former actor. The satirists did not impugn his masculinity; on the contrary, as the Duchess's stallion he even appears to have commanded a grudging respect, as if the sexually charged image which he had created on the stage spilled over into real life. While clearly disapproving of Goodman's morals, the satirists tend to talk of Cleveland being *his* whore. They allow him mastery, and tend to portray him as the lower-class rake, the buck or the stallion, and her as a pathetic rich older woman who has 'stoop[ed] to a dunghill from a Throne' (Wilson 1964: 100). Masculinity as sexual virility is played off against masculinity as social status – and comes off rather well! Even in the eyes of the court satirists, the implied sexual energy of Goodman the stud more than compensates for his abrogation of his societally dominant masculine gender role.

4.3 Rochester, Charles II and symbolic masculinity

The theatre Charles restored was not quite the one which he had in mind. The monarchy he restored was not quite the one which many of his supporters had in mind either. After the turmoil of the English Civil War, and the period of the Commonwealth, the exiled King Charles returned to widespread, if not completely universal, rejoicing. In plays, poetry and masques, the political and the religious-emotional significance of the Restoration were interwoven. Propagandists for the new Charles sought ways to identify him as the old Charles reborn, and to maintain the fiction that 'there were two restorations in 1660: the literal restoration of Charles II, and the metaphorical restoration (or retention) of Charles I as father-king-god' (Maguire 1992: 140). It was, however, a short-lived conceit. The personal character of Charles II contrasted too starkly with the mythology with which his propagandists wanted to surround him. Thus, while in the first euphoric years after the Restoration, this Royalist faction tried valiantly to represent the second Charles as the royal martyr reborn, it soon became clear that this was not convincing. Charles's own political authority was insufficient to sustain the mythology, while his human weaknesses were all too obvious. In 1662 the Venetian Resident in England reported that

> the discontent is general and everyone complains of the king, and that he allows himself to be governed by ministers while he cares for nothing,

attending only to his hunting, his lusts and other amusements, which are not
well interpreted.

(*Calendar of State Papers Venice, 1661–1664*
Quoted in Maguire, 1992: 140)

It seems to have been a great disappointment that the self-centred,
pleasure-loving, fornicating, moody and irresponsible Charles had
allowed the Stuart myth to turn sour so soon.

Once again, then, an important relationship emerges between
masculinity as sexual energy and masculinity as social status. In this
case, however, the social status, which is that of the King, has a
symbolic dimension. An important part of Royalist ideology
emphasized the possibility of re-establishing a continuity with the past.
This involved the coincidence of two diagrams – the one of patriarchal
authority, the other of Stuart idealism – which had been dominant in
the early part of the century, and which had been dislocated during the
period of the Commonwealth. The Protestant/Royalist cosmology had
involved a direct line of sanctioned authority, which led from God
downwards, via the King, to the male head of the household. This is
what we have already seen articulated in Filmer's *Patriarcha*. As the
King distributes 'to every subordinate and inferior father... their rights
and privileges' (Aughterson 1995: 163) the diagram becomes both
mutually reinforcing and elegantly circular. The earthly authority of
the father derives from the political authority of kingship which derives
from the natural authority of the father... And to lock all this in place
there is the ubiquitous Christian imagery of God as Father. Patriarchy,
and *Patriarcha*, is thus a closed system, needing no other justification
than its own 'naturalness'.

But this powerful metaphor of the King as head of the domestic
household was severely damaged by the public nature of Charles's
'lusts and other amusements'. The King as husband-lord or as father-
lord was replaced by the figure of the King as libertine. Filmer's philosophy of patriarchy becomes completely out of date in the Restoration,
and the period's attempts to negotiate the contradictions which the
figure of the new Charles presented involved rethinking questions of
both masculinity and nationhood.

4.3.1 *The Royall Company of Whoremasters:* Sodom *(n.d.)*

One play and one writer in particular illustrate some of the contradictions which the royal masculinity of Charles posed for the age. The title
page of the manuscript copy in the British Library reads: '*Sodom or the*

Quintessence of Debauchery by E of R Written for the Royall Company of Whoremasters' (Greene 1974: 187–8). There is no record of a public performance of the play, although it is said to have been acted at Charles's court, and while it is hard to date precisely, it was probably written in the mid-1670s. Majority (though not unanimous) scholarly opinion upholds the traditional identification of the play's author – 'E of R' in the manuscript – as the Earl of Rochester. In his comparatively short life, Rochester became an iconic figure in Restoration society, embodying *par excellence* the figure of the rake. And the play *Sodom* is so obscene, so misogynistic, so scandalous, that it was clear to many at the time that (whether he actually did or not) Rochester certainly *should* have written it.

If it was indeed performed at court, the play provides another example of Charles's well-chronicled tolerance towards Rochester. The earl continually lampooned the monarch, often in the bitterest terms, without ever earning himself a punishment worse than a few weeks' banishment from court. *Sodom* is both satire and pornographic fantasy, in tone something like an extraordinary mock-heroic cross between Buckingham's *The Rehearsal* and Jarry's *Ubu Roi*, with a touch of de Sade thrown in for good measure. The central character, King Bolloxinion, is all-too-clearly a satirical portrait of Charles himself. At the opening of the play he has a speech which elaborates and embellishes one of Rochester's own most famous verses about Charles, 'For which he was', as the poem's title explains, 'banished'. The poet describes the King's manhood with ironic awe: 'Nor are his high desires above his strength / His sceptre and his prick are of an equal length'. The apparent compliment to the King's virility collapses, however, into a jibe against the weakness of his political will: 'And she may play with one who plays with t'other' (Wilmot 1993: 80). Rochester's accusation was witty but hardly original: the symbolism of the sceptre was a common enough joke, and it was a repeated anxiety during Charles's reign, that the monarch's phallic power lay in his sexual potency instead of being properly transmuted from the physical into the political sphere, and that as a result of Charles's promiscuity, the royal prick continually compromised the royal sceptre.

In *Sodom*, however, a more fantastic scenario plays itself out: Bolloxinion begins by announcing that

> my Nation shall be free
> My Pintle only shall my Scepter be;
> My laws shall act more Pleasure than command
> And with my Prick, I'll govern all the land.
>
> (*Sodom* I.i.6–8)

It is a commonplace that the rake or the libertine is not a man who loves women but one who despises and/or fears them, and the rhetoric of this play proves the point. In the world of *Sodom* and its rake-king Bolloxinion, women are irrelevant except as objects of erotic commodification. Even in this context, they are portrayed not as desirable but as disgusting: the misogyny which Rochester articulates in his verse satires is here taken to extremes as he paints grotesque pictures of the female body, rife with images of disease and rottenness. The words 'cunt' and 'nasty' occur relentlessly throughout the drama, more often than not in close conjunction.

The play develops, not into a familiar satire on Charles's excessive fondness for heterosexual gratification, but into a strange satirical fantasy in which women are effectively written out of the sexual economy. The jaded King Bolloxinion is persuaded by his pimp, the 'Buggermaster General', to turn to homosexual rather than heterosexual attractions, which, once tried, delight him so profoundly that he is converted absolutely. He, his court, his army and his nation transform the country into a state in which homosexuality is not only the norm, but compulsory. One particular scene sees Bolloxinion revelling in the gift of 40 young boys sent to him by a neighbouring king, Tarsehole of Gomorrah – who represents Louis XIV of France, upon whom Charles was (in the eyes of his subjects) dangerously dependent.

> As political satire, this unusual inversion of 'normal' sexual practice undermines Charles's royal identity, subverting and feminizing the king's ostensible male authority. The 'Merry Monarch', notorious for his heterosexual promiscuity, becomes a worshiper of homoerotic delights, his masculinity transformed into an unmanliness that threatens the kingdom.
>
> (Weber 1995: 75)

It should be borne in mind that *Sodom* comes from a period when, according to most historians of homosexuality, there was as yet no consciously defined homosexual identity: this did not develop until the growth of the 'molly-house' subculture in London in the early years of the eighteenth century (see Trumbach 1977: 1991). And despite the play's title, homoeroticism is oddly underplayed in *Sodom*. While the play includes a variety of onstage representations of sexual acts, at no point do these include a depiction, or the suggestion of a depiction, of two men enjoying sex with each other on stage: in this text the pleasures of homosexuality are verbal and allusive, not physical or performative. In reality the play is about politics, not about sex. The ambiguity of its title, referring not only to sexual practices but also to the destruction of the biblical city, alerts the reader/spectator to this:

the main trope of the play is not the libertarian (or libertine) celebration of sexuality, but an extraordinarily vivid expression of the fears and anxieties which the historical Charles's heterosexual irresponsibility posed for the kingdom. The totalitarian state based on compulsory homosexuality which the play envisages is a metaphor rather than an erotic daydream, an act of Swiftian satirical imagining. Bolloxinion's choice of a self-sufficient male sexuality, his exclusion of the feminine, leads to the nation's collapse as plague begins to destroy the land. Only a return to the heterosexual order, and the consequent redressing of the procreative balance, will save the country, he is told by his counsellors. Bolloxinion, however, ignores their calls, declaring that 'I'll reign and bugger still' (V.i.57), and the country, like its biblical namesake, is engulfed in a final hellish conflagration.

This ultimately homophobic and misogynistic play dramatizes an important aspect of the peculiar tensions between masculinity and political stability which were a feature of the Restoration. Two powerful emotions seem to dominate the play – the fear of women and the fear of political anarchy. Perhaps a third could be added to this – a masculine self-loathing projected onto the figure of the King, whose pintle was his sceptre and who posed the threat that an unbridled masculine sexuality would engulf the nation once again in chaos. *Sodom* articulates these fears, first by expressing its disgust at female sexuality, then by excluding women from the equation, and then by envisaging an impossible alternative, an all-male homoerotic sexuality which turns out to be equally politically destructive. Rochester's libertine fantasy is both sexually conservative and politically moralistic.

4.3.2 *Rakes and fops:* The Man of Mode *(1676)*

To be the object of the gaze was a token of one's power and status in Restoration London, and at court the flamboyant Rochester drew attention to himself often enough. In 1676 he was the object of the gaze in another sense too, for he was generally identified as being the original of Dorimant, the rake-hero of Etherege's *The Man of Mode, or Sir Fopling Flutter* (1676). Dorimant is a sexually predatory, attractive and emotionally callous libertine. By the end of the first scene the audience has seen him announce his boredom with one lover, arrange a liaison with her best friend, pay off a prostitute, and begin to show an interest in yet another young woman, recently come to town. The complex story of the play involves the fluctuations of Dorimant's fortune in his liaisons and quarrels with three of these four women (the prostitute does not reappear), adventures which end with him on the edge of securing the hand of the young, beautiful, witty and rich Harriet – who so wins his heart that he agrees to renounce his rakish lifestyle, settle down and even abandon – for a while at least – town life and live with her in the country.

The public theatre of the period returns time after time to the figure of the rake or libertine: the sexually predatory male, whose goal is to have as many affairs in as short a time as possible, and who plays off the illicitness of the liaison against his own reputation for sexual conquest. There have been various attempts to explain the fascination which the rake-figure held for Restoration audiences. Charles himself, of course, probably had something to do with it. Another answer which has been mooted is that the rake represents a philosophical position: Virginia Ogden Birdsall, for example, sees the 'rake-hero' as constituting not only the typical protagonist of the comedies of the Restoration period, but also as personifying and celebrating the political philosophy of Thomas Hobbes. She argues that 'the rake-heroes, both as libertines and as persistent challengers who thrive on controversy, are exemplary of the Hobbesian thinking which prevailed in court circles after the Restoration' (Birdsall 1970: 39). Thus the predatory masculinity of the libertine is symptomatic of a more general mood, a rebellious and aggressive scepticism, deriving at least in part from the political theories of Hobbes, in which the old medieval and Renaissance conceptions of social moral and universal order were rejected.

There is some truth in this suggestion, although it needs qualification. Whereas Hobbes's writing was aimed at developing a political system which would restrain and channel the selfish drives of the individual for the good of society as a whole, the libertine response reverts to a hedonistic drive towards pleasure for its own sake. Moreover, while it *is* true to say that the rake's sexual pursuits were a favourite narrative in Restoration comedy, it is less clear that the hedonistic masculinity of the rake is being straightforwardly celebrated in these plays. On the contrary, the attitudes and philosophies which are expounded by such characters as Dorimant at the beginning of the plays are rarely endorsed wholeheartedly by the play's totality. There is a continual tension in these plays between form and content: between the wittily sceptical content of the lines that the heroes speak, and the trajectory towards the socially accepted stable relationship demanded by the form and structure of romantic comedy which they inhabit. Typically, Dorimant plots adultery, lives and loves promiscuously and makes denigratory remarks about fidelity and matrimony: equally typically his ultimate destination is a financially advantageous (if

geographically restrictive) marriage. Against the apparent social subversiveness of the rake-plot is to be set the conservatism of its endings.

As we have seen, in the case of Dorimant, marriage to Harriet even
involves pledging his willingness to give up city life – the very environment that creates and sustains the libertine and his lifestyle. This narrative structure suggests that there may be more to the popularity of
the rake-hero on the Restoration hero than an unquestioned endorsement of a philosophical libertine position. The libertine adventures
seem rather to be a phase through which the hero passes on his road to
the more conventional happy ending of social and sexual stability in
marriage. At the level of mimesis – the representation of the social
world to which it belongs – the rake-plot stages a tension between two
different versions of masculinity: one fully represented on the stage
itself, the other there as a future possibility. On the one hand, there is
the style of masculinity which is located in the rivalries and intimacies
of male bachelor companionship, and which is routed through heterosexual conquest. On the other hand there is the masculinity which is
expressed through financial and social status within the circles of the
gentry and/or the aristocracy, and through domestic security. At the
level of audience response it is clear that the chief theatrical pleasures,
for the Restoration comedy audience, resided in the dynamics of the
first phase rather than in the second. The marriage with which these
plays ended was the reality principle to which it was necessary to
submit – but it was the erotic chase that provided the dramatic interest.

The hedonistic freedom which the rake represents, then, is only partially Hobbesian in its energy. Moreover, it is not free-standing, but
part of a dialectic between two contradictory masculine principles.
Even so – what is the significance of this specific dialectic? Why did the
rake exert such a powerful pull on the imagination of Restoration audiences? It is, I would suggest, because the rake acts as a *compensatory*
image of masculinity in a culture which feels that its traditional models
of masculinity no longer work. It is a fantasy image, which attempts to
establish an aggressive and simplistic model of masculinity at a time
when – following the cultural and intellectual turmoil caused by the
Civil War and its aftermath, and the symbolic castrating of patriarchal
authority – the culture was attempting to reinvent itself in all spheres,
including that of gender.

The rake, moreover, makes most sense when seen in conjunction
with his usual dramatic foil on the Restoration stage: the fop, represented in *The Man of Mode* by the eponymous Sir Fopling Flutter, the
affected, ostentatious and self-regarding butt of most of the play's
jokes. If the rake is the compensatory image of an uncomplicatedly

aggressive masculinity, the anxious corollary of this is the projection of various forms of inadequate masculinity, of which the most common is the stage figure of the fop. In *The Man of Mode* Etherege makes this relationship between the two stereotypes clear. Dorimant and Sir Fopling Flutter are continually compared and contrasted in the play. Both of them are, in their way, the 'man of mode'. In dramatic presentation they are offered as complete opposites: in the first scene of the play Sir Fopling is described by Dorimant and his sparkish friends:

YOUNG BELLAIR:	He thinks himself the pattern of modern gallantry.
DORIMANT:	He is indeed the pattern of modern foppery.
MEDLEY:	He was yesterday at the play, with a pair of gloves up to his elbows and a periwig more exactly curled than a lady's head newly dressed for a ball.
YOUNG BELLAIR:	What a pretty lisp he has!
DORIMANT:	Ho, that he affects in imitation of the people of quality of France.
MEDLEY:	His head stands for the most part on one side, and his looks are more languishing than a lady's when she lolls at stretch in her coach or leans her head carelessly against the side of a box i'the playhouse.
DORIMANT:	He is a person indeed of great acquired follies.
MEDLEY:	He is like many others, beholding to his education for making him so eminent a coxcomb. Many a fool had been lost to the world, had their indulgent parents wisely bestowed neither learning nor good breeding on 'em.
YOUNG BELLAIR:	He has been, as the sparkish word is, brisk upon the ladies already. He was yesterday at my Aunt Towneley's and gave Mrs Loveit a catalogue of his good qualities under the character of a complete gentleman, who (according to Sir Fopling) ought to dress well, dance well, fence well, have a genius for love letters, an agreeable voice for a chamber, be very amorous, something discreet, but not over-constant.

(Man of Mode I.i.322–44)

This, then, is what Dorimant and the young wits mean by 'fop'. The word, in its original sense meant, simply, 'fool', a generalized sense of the word which continued well into the Restoration period: to be a fop, in the dialogue of Restoration comedy, could cover a multitude of different kinds of foolishness. But by the time of the Restoration, foppery has acquired an additional, and more specifically gendered, meaning. The fop, as a type of inadequate masculinity, becomes a figure of contempt or concern in everyday discourse as well as in the theatre. The nature of this can be seen from the outburst in Henry Bulkeley's letter to (appropriately enough) the Earl of Rochester in June 1676, the same year that *The Man of Mode* was first performed. Bulkeley complains that:

> ye Fop is the only fine Gentleman of the Times, & a committee of those able Statesmen assemble dayly to talke of nothing but fighting and fucking at Locketts, and will never be reconciled to men who speake sense & Reason at ye Beare or Coven garden. It is thay are the hopeful spriggs of ye Nation whose knowledge lies in their light Periwigges & trimed shoes ... fellowes that woud make ye World believe they are not afraid of dying, & yet are out of heart if the Wind disorders their Hair or ruffles their Cravatts;
>
> (Wilmot 1980: 125)

Bulkeley's fops are a combination of masculine stereotypes: on the one hand we recognize the aggressive male of contemporary gender studies, with his 'talk of nothing but fighting and fucking'. On the other hand, however, these fops embody a self-regard, and an obsession with their dress and appearance which Bulkeley finds both effeminate and offensive. His disgust has a political, and in particular a nationalist, dimension to it, too: these 'hopeful spriggs of ye Nation' are letting down their country as well as their gender.

Dorimant ironically echoes Bulkeley's general condemnation of the foppishness of the age: 'The young men of this age,' he says at one point, are 'generally only dull admirers of themselves, and make their court to nothing but their periwigs and their cravats – and would be more concerned for the disordering of 'em though on a good occasion, than a young maid would be for the tumbling of her head or handkercher' (IV.i.15–20). But Sir Fopling takes this to extremes. In the character of Sir Fopling, foppery also becomes a form of effeminacy: all Sir Fopling's faults involve some degree of this. Several details in the wits' description compare him to a woman, with his 'periwig more exactly curled than a lady's head newly dressed for a ball', and his looks 'more languishing than a lady's when she lolls at a stretch in her coach...'; Medley characterizes his coyness when asked to demonstrate his dancing as being 'Like a woman' (IV.i.260).

Later performances (beginning, perhaps, with those of Colley Cibber in the early eighteenth century) take this even further, locating the figure of a fop within their gallery of newly defined homosexual stereotypes. This, however, is not part of Restoration thinking about him. The effeminacy of characters like Sir Fopling Flutter did not yet imply homosexuality so much as a 'softness', a style of masculine social behaviour which the play rejects as undesirable. Indeed the 'genius for

love-letters', and his 'very amorous' nature, which Sir Fopling includes
amongst the attributes of the gentleman he perceives himself to be, are
constructed as exclusively heterosexual features which he employs
solely in the pursuit of women. As the plot unfolds Sir Fopling
becomes a rather hapless rival to Dorimant in his amorous pursuits.
Indeed, one of the main plots involving Dorimant sees the rake
attempting to 'punish' his old flame Loveit by pairing her off with Sir
Fopling – only to become genuinely jealous when she pretends (quite
against her real feelings) to be rather taken with the latter. The scene
is a significant one: earlier in the play, Dorimant, taunting Mrs Loveit,
had declared that 'I would not have a woman have the least good
thought of me that can think well of Sir Fopling' (II.ii.229–30); now, in
all seriousness, he reiterates 'She cannot fall from loving me to that?'
(III.iii.260). Sir Fopling's effeminacy is a threat to Dorimant, because it
apparently can taint his own masculinity by contagion – even at second
hand by way of Mrs Loveit.

Importantly, as well as being unmanly, Sir Fopling is also
Frenchified. His lisp is 'in imitation of the people of quality of France'
(I.i.328) from where he has newly arrived – and when we see him we
discover his language is peppered with French words. During the
period of the Stuart Restoration, France is always important as a
cultural 'other', but the meanings of that otherness are not stable.
During the 1670s, in particular, there were two currents of meaning,
which played against each other. The French cultural influences which
Charles and his courtiers had brought with them when they returned in
1660 had been found by many to be a welcome breath of
Continentalism. The theatre in particular had benefited from French
influence, as the new custom of employing actresses showed. But the
broader political influence also brought with it the inevitable English
nervousness about Catholic domination, especially in an age that saw a
marked growth in French power on the Continent – a growth in which
the francophile Charles was seen to be complicit. Anti-French feeling
grew alongside a growing distrust of the Stuart monarchy, and the
English felt an increasing need to define their own national identity in
opposition to France and Catholicism, up to the point when, in 1688,
the governing classes invited William of Orange to replace James II,
allowing the latter to flee to France.

Thus the fop is constructed as other to the shared masculinity of the
bachelor group who mock him, but this otherness contains a dimension
which is as much to do with national identity as it is with gender
identity. It also has to do with ideas of 'naturalness'. When Dorimant
observes that Sir Fopling is a person 'of great acquired follies', it is the

word 'acquired' that is picked up by Young Bellair. 'Learning [and] good breeding' are to blame, for the fop personality is a deliberately constructed one, as opposed to the implied naturalness of the (English) masculinity to which the speakers lay claim. Later in the play we are told how Flutter's transformation came about: 'He went to Paris a plain bashful English blockhead, and is returned a fine undertaking French fop' (IV.i.264–6). These binary oppositions are developed throughout the play: effeminacy, French culture and artificiality, are opposed to masculinity, English culture and naturalness.

There is one point, however, at which these apparent opposites converge. In Act IV Scene i of the play, the rake briefly *becomes* the fop. In order to fool Lady Woodvill, and to allow himself access to Harriet, Dorimant attends the dance at Lady Towneley's house under the assumed identity of Mr Courtage, 'that foppish admirer of quality, who flatters the very meat at honourable tables, and never offers love to a woman below a lady-grandmother' (III.iii.308–10). He plays the part well, duly flattering and flirting with Lady Woodvill. In a scene in which a prime topic of conversation is the confusion of rank in contemporary society, he confuses things even further with his disguise. In terms of the play's ideological structure, the fop and the rake are offered as opposites, on display to throw the other into relief. Underlying this opposition, however, is the admission that Flutter's foppery is not the opposite of masculine style, but a particular version of that style taken to excess – to the point where it rebounds ineffectually upon itself.

4.4 'In Mr. Wycherley everything is Masculine': Manlyness in the plays of Wycherley

Wycherley's first play, *Love in a Wood*, brought him to the attention of the Duchess of Cleveland (in whose list of lovers Wycherley figures between Charles II and Cardell Goodman) and thence into the circle of court wits. Throughout the 1670s Wycherley wrote the plays for which he is still known, and basked in the warmth of court favouritism, until in 1679 a politically ill-considered marriage brought him out of favour and eventually into prison. Court poet though he is, however, the court itself has less of a presence in Wycherley's plays than it does in Etherege's. The occasional court figure makes an appearance in a supporting role, and his protagonists (such as Horner) tend to live at the fashionable end of town, but the worlds which Wycherley creates are generally populated by the stereotypes of the city: merchants and aldermen, sea-captains and city-heirs. In these worlds, located at the

point where a deep-rooted Puritanism intersects with a libertine pleasure in sensuality, masculinity is, more often than not, under pressure.

4.4.1   Strong women, weak men: The Gentleman Dancing-Master *(1672)*

One of the repeated myths of Restoration comedy is the myth of the
independent woman. The contemporary belief that, since the time of
the Commonwealth, English women were particularly liberated, especially in comparison to their Continental counterparts, is repeatedly
stated. Sometimes it is heard in the self-congratulatory tones of the
proud nationalist –

> England is the paradise of women. And well it may be called so, as it might
> easily be demonstrated in many particulars, were not all the world already
> therein satisfied. Hence it hath been said that if a bridge were made over
> the narrow seas, all the women in Europe would come over hither.
>
> (Ray 1670: 94)

– and sometimes in the satiric tones of those who deplore the fact that
women have now, as the author of *The Commonwealth of Ladies*
phrased it in 1650, 'voted themselves the Supreme Authority both at
home and abroad' (cited in Fraser 1989: 250).

In *The Gentleman Dancing-Master* the character called 'Monsieur'
(actually a Francophile Englishman recently returned from Paris) is
horrified to discover on his arrival in England that social relationships
between men and women have changed: the women are now more
assertive, more active and more predatory. Prostitutes chase after their
clients, invading those inns and clubs which were once exclusive male
preserves.

WAITER:	... They'll break open the door – they searched last night all over the house for my Lord Fisk and Sir Jeffrey Jaunty, who were fain to hide themselves in the bar under my mistress' chair and petticoats.
MONSIEUR:	What! Do the women hunt out the men so now?
MARTIN:	Ay, ay, things are altered since you went to Paris. There's hardly a young man in town dares be known of his lodging for' em.
GERRARD:	Bailiffs, pursuivants, or a City constable are modest people in comparison of them.
MARTIN:	And we are not so much afraid to be taken up by the watch as by the tearing midnight ramblers, or huzza-women.

(*Gentleman Dancing-Master* I.ii.148–59)

In fact, the material conditions, and the legal and social status of women improved very little during the middle years of the seventeenth century. The legal position of women in relation to their husbands underwent no major change between the beginning and the end of the century: in both 1600 and 1700 the husband's authority over the wife was absolute. The Restoration was hardly a progressive period as far as the place of women in English society was concerned – indeed, many modern commentators have found it 'the nadir of the collective fortunes of the female sex' (Roberts 1989: 5). The jingoistic claim that England was a 'paradise of women' masks the fact that one of the ideological projects of the Restoration was to undo such advances in women's freedoms as *had* taken place, especially in the religious sphere, during the Commonwealth.

Nonetheless, during the second half of the seventeenth century we do begin to see the emergence of a few exceptional women in public life. These years produced several major women writers, a few prominent businesswomen, and, of course, the actresses in the new theatrical culture which offered visibility as well as employment to women. Female literacy increased during the period, while the notion that women were not necessarily men's intellectual inferiors was gaining wider acceptance. New marriage settlement laws occasionally worked to the advantage of women, allowing for some financial empowerment in widowhood, if not before, and the appearance on the London stage of type-characters such as Etherege's Widow Rich, and Wycherley's Widow Blackacre signals the growing significance of widows who are empowered over men by virtue of their marriage contracts (see Munns 2000: 142–57). Perhaps more important than any real changes in women's social, legal and material positions, however, was the widespread male belief, by the time of the Restoration, that old prerogatives and privileges were under threat.

These comparatively slight shifts in gender roles are exaggerated for comic effect by Wycherley. In his plays, masculinity is repeatedly seen as a problematic issue and is presented, in one way or another, as being ineffectual. In *The Gentleman Dancing-Master*, as we have seen, the newcomer to London is presented with a new set of rules for the interaction between the sexes. A few moments after the dialogue quoted above, the stage is invaded by the comic double-act of Flounce and Flirt – two ladies of the town, – who then proceed to take over the stage completely, eclipse all the male characters present, and dominate the rest of the scene. It ends with a farcical 'abduction', as Flounce and Flirt carry Monsieur off to their 'lodging', the brothel at the sign of the Crooked Billet.

FLOUNCE: Fie, fie, come along
MONSIEUR: Beside, I am to be married within these two days; if you
            should tell now –
FLIRT: Come, come along; we will not tell.
MONSIEUR: But will you promise then to have the care of my honour?
            Pray, good madam, have de care of my *honneur*, pray have de
            care of my *honneur*. Will you have de care of my *honneur*?
            Pray have de care of my *honneur*, and do not tell if you can
            help it.
            Kneels to 'em.
            Pray, dear madam, do not tell.
                                      (*Gentleman Dancing-Master* I.ii.337–435)

The reversal of gender roles in this scene is very thorough-going.
The 'masculine' sexual aggression of Flounce and Flirt is counterbal-
anced by the delighted semi-protestations of Monsieur as he responds
by assuming a stereotypically submissive role. Kneeling before his
abductors, pleading for them to have care of his honour, expressing his
concern for his chastity on the eve of his marriage – Monsieur's words
and actions are all encoded in terms of the feminine.

The scene of Monsieur's abduction is watched with amusement by
his companions, Gerrard and Martin, the hero and his friend, who
represent a more traditional form of masculinity. The audience,
indeed, is unlikely to be very surprised by Monsieur's capitulation. He
has, after all, already been placed for them in the 'fop' tradition.
Appearing on the London stage four years before Etherege turned the
type into a caricature of mythical proportions, Monsieur is clearly a
predecessor of the francophile Sir Fopling Flutter. Like him, Monsieur
'went to Paris a plain bashful English blockhead, and is returned a fine
undertaking French fop' (*The Man of Mode* IV.i.264–6). Like Sir
Fopling, too, Monsieur's attachment to his French clothes is extreme
and absurd. When ordered by his uncle to abandon them or face the
cancellation of his wedding, his reluctant and gradual compliance takes
place over a series of scenes whose comedy is based on his dress
fetishism:

MONSIEUR: Vil you not spare my pantaloon, begar? I will give you one
            little finger to excuse my pantaloon, *da!* ... Auh, *chères* pan-
            taloons! – Speak for my pantaloons, cousin; my poor pan-
            taloons are as dear to me as de scarf to de countree
            capitaine, or de new-made officer. Therefore have de com-
            passion for my pantaloons, Don Diego, *mon oncle; hélas,
            hélas, hélas.*
            Kneels to Don Diego.
                                        (*Gentleman Dancing-Master* IV.i.41–6)

Once more Monsieur ends up on his knees – pleading this time for his clothes rather than his sexual reputation.

The effeminization of the Frenchified fop is, of course, a familiar enough trope in Restoration comedy. In *The Gentleman Dancing-Master*, however, Wycherley takes a rather broader view of masculine ineffectuality. In Etherege's *The Man of Mode*, we have already seen 'natural' Englishness contrasted with artifical and foppish Frenchness, and a similar pattern is obvious here in Wycherley's slightly earlier play. Here, however, it is given a further dimension. As well as Monsieur, who has rejected the codes of English masculinity in favour of the French, Wycherley gives us the character of Monsieur's uncle (and the father of the heroine Hippolyta). James Formal has also lived abroad, and has consequently constructed *his* identity according to a Spanish model of masculine dress and behaviour. The popular national stereotype of the time attributed to the Spanish male a strict and grave formality, coupled with a fierce sense of family honour:

> DON DIEGO: Now in Spain he is wise enough that is grave, politic enough that says little, and honourable enough that is jealous. And though I say it that should not say it, I am as grave, grum, and jealous as any Spaniard breathing ... and I will be a Spaniard in everything still, and will not conform, not I, to their ill-favoured English customs, for I will wear my Spanish habit still, I will stroke my Spanish whiskers still, and I will eat my Spanish *olio* still; and my daughter shall go a maid to her husband's bed, let the English custom be what 'twill.
>
> (*Gentleman Dancing-Master* II.i.33–6, 38–42)

The diagram which Wycherley is drawing appears to be a straightforward one. He offers two 'deviant' and rather absurd models of masculine behaviour: the excessively flowery, effeminate and decadent French model, and the excessively strict, 'grave, grum and jealous' Spanish one. It seems clear that the middle ground is just waiting to be filled by a positive model of natural, unaffected English masculinity.

The *way* in which this happens is not quite what an audience might expect. The main narrative of *The Gentleman Dancing-Master* is one in which gentlewomen, too, 'hunt out the men' – and in the process resist male parental authority. The central courtship plot involves the familiar structure of the avoidance of an arranged marriage. The heroine is the quick-thinking 14-year-old heiress and marriage prize Hippolyta, who is supposed to marry Monsieur, but who prefers Gerrard. Gerrard initially looks set to fill the role of rake-hero. We are told that he has been showing an interest in Hippolyta before the play begins, and when he is characterized as a tall, witty, handsome, brave and very *English* gentleman-about-town, it seems that we know what to expect. The contrast between the ineffectual French fop and the dashing English hero is clear. There is, however, a twist: when he actually appears on-stage Gerrard turns out to be passive in comparison to Hippolyta, whose Amazonian name well suits her forceful personality. It is her improvisatory skills, not Gerrard's, which drive the plot. She chooses him rather than *vice versa*, and far from initiating and actively pursuing the courtship, he does little but respond to her cues – usually rather more slowly and dully than she requires. Hippolyta makes all the running, both emotionally and dramatically, in the plot, and like Flirt and Flounce in the tavern, it is she who, effectively, carries off Gerrard. While the men in the play are repeatedly seen as ineffectual, Hippolyta takes centre stage, concocting all the lies and excuses, making all the decisions, and planning all the stratagems.

The key stratagem is the pretence, thought up on the spur of the moment to cover the imminent discovery of Gerrard in her room, that Gerrard is in fact her dancing-master, hired by Monsieur to teach her some French style. The play is deliberately farcical in its construction, and much of its humour derives from the protagonists' repeated attempts to prevent the authoritarian father from discovering Gerrard's utter incapacity at dancing – a characteristic, incidentally, which had been listed among his very 'English' attributes early in the play (I.i.127). (There may have been a theatrical in-joke here, too, since the part of Gerrard was probably first played by Thomas Betterton, whose own incompetence as a dancer was legendary in theatrical circles.) Gerrard's access to his erotic goal is dependent upon his adopting the *persona* which is, to some extent, unmanly. At various points in the play dancing-masters are presented as a class of eunuch, excluded from the list of eligible love-objects on grounds of class and breeding ('he debases ... civility and good breeding more than a City dancing-master', complains Hippolyta in the first minutes of the play (I.i.42–3)); and on grounds of stereotyped national characteristics and on grounds of affectation, cowardice and general effeminacy ('those tripping outsides of gentlemen are like gentlemen enough in everything but drawing a sword', II.ii.238–9).

Thus while it is up to Gerrard to occupy the middle ground of English masculinity which the play's structure offers, he does so unsatisfactorily. On the level of character, he is relegated to the unmanly role of dancing-master for most of the play. On the level of action, he plays second fiddle to Hippolyta to such an extent that, even when he *is* acting the more conventional role of the lover, he is doing so ineffectively. For most of the play he is a bumbling amateur, whose attempts at intrigue, courtship, disguise and dancing are offered to the audience as a source of affectionate amusement. While the more typical rake-hero which Dorimant represents drives the action of a play through his scheming, and dominates the dialogue with his wit, Gerrard is generally attempting to keep up with Hippolyta on both scores!

The Gentleman Dancing-Master is a play in whose world female dominance is the norm. The assertiveness shown by Flounce and Flirt, women at the lower end of society, is echoed by the assertiveness of women in the moneyed classes. This link between the two is made explicit in the play's Epilogue, spoken by Flirt, who acknowledges that Hippolyta is 'like one Of us bold flirts of t'other end o'th'town' (Epilogue 12–13). That last phrase of Flirt's is significant. 'T'other end o' th'town' is the West End, where the prostitutes would have gathered, and where, up until that point, the theatres of Restoration London had also been located. But *The Gentleman Dancing-Master* was first performed in the Duke's Company's 'new theatre near Salisbury Court', the Dorset Gardens theatre, close to St Paul's in the City. Geographically not much more than half a mile apart, the two venues were expected to cater to rather different audiences. The Lincoln's Inn Fields and Drury Lane area was the more fashionable of the two, and when the new theatre opened in Dorset Gardens, it seems that the Duke's Company were unsure what sort of audience it would attract. They do not seem to have been certain whether, at the Dorset Gardens playhouse, they would continue to attract the court-circle wits whose natural habitat was the West End, or whether their audience would now be limited to the neighbouring 'cits' – the citizens of the mercantile class. These were the spiritual heirs of those aldermen of Elizabethan London whose suspicion of the theatre is so well documented, and they were probably a hard audience to play.

The *milieu* of *The Gentleman Dancing-Master*, its settings and characters, are those of the City. The affectations of characters such as Monsieur and Formal are all the more marked for being the affectations of merchants, not those of aristocrats. In both the Prologue and the Epilogue, Wycherley speaks directly to his audience, which he assumes – or pretends to assume – is predominantly composed of merchants and their households. He addresses them in mock-flattering terms, praising them for their tolerance:

> For you to senseless plays have still been kind,
> Nay, where no sense was, you a jest would find;
> And never was it heard of, that the City

> Did ever take occasion to be witty
> Upon dull poet, or stiff player's action,
> But still with claps opposed the hissing faction.
> (*Gentleman Dancing-Master* Prologue 12–17)

Wycherley is both wooing and teasing an audience whose tolerance, he suggests, is not entirely unconnected with a certain dullness and lack of discernment. In the Epilogue Wycherley offers an apology for any imputation of sexual silence among the citizen classes and solemnly denies that any real-life merchants' daughters might be as bold and forward as Hippolyta. The seriousness of this apology is undermined, however, by the fact that it is immediately followed by 'Flirt's' direct invitation to the 'good men o'th' Exchange' to step backstage and partake of the sexual favours of the actresses, who (she assures them) will much prefer 'Your velvet jumps, gold chains and grave fur gowns' (Epilogue 33) to the laced coats and belts of their more usual courtly visitors.

The Gentleman Dancing-Master was Wycherley's one box-office flop in an otherwise very successful decade. There may have been something in the play's gender politics which its audience found uncomfortable; Wycherley may well have touched a nerve with Hippolyta's final couplet,

> When children marry, parents should obey,
> Since love claims more obedience far than they
> (*Gentleman Dancing-Master* V.i.711–2)

This image of the collapse of parental authority, in a comedy which puts such power into the hands of its heroine, may have been too near the knuckle, even in jest. But perhaps more disturbing than the witty and attractive heroine was Wycherley's picture of a citizen class in which masculinity is at a loss to know how to act, which is comically reaching for foreign models or submitting to the assertiveness of women.

Monsieur ends up being blackmailed by Flirt into a contract by which he will publicly maintain her, on lavish terms, as his mistress. Their agreement is an ironic take on one of Restoration comedy's most enduring conventions: the proviso, or covenanting scene. The most famous example of this is probably the scene between Mirabell and Millamant in *The Way of the World* (1700), but the convention of the proviso scene in which 'the young couple work out their own personal agreement over the distribution of power in the relationship' (Munns 2000: 144), has its origins in Dryden's early comedies, such as *Secret*

Love (1667), and became a stock device of Restoration courtship and marriage comedies.

The broader significance of the proviso scene's popularity relates to an important aspect of gender debates in the second half of the seventeenth century. As we have already seen, Sir Robert Filmer's model of patriarchy, which locates the natural source of authority in the 'father', both on a literal and metaphorical level, had become increasingly untenable under Charles II. The granddaughters and great-granddaughters of Katherine Minola would have some recompense, for even as it articulates the theory of patriarchy, Filmer's text – a work of political theory in support of a doomed King – essentially marks the point at which it ceases to be effective as the basis for practice, at least in the sense of the word that Filmer himself would have understood. In the years after Filmer's death in 1651 the gender diagram would be redrawn in terms of social contracts – and a new understanding of masculinity would emerge.

Thomas Hobbes's massive work, *Leviathan*, was published in the same year that Filmer died, and was the earliest major statement of political theory based upon the idea that the basis of society lies not in a divinely ordained natural order but in the network of explicit and implicit contracts between the people who make up that society. If Filmer articulates the point of view of the traditionalist, that society is naturally ordained along patriarchal principles which it is dangerous to ignore (and the chaos of the Civil War gave him sufficient reason for thinking this right), Hobbes represents the modern point of view – that society is socially constructed.

Both Hobbes and Filmer believed in the importance of a strong monarchy. Filmer, writing as the Civil War begins, insists that this is rooted in a predestined natural order. For Hobbes, writing in exile amidst a discouraged and disempowered court, such confidence is misplaced; he constructs a more elaborate set of arguments to prove the paradox that it is only through chosen submission to political authority that society is possible, and that this submission is therefore an act of freedom. Similarly, the relationship between men and women is not simply attributable to unchanging natural order, but to an organic set of agreements and contracts which make male/female relationships possible and which in the long run lead to increased happiness. Filmer demands submission to a natural law; Hobbes encourages signing up to a social contract – without necessarily reading the fine print.

James MacInnes goes so far as to argue that the concept of masculinity as we now understand it has its genesis in this shift from a patriarchal to a modern 'contractual' world-view:

Because it inherited the material and ideological legacy of the patriarchal era, modernity presented men (and women) with the novel problem of rationalizing and explaining men's greater power, resources and status without recourse to the straightforward patriarchal assertion that men's *natural* difference to women gave them a *natural* right to rule them. The concept of masculinity (and the corresponding concepts of gender and femininity) was their solution to this problem.

(MacInnes 1998: 7)

Hobbes and the contract theorists, then, argued that men and women are different because they are socialized into so being. The division of labour which this entails, the attainment of their differing gender identities, the ensuing differences of 'power, resources and status' are the result of social processes, not natural laws. To explain why men are superior to, or privileged in comparison to, women, they developed, without ever using the words, concepts of masculinity and femininity.

Yet the argument in the end was difficult to sustain without referring at some stage to some imagined natural law, since,

the contract theorists faced an insurmountable problem. If social relations were constructed by contract rather than nature, how could the two sexes come to occupy such different positions; why did they make such different contracts?

(MacInnes 1998: 8)

At this point the most committed social contract theorist begins to gesture towards residual notions of *natural* male superiority. In order to address the ensuing contradiction that, on the one hand, all people are essentially equal, and that, on the other hand, men are essentially superior to women, Hobbes and later contract theorists were forced into the position of arguing that masculinity is somehow *both* socially constructed and *also* derived from the natural order of things.

The popularity of the proviso scene in Restoration romantic comedy is significant, then, because it provides a visual and dramatic representation of this changing sense of the relationships between men and women. It is a perfect metaphor for an age in which the notion of contract was becoming increasingly important on several levels. Just as, a few years later, the Glorious Revolution of 1688 would replace an absolute monarchy with a parliamentary one, whose authority was to be vested in a contract between Parliament and the Crown rather than in an appeal to a pre-ordained chain of being, so an essentially Royalist model of patriarchal gender relations was giving way to one which is more mercantile in its tenor, and whose dominant metaphor was the negotiated contract. In its romantic mode the proviso scene provides a kind of reassurance for the audience: the hero and heroine, it implies, are entering into an agreement which is mutually arrived at, and which defines the balance of power in a way that satisfies them both; by implication it reassures the audience of the essential rightness of the dominant social contracts between men and women. Wycherley's parody of the convention, however, turns the world upside down. It exposes some of the contradictions of the social contract by implying that it might be arranged otherwise, and that women *might* negotiate the contract to their advantage. It is up to men to be manly enough to ensure that they do not do so – but in *The Gentleman Dancing-Master* there is a masculine power vacuum.

4.4.2 *'As bad as a Eunuch!':* The Country Wife *(1675)*

Gerrard gains access to his erotic goal by adopting the unmanly persona of the dancing-master, but he pays the price of becoming merely a pawn in the game of love which is played by Hippolyta. In *The Country Wife*, the trickster-protagonist Horner also trades in his masculine reputation in order to facilitate his erotic pursuit. Horner, in fact, goes further than Gerrard. He renounces the identity by which he is known – that of a sexually predatory rake – and has the rumour spread about that he is now permanently impotent, 'as bad as a eunuch' (I.i.5), as a result of having taken the cure for the pox in France. The ruse gains him private access not just to one woman but to several; it allows him to act the libertine in secret while making all the men believe that he is harmless. Unlike Gerrard, moreover, Horner remains in control of his own stratagems, which are the main agents that drive the plot.

Eve Kosofsky Sedgwick, famously, reads *The Country Wife* as an 'anatom(y) of male homosocial desire' (Sedgwick 1985: 49). The 'homosocial', as Sedgwick defines it, goes beyond the simple notion of male bonding. It involves an unstable triangular pattern of power relationships, rivalries and (non-sexual) intimacies between men, a pattern which is central to the workings of patriarchal power (or at least of male dominance). Homosociality, in this sense, works in such a way as to exclude, commodify and/or idealize women. At the same time it proscribes explicitly sexual relationships between men: homophobia is central to homosociality.

Sedgwick's characterization of homosociality has been very influential, and it is a very useful concept. Up to a point, her reading of *The Country Wife* in terms of this model of masculine power relationships works well. The obsession with cuckoldry, which is so central to the play, is a particularly intense, competitive and hierarchical form of homosociality, in which women figure largely as a channel through which to route the male/male relationships which are the most important dimension of the play's emotional life. I think she is right in attributing to the cuckolding world of libertine comedy an essential homosociality that prizes the masculine interactions above the heterosexual conquest itself, and certainly above any genuine male/female emotional interaction. Indeed, the basic mode in which the play operates, the codes which comprise the conventional 'world' of Restoration comedy in general, may well be described in this way: the same point can be made about *The Way of the World*, *The Man of Mode* and so on.

The Country Wife, however, is a more problematic case. Horner gains for himself privileged access to the married women in the play, whose husbands are no longer concerned at leaving them alone with Horner. He does so, however, at the price of his own masculine reputation. Sedgwick argues that

> Far from renouncing or subordinating the male-homosocial destination, Horner has actually elevated it to a newly transcendent status. If he gives up the friendship and admiration of other men, it is only in order to come into a more intimate and secret relation to them – a relation over which his cognitive mastery is so complete that they will not even know that such a bond exists.

> (Sedgwick 1985: 56)

On a level of motivation, this rings partly true. Horner's sexual predations have little to do with love of women, or even, perhaps, with sensual gratification. The preening pleasure he takes in the ascendancy he gains in his own mind over his fellow-males shows that he is clearly still playing a game, in which women are the pieces on the board and his opponents are the other men in the play. But is being in *cognitive* control of the systems of exchange enough? Sedgwick would say it is, but I am less sure. By announcing himself to be sexually incomplete (not a 'real' man), Horner is removing himself from the masculine cameraderie on which the rich model of homosociality, which Sedgwick delineates elsewhere, actually thrives. The only audience he has left is the Quack to whom, at the end of Act I Scene i, he explains his strategy – a temporary confidant and a poor substitute for the recognition of his peers.

This is closely related to the shifting meanings of the word 'honour'. Honour codes had been an essential element of the homosocial in the earlier part of the seventeenth century, and in some spheres of

Restoration London they still were. We saw in the last chapter how notions of a masculine honour code are parodied in *Henry IV Part 1*. However, in the world of Wycherley's plays the word 'honour' has become completely corrupted. In *The Gentleman Dancing-Master* we have seen it tortured into meaninglessness by Don Diego, on the one hand, and Monsieur, on the other. Once again, here in *The Country Wife* the debasement of the word is central to the play. The multiple puns within the name of the central character signal the breakdown of meaning: 'Horner' is a homophone of 'honour', as well as being animalistic, phallic, cuckolding, 'a goat, a town-bull ... a satyr ... a eunuch' all at the same time. (Wycherley spells out some of the 'clandestine obscenity in the very name of Horner' in *The Plain Dealer* II.i. 407–12.)

Throughout the play, continual reference is made to the notion of honour, as it relates to both men and women. Lady Fidget and her friends articulate its debasement. Pondering on the various ways in which a *woman's* honour may be damaged, they complain first about men who 'report a man has had a person, when he has not had a person' (II.i.374–6). They conclude that deceiving a husband with a 'private person' is less injurious to honour than doing so with a person of quality, since 'a woman of honour loses no honour with a private person' (II.i.395). The kind of satire that is implicit in their casuistry is familiar enough. The meaning of 'honour' becomes increasingly limited until it means little more than 'having the reputation of being sexually chaste'.

Male honour, too, is a debased concept, though in a rather different way. Later in the scene, Lady Fidget finds out about Horner's plan:

LADY FIDGET: (*apart to Horner*)   But poor gentleman, could you be so generous? So truly a man of honour, as for the sakes of us women of honour, to cause yourself to be reported no man? No man! And to suffer yourself the greatest shame that could fall upon a man, that none might fall upon us women by your conversation. But indeed, sir, as perfectly, perfectly the same man as before your going into France, sir? As perfectly, perfectly, sir?

HORNER: As perfectly, perfectly, madam. Nay, I scorn you should take my word; I desired to be tried only, madam.

LADY FIDGET: Well, that's spoken like a man of honour; all men of honour desire to come to the test.

(*Country Wife* II.i.536–46)

If Lady Fidget cannot see much beyond the notion of public reputation in her discussion of women's honour, in her assessment of Horner she is able to entertain something more complex, though in the end equally contradictory. In her first speech quoted above, she attempts to make sense of it: the 'honour' that Horner displays in putting about his false information has, to her mind, something genuinely noble about it. He has sacrificed his reputation as a man, so that their reputations as 'ladies' will not be compromised. In another context this might well have been a genuinely honourable gesture. The audience, however, is invited to see beyond Lady Fidget's understanding of what constitutes honour. By the time Lady Fidget uses the term again it has changed once more. Horner, she says, speaks 'like a man of honour', and taking that cue, Lady Fidget reverts to an inappropriately pseudo-chivalric frame of reference: 'all men of honour desire to come to the test'. The test which Lady Fidget is thinking about, however, is the test he will take in her bed, in which he is expected to prove that he is, after all, every bit as much of a rake as he was before he went to France. The shallowness of Lady Fidget's definition of honour leads her to represent Horner's calculated self-serving as nobility of character, and to turn the whole notion of honour inside out. We may read this simply as a mark of character – Lady Fidget is so stupid, or so corrupt, that honour has ceased to be meaningful for her. But it goes further than that: she is simply the most extreme spokesperson. The breakdown in meaning which the concept of honour has undergone affects and infects the whole world of the play. The homosocial background against which the main plot is set is affected by this breakdown in the codes of honour. Consequently, the rules of the game have changed. Horner is playing to the gallery, and the isolation which his role imposes upon him has a price. A social relation which is so 'intimate and secret' that the majority of those involved in it do not even know that it exists looks less like homosocial desire than it does like narcissism.

In Rochester's *Sodom*, an attempt to exclude the feminine led, not to homoerotic excess, but to a destructive masculine sterility. The story has its classical counterpart in the myth of Narcissus, which tells how the beautiful but emotionally stunted youth, unable to love the nymph who adored him, eventually fell in love with his own reflection, glimpsed in a pool. Sometimes used as a simple image of male homo- or auto-eroticism, classical psychoanalytic theory gives the myth a central place in its account of ego development. Primary narcissism refers to a particular stage of infant development when the child believes itself to be self-sufficient – a stage which, in Freud's libidinal model, precedes object-relatedness and the castration anxieties of the Oedipal phase. Secondary narcissism, says Jeremy Holmes, covers the range of different conditions ... in which people are pathologically self-preoccupied; unable to relate; approach others not as ends in themselves but as means to selfish ends; resort to 'self-soothing' behaviours such as drug addiction, deliberate self-harm or promiscuous sex; become self-defeatingly self-reliant, and so on.

(Holmes 2001: 36)

On a number of other levels the myth of Narcissus provides a valuable metaphor whereby to view the staged masculinities of the Restoration theatre. 'In men,' Holmes adds 'there may be a huge preoccupation with the penis' (Holmes 2001: 15).

In *The Country Wife*, Horner's sexual strategies end in a narcissistic isolation from his own sex and a purely predatory relationship to the opposite one. His final lines to the audience, following the 'dance of cuckolds' which ends the play's action, appear to be the play's Epilogue:

> Vain fops but court, and dress, and keep a pother,
> To pass for women's men with one another.
> But he who aims by women to be prized,
> First by the men (you see) must be despised.
>
> (*Country Wife* V.iv.422–5)

Sedgwick argues that Horner had 'elevated [male homosocial desire] to a new transcendent status'. I would suggest that he has simply played himself out of the game. In this final speech Horner, as he has done throughout the play, rejects male sociality, which he sees as false in any case, in favour of being 'prized' by women, whom he equally despises on all levels but the physical. Horner, as both rake and fop, has addressed the castration anxiety, and has triumphed over his male rivals; the price, though, is that in doing so he has become trapped in a new kind of isolation. It is one which he appears, in these final few lines, to celebrate. However, Horner's speech is not, after all, the play's last word. This belongs, in the playhouse at least, to Elizabeth Knepp (Pepys's old favourite) who by now is playing Lady Fidget. She steps forward to deliver the actual Epilogue, which ends with the following lines:

> But, gallants, have a care, faith, what you do;
> The world, which to no man his due will give,
> You, by experience, know you can deceive,
> And men may still believe you vigorous;
> But then, we women – there's no coz'ning us.
>
> (*Country Wife* Epilogue 29–33)

With an adroit move the Epilogue reverses everything which the play
has suggested. Horner says that he will suffer being despised for his
supposed impotence by his fellow-men in order to enjoy the benefits of
being prized sexually by the women. But Knepp/Fidget, with that wink
to the audience which Pepys found so endearing, warns the young
playhouse gallants that however much they may boast about their
sexual prowess amongst their male friends, 'we women' will know
whether or not they are really any good in bed. The only final
guarantee of masculinity is sexual performance – and only a woman, as
she leeringly tells the audience, can judge *that*. Horner's masculine
fantasy of narcissistic self-sufficiency has its limitations – and castration
anxiety meets performance anxiety.

4.4.3   *The importance of being Manly:* The Plain Dealer *(1676)*

There is a famous scene in *The Plain Dealer*: two characters, Olivia and
Eliza, are discussing different notions of scandal; their conversation
turns into an argument about the merits of *The Country Wife*, and the
character of Horner in particular. They inhabit, this scene implies, the
same reality as the playgoers who are actually watching them in *The
Plain Dealer*: they too are members of Wycherley's audience. Then, in
a neat *coup de théâtre*, Eliza announces that she is off to watch *another*
play by Wycherley, 'which is acted today' (II.i.143). She makes her exit
from the stage of *The Plain Dealer* in order to go and join the audience
in watching the play! It is a moment that is emblematic of the relationship – both intimate and unstable – which the play as whole establishes
with its audience.

Of all the Restoration comedies, *The Plain Dealer* promises most in
terms of a study of Restoration masculinities. Its central character is
named Manly, the 'Plain Dealer' of the title – the stereotypical plain-
speaking, blunt man, who refuses to involve himself in the flatteries
and artificialities of a society which he regards as hypocritical. The play
draws on a familiar trope: 'plain dealing' is one of the traditional
seventeenth-century traits of a healthy manliness. The character-books
and conduct-books, which draw up patterns of masculine behaviour,
repeatedly commend plain dealing. Joseph Hall's character of the
Honest Man, for example 'loves actions above words ... hates
falsehood worse than death' (Aldington 1924: 56) and contrasts the
plain dealer with the flatterer, the fawner, the liar, the dissembler, the
hypocrite and so on. Plain dealing is, moreover, characterized as a
particularly masculine virtue, not only because of traditional

misogynistic associations between women and duplicity, but also because of the way in which plain dealing is located as a way of negotiating the public world of men's affairs, of business and politics. There is, however, a perceptible shift in the value of plain dealing in the second half of the century. While it continues to be praised as a masculine virtue through into the reign of Charles II, the later writers generally allow for rather more flexibility than their Jacobean predecessors. In keeping with the general notion of 'affability' and 'civility' (see above) they tend to recommend that plainness of manner be tempered with a few of the 'civilizing' qualities. Thus, for example, Charles II's physician William Ramesey, in his conduct-book *The Gentleman's Companion* (1672), cautions his reader not to 'flatter, lye or dissemble', but he concedes that 'a little Vanity, and Opinion ... may be allowed, especially in such natures whose Bark is ballasted with Solidity, and Reason' (cited in McCarthy 1979: 76).

By the 1670s, then, plain dealing seems to allude to a slightly old-fashioned stereotype of masculine virtue – and perhaps, therefore, one all the more suited to take a satirical look at the follies of the present age. Manly, in Wycherley's play, appears, on one level at least, to represent the stable values of a play which seem to articulate a model of masculinity rather different from that of the usual world of Restoration comedy. Historically, in fact, Manly has frequently been identified directly with Wycherley himself. The character seemed to expand beyond the page or the stage and to take over his creator, and it became axiomatic among his contemporaries that Wycherley *was* the Plain Dealer. Wycherley himself propagated the idea, which he came to hold with increasing seriousness. He started to sign himself 'The Plain Dealer' in his letters. Any irony that may have been intended at first was soon lost as his friends responded by taking up the notion in turn. Thus George Granville, Lord Lansdowne, wrote 'A Character of Mr. Wycherley' in which he asserts that

> In *Mr. Wycherley* everything is *Masculine*. .. Like your Heroes of Antiquity, he charges in Iron and seems to despise all Ornament, but intrinsick Vertue; and like those Heroes, has therefore added another Name to his own: and by the unanimous Assent of the World is call'd The *Manly Wycherley*.
> (Cited in Boyer 1701: 256)

Wycherley's own personal character becomes an icon of masculinity, based on his own quality of plain dealing (the eschewing of 'all Ornament but intrinsick Vertue'); and the word 'Manly' is used both as proper noun and as adjective. In a way which is typical of its age, Lansdowne's version of the masculine Wycherley smooths over all complexities and contradictions, and presents us with a package which is validated 'by the unanimous Assent of the World'. The two terms of manliness and plain dealing set up a seamless circulation of meaning.

The play itself, however, presents a more complex picture. In the playhouse, the audience's first experience is the Prologue, spoken by the actor James Hart, who was cast as Manly. Hart's first lines,

> I the Plain Dealer am to act today
> And my rough part begins before the play
> (*Plain Dealer* Prologue 1–2)

immediately create a state of dual awareness: the speaker is both Hart the actor, and Manly, the character he is about to play (or is he playing Manly already?). Prologues, of course, traditionally create a liminal space, somewhere between the world of the play and the world of the audience, but this one exploits that ambiguity more intensively than most. It allows the speaker to use his plain-speaking persona as an ironic disclaimer and launch a particularly aggressive attack on the audience, dividing it up into its various component parts and antagonizing each in turn. But already there is a query about the nature of this actor/character's plain-dealing. The complexity increases when Hart tells the audience:

> Plain-dealing is, you'll say, quite out of fashion;
> You'll hate it here, as in a dedication.
> (*Plain Dealer* Prologue 24–5)

What the audience may or may not know, however, is that the play, in its published version, does indeed have a dedication by Wycherley, which he signed not in his own name, but (once again) as 'The Plain Dealer'. There are, it seems, *three* 'Plain Dealers': there is Manly the character in the play; Hart/Manly, the speaker of the Prologue; and Wycherley/Manly, the signatory of the Dedication.

Dedications (as the Hart/Manly Plain Dealer of the Prologue implies) sit uneasily with 'plain dealing' in the first place: they smack too much of flattery and fawning. But here, in fact, the reader is immediately wrong-footed, for the dedicatee, 'my Lady B—', turns out not to be (as might have been expected, and as it had been in *Love in a Wood*) Wycherley's former lover Barbara, Duchess of Cleveland, indeed not a rich patron at all, but 'Lady' or 'Mother' Bennett, a well-known London bawd. The mock-respectful tone of the Dedication to *The Plain Dealer* contains complex ironies which parody both the form and practice of Dedications. On one level, then, the dedication keeps up its promise of plain dealing: it is not, after all, a document of flattery. On another level, however, we are already aware that what is going on rhetorically is nothing like 'plain dealing', but is, on the contrary, part of a multi-layered discourse. Who is speaking in this prologue? Who is speaking the ironic dedication? The relationships between author and actor, actor and character, author and character, text and performance, the world of the audience and the world of the play are all problematized, and the plainness of the play's own dealing is compromised before the action even begins.

The play's central plot appears simple enough: Manly, a sea-captain and avowed plain speaker, disdains the shallowness of the world and puts his trust in only two people: Olivia, whom he loves, and his friend, Varnish. Both of these collude to betray him, however, and he revenges himself upon them both. In the process he discovers true love in the person of Fidelia, who has been his constant companion, but in disguise as a young man. In a sub-plot Manly's lieutenant Freeman pursues, and eventually wins, the unpleasant but wealthy Widow Blackacre. But things are more complex than they seem. 'Art' and 'Nature' are contrasted in the moral and gender schemes of the play, and are also played off against each other in the structure of the play's narrative. *The Plain Dealer* holds a mirror up, not only to nature, but also to art. While still being set in the 'real' world of Restoration London, it weaves together a web of intertextual references: to Shadwell's Don Juan play, *The Libertine*, to Wycherley's own *The Country Wife,* to Molière's *Le Misanthrope*, which is its partial inspiration, and, most importantly, to *Twelfth Night*, against whose central situation its own action is mapped. Manly's Olivia is a much more unpleasant character than Orsino's, but like her Shakespearean predecessor she gets involved in gender confusion when she falls for Fidelia, who is acting as go-between for Manly. Fidelia is, of course, a parody of Shakespeare's Viola, and the notion 'faithfulness' which her name implies is given a comic spin by the simultaneous pun on fiddle/viol. The play itself is a wreath of double-meanings, ironic ploys and counter-ploys.

Manly the character starts off in a straightforward enough way. His extended self-description, which could almost be taken directly out of a character-book, is a traditional character of a Plain Blunt Man:

> I, that am an unmannerly sea-fellow, if I ever speak well of people (which is very seldom indeed) it should be sure to be behind their backs, and if I would say or do ill to any, it should be to their faces. I would jostle a proud, strutting, overlooking coxcomb, at the head of his sycophants, rather than put out my tongue at him when he were past me; would frown in the

arrogant, big, dull face of an overgrown knave of business, rather than vent my spleen against him when his back were turned; would give fawning slaves the lie, whilst they embrace or commend me; cowards, whilst they brag; call a rascal by no other title, though his father had left him a duke's; laugh at fools aloud, before their mistresses; and must desire people to leave me, when their visits grow at last as troublesome, as they were at first impertinent.

(*Plain Dealer* I.i.45–57)

This last remark is addressed directly to his own visitor, and his antagonist in this first scene, the foppish Lord Plausible, who will 'speak well of all mankind' (I.i.31). Manly's description of himself, as 'an unmannerly sea-fellow' contains a clue to the pun which illuminates his own name: 'Manly' is the opposite of its near-homophone 'mannerly', and Manly's first speech is a rejection of the

decorums, supercilious forms and slavish ceremonies, your little tricks which you, the spaniels of the world, do daily over and over, for and to one another – not out of love or duty, but your servile fear.

(*Plain Dealer* I.i.1–5)

Manly's moral diagram is clear: plain dealing is opposed to social hypocrisy. He earlier compares Lord Plausible and his kind to 'common whores'. He sets up a familiar opposition between artificiality and naturalness, with masculinity aligned with both naturalness and courage, while the decorums, forms and ceremonies of society are based on servile fear and associated with the debased femininity of the 'common whores'. One of the charges Manly levels at his hypocritical opponents is that they are 'effeminate' (II.i.623). If one of the problems of Restoration models of masculinity was that the social virtues of civility and affability might be taken too far and revert to an un-masculine self-regard, Manly's response to this is to reject all such forms.

Fidelia – dressed, like Viola, in boy's attire in order to be near the man she loves – constantly professes her devotion to Manly, who repeatedly rejects her as 'a maudlin flatterer ... [a] little milksop' (I.i.350–1), a 'coward' (I.i.363), a 'handsome spaniel' (III.i.52), and so on. 'Go, prithee, away', he tells her. 'Thou art as hard to shake off as that flattering effeminating mischief, love' (III.i.63–4). Behaviours which in a woman might have been read as signs of genuine love, in the 'male' Fidelia are read as signs of insincerity, flattery or effeminacy. In *Twelfth Night* the heroine had hit upon a winning tactic, for Orsino seems to have found the androgyny of Viola/Cesario attractive. By way of contrast, Manly finds Fidelia repulsive. His own masculine self-image is predicated upon the notion that manliness (which he considers synonymous with plain dealing) is in itself a virtue. Correspondingly, behaviours such as flattery, cowardice and the showing of emotion are both vices and 'effeminate'. Inevitably, then, he finds his young companion disgusting precisely because of those traits which announce Fidelia's effeminacy – or to be more accurate, her femininity. It is not until Fidelia's true female identity is announced that he undergoes the reversal that allows him to give her his heart (in exchange, he fortuitously discovers, for the large and hitherto unmentioned fortune to which she is heir!) In *The Plain Dealer*, then, as in *Twelfth Night*, the cross-dressing plot leads to a series of confusions concerning the codes of masculine and feminine behaviour. In *The Plain Dealer*, however, Manly's response to that confusion is to reject its source: he needs to keep the codes quite separate, and has no room for the playful ambiguities that enrich Shakespeare's comedy.

Indeed, it is at the point when the play is employing that particularly Shakespearean plot device, the bed-trick, that the lack of playfulness, and the brutality of Manly's masculine code, are most apparent. Seeking vengeance for his rejection and betrayal by Olivia, Manly decides that his 'revenge shall only be upon her honour, not her life' (IV.ii.254–5). Enlisting the collusion of the abject Fidelia (whom Olivia also believes to be a boy) Manly bullies her into arranging a sexual assignation with Olivia and then substitutes himself under cover of dark. 'So much she hates me,' he tells Fidelia, 'that it would be a revenge sufficient, to make her accessory to my pleasure, and then let her know it' (IV.ii.259–61). Rape is a crime of hatred, not of lust, and Manly effectively rapes his former lover with a view to publicizing the fact at a later date in order to shame her.

For Fidelia, her co-operation in Manly's bed-trick is also an act of abject self-humiliation whose only justification is her own desire for Manly. What Manly (mis)reads as the young man's collusion (albeit reluctant) in male revenge against woman is actually nothing of the kind. It is one of the play's jibes against him that Manly – for all his claim to see and act plainly – continually misreads the relationships in which he finds himself. His one positive model of male companionship, for example, is equally illusory. Nearly always the outsider in his own society, he is not – in his own mind at least – entirely alone. There is one friend in whom he places his trust:

> a true heart admits but of one friendship, as of one love; but in having that
> friend I have a thousand, for he has the courage of men in despair, yet the
> diffidency and caution of cowards; the secrecy of the revengeful, and the

constancy of martyrs: one fit to advise, to keep a secret, to fight and die for
his friend. Such I think him, for I have trusted him with my mistress in my
absence ...

(Plain Dealer I.i.199–204)

Manly's belief in the depth of this friendship both qualifies and vali-
dates his otherwise misanthropic outlook on life. As the final phrase
shows, this intimate relationship with the trusted friend involves a
commodification of women which fits in with Sedgwick's notion of a
'strong' homosociality. In fact, it is here (rather than in Horner from
The Country Wife) that we see a genuinely 'transcendent' level of the
homosocial bond, for Manly has fetishized this one friendship, project-
ing into it an idealization of the male/male relationship. Indeed, it is
this idealization that allows him so confidently to scorn the reality of
male social interaction in the hated real world. For Varnish does not
appear in the play until Act IV, and when he *does* appear, he turns out
(not surprisingly) to be the greatest hypocrite of them all, and the one
who has most thoroughly fooled and betrayed the trusting Manly.

In *The Country Wife*, I suggested, male homosociality is replaced by
narcissism. In this play the two states have a slightly different relationship to each other. Manly's plain dealing involves a rejection of social
mores and social values, and indeed social existence. In the Dramatis
Personae he is described as 'choosing a sea life only to avoid the world'
(Wycherley 1996: 289). His desire to cut himself off from the artifice of
English society is repeated continually throughout the play, both by
himself and by others. 'I can walk alone' (I.i.9), he says, and this is his
character-note. His original plan had been to go into perpetual self-
exile, to 'settle himself somewhere in the Indies (and) ... never to
return again' (I.i.111–13) – a design which he maintains until the last
moments of the play. Yet this rejection of society, combined with his
inappropriate idealization of his friendship with Varnish, and his own
solipsistic morality which ignores the values of social intercourse, leads
him to construct for himself an ethically isolated cocoon of meaning.
Paradoxically, the preening flatterers of the world whom Manly rejects
are, in their way, less self-regarding than the Plain Dealer himself:
plain dealing itself turns into another form of narcissism.

On a number of levels, then, the Restoration theatre's staging of
masculinities is dominated by the myth of Narcissus. On the most
obvious level, it describes the preening self-regard of a fop such as
Monsieur or Sir Fopling Flutter. Like the fops whom Bulkeley
describes so contemptuously to Rochester, obsessed with their hair and
cravats and their 'Periwigges & trimmed shoes', Monsieur and Sir

Fopling demonstrate a concern for style and appearance in which masculine self-fashioning, taken to excess, turns back upon itself and becomes narcissistic. Similarly, there is always an element of narcissistic pleasure about the rake, whose drive towards sexual conquest is as self-contained in its way as the fop's and (usually) draws a similar attention to itself. It is fitting that when we first meet the libertine Dorimant in *The Man of Mode*, he is in his dressing-room, surrounded by clothes, toiletries and mirrors.

The mirror has always been an important metaphor for the theatre. Hamlet's notion of the theatre as a mirror up to nature has been echoed, expanded and qualified in countless epilogues and prologues. Moreover, the Restoration comic theatre is a more narcissistic mirror than most. On the one hand, it displays a whole range of individual narcissists, such as Dorimant, Flutter, Horner, Manly and – in his way – Bolloxinion. Perhaps these have a common source: it is one of the paradoxes of Restoration drama that while the social context, the theatres and the audiences were changing with the times, many of the playwrights were not. Long after the theatre as an institution had come to terms with the fact that the court would no longer be its main raison d'être, the plays on which it flourished were still largely being written by playwrights who were attached to, or who were trying to become attached to, court circles. Hence the contradiction that these plays, with their 'imagined societies ... in which private life happens on the fringes of the Court and is directly determined by events at the centre, are fantasies of royal cultural hegemony which no longer coincide with the reality of London' (Shepherd and Womack 1996: 145). These fantasies of royal cultural hegemony – which the Restoration playwrights still entertained – meant that one of the images which loomed in the multi-faceted mirrors of the Restoration theatre was that of Charles himself, the Royal narcissist whose masculine excesses were reflected and refracted through courtier-playwrights such as Rochester, Etherege and Wycherley, and their creations.

On another level, too, the theatre itself is narcissistic. Freudian and Lacanian theories ascribe the human tendency to take pleasure in looking at things (scopophilia) to a form of narcissism. According to Freud, 'The primary stage of the scopophilic instinct, in which the subject's own body is the object of scopophilia, must be classed under narcissism' (Freud 1986: 210). Thus the pleasures of theatrical spectatorship may themselves be grounded in 'the early phase of the development of the ego, during which its sexual instincts find auto-erotic satisfaction [and which we call] "narcissism"' (Freud 1986: 210). Again, this is particularly true of the Restoration theatre, whose own social, economic and aesthetic relationships with its audience embody a kind of social narcissism in themselves. Whereas Tragedy in the Restoration theatre typically transports its audience to distant times and exotic settings, its Comedy continually implies that the world which the audience sees on the stage is a direct reflection of its own. It is made up of familiar costumes, manners, settings, language and concerns, and contains abundant references to places such as Whitehall, the Exchange, Westminster Hall, specific taverns and coffee-houses; to events such as the publications of certain books, performances of certain plays, the passing of certain laws; to the codes of manners and dress, etcetera, which were all part of the play's immediate web of social meanings. (It is this insistent continuity between stage and audience which allows Wycherley his self-referential jokes about *The Country Wife* and the fiction that Eliza is about to go and watch herself in her own play.) To be sure, the audience neither expected nor got mimetic realism in the staging, and there was plenty of room for caricature, stylization and artifice in the acting – but these only make more evident the extent to which the Restoration comic theatre drew on the details of a certain class of contemporary London life for its vocabulary. The implied contract between stage and audience for comedy in the 1670s was that the audience should see 'itself' – or an image of aspects of itself – on stage. Few theatres, before or since, have been so insistent on this continuity, and few have been, at the same time, so obsessive in their treatment of a limited range of masculine stereotypes. Hamlet's mirror up to nature becomes the pool in which the young man sees and becomes obsessed by his own reflection.

5

Outlaws and Sentiment: Masculinities in the Eighteenth-Century Theatre

5.1 Introduction

Male conduct-books of the Restoration and late seventeenth century, books such as Richard Allestree's *The Gentleman's Calling* (1660) and Jean Gailhard's *The Compleat Gentleman* (1678), redefined masculinity in terms which stressed civic virtues such as affability and temperance. By the early eighteenth century, these had effectively become the dominant terms of hegemonic masculinity. The Hanoverian man of civility possessed a sense of inner authority and self-control, which manifested itself externally in the way he spoke, behaved, dressed and acted towards others. 'Civility', in fact, had been a virtue exalted by writers of conduct-books from the Renaissance onwards. However, as the aristocracy waned in influence, and the gentry and mercantile classes grew in importance and self-confidence, the virtues of civility became increasingly divorced from the aristocratic honour codes of earlier generations and 'manners became the centrepiece of both the social and the gender hierarchies, as masculinity in the upper ranks was more closely and deliberately defined and constructed than it had ever been previously' (Fletcher 1995: 323).

The making of a gentleman continued to be the subject of conduct-books, manuals, letters and philosophical treatises throughout the early eighteenth century. On the stage, however, the most important and influential plays of the period dealt not with polite society, but with thieves, whores and murderers. In this chapter, I want to explore the relationship between the emerging eighteenth-century concepts of gentry and mercantile masculinity, and the fascination which the culture showed for tales of crime and punishment. I will be drawing primarily on three major sources, all of which, in different ways, have frequently been taken as key texts for an understanding of eighteenth-century society and culture: John Gay's *The Beggar's Opera*; the journal writings of James Boswell, and George Lillo's *The London Merchant*. The starting-point is the character of Macheath in *The Beggar's Opera*, as an example of 'the outlaw masculine'.

5.2 The outlaw masculine

By the phrase 'outlaw masculine' I mean two things. Firstly, on a literal level, the figure of the outlaw-hero, which was so important in the popular culture of the eighteenth century. Secondly, I mean a kind of masculine energy which undermines the social consensus that was being created in the bourgeois sphere, and which reveals the developing double standard in Hanoverian ideology, and particularly in Hanoverian gender construction. The first of these categories, the literal outlaw figure, was a current and available stereotype for the popular imagination well before Gay's phenomenal success turned Macheath into its foremost exemplar. It could be found, in particular, in the impressive tradition of criminal literature which lies behind *The Beggar's Opera*: gallows speeches, sermons, pamphlets and ballads of contrition, in the Accounts of the Ordinary of Newgate, in Captain Alexander Smith's famous *A Complete History of the Lives of the Most Notorious Highwaymen* (1713) or the *Lives of the Convicts*, which Boswell admitted to having read so avidly. These are, of course, writings which are presented as warnings against vice: the repeated narrative that they present is that of the careless youth led by easy steps into ever more serious antisocial behaviour, and eventually to the gallows where he (or sometimes, but much less frequently, she) is brought to a pathetic but just end. Their primary and avowed purpose is to caution their readers against just such a fate, and to reassure that Good will triumph over Evil and Order over Disorder. 'It is,' argues John Brewer, 'the story, not the hero, who matters' (Brewer 1997: 438). And so it may, in theory. But narratives being what they are, the hero can sometimes exceed the narrative structure, and more often than not these writings have an equivocal effect. They set up an uneasy tension between presenting their subject matters as moral emblems, on the one hand, and the attractive heroes of a pseudo-tragic narrative, on the other. It is a tension which skilled writers such as Daniel Defoe used to great effect both in novels such as *Moll Flanders* and in documentary narratives such as *The History of the Remarkable Life of John Sheppard*.

Sheppard, of course, had already attained legendary status during his lifetime, and he continued to be mythologized after his death. Tales of his exploits, his burglaries, arrests and escapes (particularly his escapes) abounded: *A Narrative of All the Robberies, Escapes &c of John Sheppard* (1724) was written anonymously, brought out before Sheppard's execution, and entered its sixth edition within a year of publication. Several other biographies soon followed. Sheppard was himself an expert in self-specularization: his final recapture came about purely as a result of his love of an audience: aware of his fame, and revelling in it, he spent 'the last [day] of his free life parading himself through the ale-houses and gin-shops of Clare Market to an audience of hundreds of curious and attentive ears' (Linebaugh 1991: 37). Awaiting execution in a Newgate cell, his portrait was painted by James Thornhill, the official court painter to George I, and when he was brought before the King's Bench which sentenced him, he offered to perform a demonstration, Houdini-like, of his skill at escaping from handcuffs. With his death, the performative dimensions of the Sheppard legend became even more sharply defined.

Jack Sheppard, of course, is a prime example of the way in which the hero of a criminal narrative might exceed the exemplary moral closure of that narrative. And even in the most unsophisticated of ballads, a simple and predictable slippage of meanings may take place whereby, whether intentionally on the part of their authors or not, the criminal becomes glamourized. The romanticization of the criminal is an inherent ingredient of crime literature.

In a similar way, the ritualistic spectacle of the public execution could cast the condemned man in the role of tragic hero or victim, or even – as Gay has Mrs Peachum affirm in *The Beggar's Opera* – an eroticized object:

> Women indeed are bitter bad judges in these cases, for they are so partial to the brave that they think every man handsome who is going to the camp or the gallows ...

> Beneath the left ear so fit but a cord
> (A rope so charming a zone is)
> The youth in his cart hath the air of a lord
> And we cry, 'There dies an Adonis'

> *(Beggar's Opera* I.i.8–12, 17–20)

Note that Mrs Peachum still requires the condemned youth to be brave, and what she finds attractive includes his 'air of a lord'. The eroticized outlaw masculine transcends his abject status to combine an aristocratic air of social authority with the 'civil' virtues of restraint and decorum.

In 1724, only two weeks after his own final performance before a crowd of 200,000 spectators at Tyburn, Jack Sheppard came back to life again in a burlesque play entitled *Harlequin Sheppard*. Written by John Thurmond, it played briefly at the Theatre Royal, Drury Lane and featured, among other attractions, a song by John Gay entitled 'A Newgate Ballad', which was sung, as the songs in *The Beggar's Opera* would be sung, to a traditional English tune – in this case the tune of Packington's Pound. From Jack Sheppard, to *Harlequin Sheppard*, to *The Beggar's Opera* is, then, no great leap. Sheppard the legendary criminal of Newgate becomes Sheppard the tragic victim performing in the spectacle of his own execution at Tyburn, becomes Harlequin Sheppard at Drury Lane, becomes Macheath at Lincoln's Inn Fields. The performer had been turned into the subject of performance.

The much-quoted contemporary witticism that *The Beggar's Opera* (1728) 'made Rich [the manager of Lincolns Inn Fields] very Gay and will probably make Gay very Rich' (Guerinot and Jilg 1976: 161) was not without its foundation. The ballad opera was a box-office success of a kind not seen before in London. Pope, in a note to the *Dunciad*, stated:

> The vast success of it was unprecedented, and almost incredible ... It was acted in London sixty-three days uninterrupted; and renew'd the next season with equal applauses. It spread into all the great towns of England, was play'd in many places to the 30th, and 40th time, at Bath and Bristol 50 &c.
>
> (Quoted in Guerinot and Jilg 1976: 160)

The hero of the Beggar's tale, Macheath, is an outlaw (like Sheppard) in the literal sense of the word. A highwayman, he is the lover of Polly, the daughter of his criminal associate, the villainous Peachum. He secretly marries Polly, but Peachum is not only a receiver of stolen goods but also (unbeknown to Macheath) an informer, and being violently against the match for purely commercial reasons, he informs against Macheath, who is arrested and imprisoned in Newgate to await execution. There, however, Macheath seduces the jailer's daughter, Lucy Lockit, who helps him to escape. He heads straight to a brothel in order to celebrate, but there he is betrayed and quickly recaptured. Just before his execution, however, the Beggar – who has been the play's narrator – intervenes as a *deus ex machina* to declare that the play must have the ending which the taste of the town demands. Macheath is arbitrarily pardoned and the play ends in ironic celebration of the triumph of poetic justice over legal.

The record run which the play enjoyed in its first season was not challenged for nearly 50 years. Phenomenally popular in its own time, a close analysis of the plays presented at the patent theatres between 1747 and 1776 show that it was the most frequently performed of all theatre pieces during those years, and it continued to be revived successfully throughout the last quarter of its century (Stone 1960: clxii–clxv). It provides, too, what is perhaps the first English example of large-scale tie-in marketing. *Beggar's Opera* screens, *Beggar's Opera* fans, *Beggar's Opera* playing cards, *Beggar's Opera* mezzotints, prints and paintings, books of the sayings of Polly Peachum, and of the Memoirs of Captain Macheath became all the rage. The figures of both Polly and Macheath became cultural icons. Thomas Walker, who first played Macheath, became a star almost overnight – and like so many after him, was ruined by the dual effects of typecasting and an inability to cope with sudden celebrity. William Cooke records that

> the applause which he obtained in Macheath, checked his progress as a general actor. His company, from this circumstance, was so eagerly sought after by the gay libertine young men of fashion, that he was scarcely ever sober insomuch that we are told by the contemporary writers of that day, that he was frequently under the necessity of eating Sandwiches (or as they were then called, anchovy toasts) behind the scenes, to alleviate the fumes of the liquor.
>
> (Guerinot and Jilg 1976: 180)

So in this transformation from the glamourized criminal hero of popular ballads to the cultural icon, Macheath of *The Beggar's Opera*, what happens to the representation of the 'outlaw masculine'? For Macheath may be a figure in the same tradition as Jack Sheppard and the gallows heroes of Tyburn, but the Foucaultian spectacle of the gallows has now been incorporated into the patent theatre itself. And whereas *Harlequin Sheppard* lasted only one night at Drury Lane, and *The Quaker's Opera,* the most substantial of the Jack Sheppard plays in the early eighteenth century, played in the low-art venue of Bartholemew Fair, Gay imports the action onto the mainstream stage of Rich's theatre at Lincoln's Inn Fields, in a play which mounts a challenge to the 'highest' art form (Italian opera) for serious attention, and which became the most popular play of the century. In doing so, Gay both exploits and confirms the cultural centrality of the outlaw masculine figure, Macheath.

But what, if anything, has happened in the process? What is the effect of the mediating institution of the theatre itself on the way in which the outlaw masculine figure is presented and received? First of all, the transition involves the accumulation of meanings which are encoded in the traditions of the theatre itself. Thus, if the role of Macheath owes something to contemporary outlaw figures such as Sheppard, it also inherits much from the aristocratic rake-heroes of the Restoration stage. But Gay reinvents and revitalizes that now rather outdated dramatic stereotype by transposing him from the world of the aristocracy to the criminal underworld.

The effect is to create in Macheath a figure who embodies what contemporary sociologists of gender have called 'protest masculinity'. Analysing certain contemporary patterns of behaviour among young men involved in crime ('violence, school resistance, minor crime, heavy drug/alcohol use, occasional manual labour. Motorbikes or cars, short heterosexual liaisons'), R. W. Connell concludes that 'Protest masculinity is a marginalized masculinity, which picks up themes of hegemonic masculinity in the society at large but re-works them in a context of poverty' (Connell 1995: 110–14). In a similar way, Gay's outlaws rework the dominant themes of eighteenth-century masculinity in the context of Newgate. There may be a certain kind of realism in this: the criminal literature of the day does suggest a congruence between the behaviours and customs of the real-life criminal fraternity and those of the upper classes. Gay, however, is using the parallels between the underworld and the world of 'society' for his own specific rhetorical ends. The political satire against the Walpole administration (the impetus which initially drives the play) soon turns into a broader satire on social behaviours and values. The man of civility, that idealized self-image of eighteenth-century manhood, embodies social and gender authority and exhibits such socially visible virtues as affability, social responsibility and equanimity of demeanour. But this highly controlled (and emotionally repressed) civil masculinity has its shadow side – an image of masculinity characterized by licence, excess, and naked self-interest. And eighteenth-century readers and audiences appear to have been genuinely fascinated by it.

The outlaw masculinity of Macheath, however, is ambiguously figured in the play, and *The Beggar's Opera* offers its audience different kinds of meaning depending upon how they respond to this ambiguity. The dominant aesthetic theory of early eighteenth-century theatre, its basic understanding of how theatre worked, was founded on a fairly simple model of spectatorial *identification* – which would imply one response and one kind of meaning. Gay, on the other hand, seems to be asking the audience to engage in a different, more complex, ironic model of spectatorship which seems to correspond more closely to the urbane political and social satire that was central to his project.

To expand on this: early eighteenth-century English periodicals such as Addison and Steele's *Spectator* and *Guardian* had attempted to incorporate the theatre into the realm of polite culture – to argue that it should be seen as a civilized and civilizing place, a fit place for the man of civility to be seen, and indeed to improve himself. As Shepherd and Womack have argued (1996), at the centre of this cultural shift was a model of spectatorship in which primary emphasis was placed on the concept of *identification*. The drama, according to this model, operates by means of providing models of behaviour with which an audience identifies. To become respectable, the theatre needs to provide models which are themselves morally exemplary, in such a way that

> envy and detraction are baffled, and none are offended, but all insensibly won by personated characters, which they neither look upon as their rivals or superiors; every man that has any degree of what is laudable in a theatrical character, is secretly pleased and encouraged in the prosecution of that virtue without fancying any man about him has more of it.
>
> (Steele 1982: 174)

A theatre which sincerely believes in the identification theory of spectatorship will always have trouble with the multiple ironies of a play like *The Beggar's Opera*. If an audience is believed to be simply the passive receivers of a message, which then goes on to directly affect their behaviour, then a hero like Macheath will be problematic. The natural inheritor of Steele's programme was Colley Cibber, whose rise to respectability as Laureate (which earned him en route such scorn from Alexander Pope) fulfilled at least in part Steele's aims for a theatre of respectability which was later consolidated by Garrick. Significantly, when Gay had first offered *The Beggar's Opera* to him, Cibber had turned it down.

Gay's text, in any case, is calculated to put the audience through a process which is more complex than Steele and Cibber's model of theatrical spectatorship can account for. It is no accident that Bertolt Brecht was fascinated with *The Beggar's Opera*, for Gay employs many of the ironizing and alienating devices which Brecht himself later made famous. Gay's play, too, offers insights into the workings of power with which Brecht (from a very different political perspective) could have had close sympathy. In fact, just as Brecht developed a dramaturgy aimed at discouraging identification between audience and stage, so Gay seems to have worked every bit as hard to prevent naïve identification on the part of his audience. In Gay's opera there is, in the first place, the framing device of the

Beggar himself, the fictional author whose presence implies an authorial voice which we know to be other than the voice of the real-life author John Gay. The ironic relationship between the songs and the main action, and often between the words and the music of the songs allows them, too, to function as Brecht wanted *his* songs to function. Brecht talked about the way his songs should wake an audience up, challenge them, unlike the use of song in opera, which encouraged audiences to suspend their critical faculties and wallow in emotion. But Brechtian *avant la lettre* though Gay may have been, what is special to him is his ability to use in a theatrical context the same ironic vision that Pope and Swift employed so effectively in prose fiction and mock-heroic verse, whereby the audience finds itself trapped between twin distorting glasses in a discursive space where what is said is rarely what is meant – even though it may be true all the same.

Thus when, in the very first song of the play, Peachum the professional criminal laments that 'The statesman, because he's so great, / Thinks his trade as honest as mine' (I.i.7–8) the audience is expected to follow the ironic thread through a complex series of twists and turns, involving the recognition of several voices simultaneously. To locate only the most prominent:

(a) *Peachum's voice*, which is speaking from the self-interested perspective of the professional criminal, and which, while recognizing his own criminality, appears simultaneously to use himself as a positive standard for worldly honesty;

(b) *the statesman's voice*, which Peachum (mis)represents as thinking himself honest as Peachum; there is a *secondary voice* in here, too, since the audience is asked to reconstruct from Peachum's version of the statesman's voice another, real-world statesman who presumably believes no such thing, or at least admits to believing no such thing, but who sees himself as far superior to Peachum in terms of honesty and respectability;

(c) *the voice of the implicit author, the authorial persona* of the Beggar, who takes as natural and true all the 'outrageous' propositions spoken by the criminal fraternity in the play;

(d) *the voice of the actual author*, John Gay, who believes none of these propositions literally, but who, by juxtaposing the worlds of the criminal and the politician in such a paradox, is challenging the audience, asking it to look afresh at their own assumptions about societal morality, to ask, indeed, who is the greater criminal, the statesman or the fence.

In terms of the experience of the play in performance, we probably need to add to this list the 'voice' of the specific actor himself, who may bring a particular identity to the part and add particular overtones to the line; and the 'voice' of the musical discourses concerned – both the Italian operatic tradition whose vogue was being parodied, and the native English ballad tradition which was being used to parody it.

Even the play's ironies were explained ironically. An article written by the pseudonymous Phil. Harmonicus, which first appeared in the anti-government periodical *The Craftsman* on 17 February 1728, and which was later reprinted and sold under the title of a 'A Key to *The Beggar's Opera*', explains, in tones of mock-horror, some of the not-so-hidden satirical meanings of the play. The 'Key' pretends to be appalled at the way in which the play lampoons the government and great men, concluding, with its tongue firmly in its cheek, that

> though I am far from wishing ... to see the Liberty of the Stage intirely abol-
> ished, yet I think such licentious Invectives on the most polite and fashion-
> able Vices require some immediate Restraint; for if they continue to be
> allowed, the Theatre will become the Censor of the Age, and no Man, even
> of the first Quality or Distinction, will be at Liberty to follow his Pleasures,
> Inclinations or Interest (which is certainly the Birthright of every free
> Briton) without Danger of becoming the May-game of the whole Town.
>
> (Guerinot and Jilg 1976: 92)

Thus when Gay juxtaposes the worlds of the criminal fraternity and the worlds of 'great men' he invites his audience to interpret the play by negotiating a complex set of ironies, consisting of different voices, each adding a different level of meaning. They are being asked to participate in a model of spectating which is challenging, intellectually engaging and involves a very active kind of meaning-making.

These are two possible models, then – possibly even contradictory models – of what Macheath may have meant to an eighteenth-century audience. On the one hand, the complex ironic and indeed moralistic mode of Gay's opera implicates Macheath in the heartless world of these 'great men' criminals: selfish, dishonest, manipulative and corrupt. The ethical scheme of the play positions him as one of the objects of the political satire, just as Peachum and Lockit are. Yet on the other hand, there is also an opposite pull: the play's narrative structure positions Macheath as the romantic hero, who gets the girl and is saved from the jaws of death at the last moment. This is how, in the 1952 Peter Brook film of *The Beggar's Opera*, Laurence Olivier played Macheath. An enduring image is of Olivier, looking particularly dashing in his highwayman's costume, astride what appeared to be a

stuffed horse, doing a cinematic gallop past a projected backdrop landscape, and singing 'Over the Hills and Far Away'. In retrospect it is all
rather ludicrous, but it illustrates the way in which Macheath can be
positioned quite simply as romantic hero. Naïve or not, the movie was
working hard to encourage a mode of identification with Macheath.

In an act of literary analysis it is good practice (or at least common
practice) to privilege the complex reading over the simple one: in this
case, to reject simple identification with the hero in favour of an appre-
ciation of the complex meanings generated by the many levels of irony
in the play. In considering the performative effect of *The Beggar's
Opera*, however, this does not quite work. The theatrical experience
need not be 'either/or': it can be 'both ... and'. The framing intellectual
irony of the play's dramatic structure need not prevent the outlaw masculine from also becoming an object of desire – which is why Walker,
who first acted the part, 'was so eagerly sought after by the gay libertine young men of fashion, that he was scarcely ever sober' (Guerinot
and Jilg 1976: 180).

The powerful moralistic reaction *against* the play which came in the
wake of its popular success was based on the genuine contemporary
fear that – whatever the play's deeper moral and political message –
the outlaw masculine, in the figure of Macheath, was so attractive that
he would become a subject for emulation. And so sermons were
preached against the play. In 1728, for example, Thomas Herring,
chaplain to the King, preached in Lincoln's Inn Chapel – only a stone's
throw from the theatre where *The Beggar's Opera* was playing – that
Gay's depiction of criminal low-life was tantamount to an encouragement to crime, and that 'several Thieves and Street-robbers confessed
in Newgate, that they raised their courage at the Playhouse, by the
songs of their Hero Macheath, before they sallied forth on their desperate nocturnal Exploits' (Guerinot and Jilg 1976: 120–1). The theory
of naïve identification had, of course, been used as a stick with which to
beat the stage since its earliest days: the Elizabethan period, for
example, is replete with anti-theatrical pamphlets warning that depic-
tions of vice on the stage would lead to a breakdown in societal morality. But in the past these attacks had largely been made by the enemies
of the theatre *as such*. In the case of *The Beggar's Opera* the argument
is being made not so much by those opposed to the theatre in general,
as by those who deplored this particular *use* of the theatre. The attacks
took many forms, and were not always disinterested. For example,
given the play's anti-government politics, it predictably attracted much
criticism from Walpole's partisans – whose motives may have had less
to do with a genuine belief in the vice-encouraging effects of the play,

and more to do with attempting to neutralize a successful cultural phenomenon which was being used effectively against the Prime Minister. But the repeated note which is sounded is that the play's glamourization and romanticization of criminal behaviour will encourage the like behaviour in real life. Gay's most recent biographer, David Nokes, notes that,

> Perhaps the most unlikely voice in this moralistic chorus was that of Daniel Defoe, who complained that *The Beggar's Opera* had presented thieves in 'so amiable a light ... that it has taught them to value themselves on their profession, rather than be ashamed of it'. Defoe traced a direct link between the popularity of *The Beggar's Opera* and the recent increase in street crime: 'Every idle fellow, weary of honest labour, need but fancy himself a Macheath or a Sheppard, and there's a rogue made at once'. This is pretty rich from the author of *Moll Flanders.*
>
> (Nokes 1995: 443)

Or indeed from the writer who had published in 1724 *The History of the Remarkable Life of John Sheppard*, and who, as Nokes also points out, had done more than anyone to turn Jack Sheppard into a folk hero (Nokes 1995: 443).

However, the point is that commentators were genuinely worried about it. The outlaw masculine might become a prevalent model – what will happen to our kids then? Perhaps the most direct elaboration on this theme comes in a pamphlet entitled *Thievery à la Mode, Or The Fatal Encouragement* – a more or less typical criminal biography, complete with deathbed repentance scene, published in the year of the *Opera*'s first success, 1728. Typical, that is, apart from the fact that the blame for the hero's descent into crime is assigned to the fact that he went to see a performance of *The Beggar's Opera* and saw how popular and fashionable crime had now become. As he robs one of his victims, he recognizes him as a fellow audience-member from the playhouse, and one of those who had

> burst out into such extravagant Encomiums upon *The Beggar's Opera*. It came presently into his head to retort upon him in a merry way, which he did in these words. This, sir, is but the sequel of *The Beggar's Opera,* and I hope no Gentleman will be offended at the Reality, who was so delighted with the Representation.
>
> (Guerinot and Jilg 1976: 133)

Thievery à la Mode, although presented as true-life story, is clearly fictional and almost certainly itself ironic. Yet it provides an interesting fantasy about how the outlaw masculine might become realized, about the possible effects of misreading the text, the performance, or the cultural phenomenon which the play had become. As we shall see in the following section, it was a fantasy not entirely without basis.

5.3   Acting out the outlaw masculine

Just as *The Beggar's Opera* continued to be popular well into the second half of the century, so debates about its moral effect also continued. Boswell records a conversation with Doctor Johnson:

> *The Beggar's Opera,* and the common question whether it was pernicious in its effects, having been introduced: JOHNSON. 'As to this matter, which has been very much contested, I myself am of opinion that more influence has been ascribed to *The Beggar's Opera* than it in reality ever had; for I do not believe that any man was ever made a rogue by being present at its representation. At the same time, I do not deny that it may have some influence, by making the character of a rogue familiar, and in some degree pleasing.' Then collecting himself, as it were, to give a heavy and comprehensive stroke: 'There is in it such a *labefactation* of all principles, as may be injurious to morality.'
>
> (Ryskamp and Pottle 1963: 151–2)

Thus the eminent Doctor appears to sit firmly on the fence on this one, denying the play's injurious effect at one moment and acknowledging its possibility the next.

Elsewhere in Boswell's journals, however, we might find some indication as to the way in which Gay's outlaw masculine is inscribed in the psyche of at least one avid eighteenth-century theatre-goer. Boswell is a particularly interesting figure in this context of a discussion of eighteenth-century constructions of masculinity, since the nature and extent of his journals and letters give a particularly full account of a figure who was speaking from close to the cultural centres of the eighteenth century, and also – particularly in the early years – meticulously constructing his own identity, repeatedly observing himself and setting standards of manliness against which he judged himself. The journals in fact give us a double insight into this process; they show him making various resolutions as to the sort of identity he intends to construct for everyday life, while at the same time *actually* constructing the verbal construct which becomes James Boswell. One of the fascinating aspects of his journals is the self-awareness with which he goes about these constructions. Soon after arriving in London, as he begins to reinvent himself as a cosmopolitan man-about-town, he congratulates himself:

Since I came up I have begun to acquire a composed, genteel character very different from a rattling uncultivated one which for some time past I have been fond of. I have discovered that we may be, in some degree, whatever character we choose.

(Pottle 1950: 52)

This ability to 'be, in some degree, whatever character we choose' is of particular interest when Boswell chooses to be the character of Macheath.

Boswell, as scholars have noted, seems to have been particularly fascinated by the figure of Macheath (see Friedman 1991; Carter 1999). In his definitive Yale edition of *Boswell's London Journal 1762–1763*, which dates from Boswell's second sojourn in London at the age of 22–3, when he was trying to establish himself as a man-about-town, and trying to determine his future career, Frederick Pottle states that 'in one way or another the figure of Macheath dominates this entire journal' (Pottle 1950: 252n.). It is a suggestive assertion, even if it does rather overstate the case. In fact, Boswell is very much taken with the theatre in general. An intimate of several actors – and very intimate with several actresses – as well as the companion of writers and even at one point a putative stage-author himself (see Pottle 1952: 187), it is not surprising that Boswell's journals are laced with reference to the stage. *The Beggar's Opera* is one play among many to which several allusions are made. Nonetheless, it is true that there *are* many references which Boswell makes, throughout his journals, both to the character and to the play, which seems to have held a particularly important place in his imagination. For example, in his journal entry for 21 February 1768, when Boswell was languishing in Edinburgh and missing London life, he records that 'At night I was with Lady Crawford at *The Beggar's Opera*, which quite relieved any gloom. The songs revived London ideas, and my old intrigues with actresses who used to play in this opera. I was happy in being free of Miss Blair' (Brady and Pottle 1957: 141). This claim, that the play for him always brought back memories of his time in London, occurs elsewhere in the journals. Together with the mention of the intrigues with actresses who used to play in the opera – which Pottle suggests refers to Mrs Love – it shows how the play comes to be associated with his times of freedom, comparative youth and eroticism.

The play was in fact an integral part of the young Boswell's erotic language. The Miss Blair, from whom he was happy to be free, was one Kate Blair, briefly an object of Boswell's amorous attentions and about whom he had written on 29 July 1767, seven months earlier, quoting from Macheath's song in Act I, 'for here every flower is united'. In a

letter written a few months after that visit to the Edinburgh performance of *The Beggar's Opera* we find Boswell once more congratulating
himself on 'having escaped the insensible Miss Blair', and in the same
paragraph quite unself-consciously using the same quotation with
which he had hymned her perfections, to praise a new object of his
affections, Miss Mary Ann Boyd, in whom, too, it appeared that 'every
flower [was] united' (Brady and Pottle 1957: 191).

Elsewhere we find Boswell debating the influence of the play with
Dr Johnson on 18 April 1775, and talking about the meaning of various
specific lines with a fellow lawyer on 14 March 1772. He talks directly
about visiting – or in some cases just missing several specific performances of it – on 21 February 1768, 15 February 1775, 7 March 1775,
and 15 April 1780. He attempts to see the play again in Edinburgh on
7 February 1776. He notes the fact that he has referred to it for various
reasons, in order to make a discursive or conversational point, on 23
February 1769, 31 March 1775, 4 April 1775, 20 March 1776, 16 April
1779, 15 April 1781.

Perhaps the most notable thing, however, is the *way* in which he
makes use of the play, and of the figure of Macheath. The following
entry, for 19 May 1763, is a famous one. Boswell has decided to go out
on the town, in search of debauchery. He has been frustrated in paying
court to one young woman, but then, in the streets, meets two others.
Taking them back to a tavern – appropriately enough, one near
Newgate –

> We were shown into a good room and had a bottle of sherry before us in a
> minute. I surveyed my seraglio and found them both good subjects for
> amorous play. I toyed with them and drank about and sung *Youth's the
> Season* and thought myself Captain Macheath, and then I solaced my exis-
> tence with them, one after the other according to their seniority. I was quite
> *raised* as the phrase is: thought I was in a London tavern, the Shakespeare's
> Head, enjoying high debauchery after my sober winter. I parted with my
> ladies politely, and came home in a glow of spirits.
>
> (Pottle 1950: 264)

In an interesting article on this topic Philip Carter shows how concerned Boswell is, throughout his London journal, with the notion of
manliness. By manliness Boswell means being (or having the reputation of being) both a 'man of dignity' and what he calls a 'pretty man':
inwardly assured and full of worldly wisdom, outwardly self-controlled
yet fashionably and politely sociable. In other words, a thoroughgoing
eighteenth-century man of civility and one for whom 'politeness [w]as
central to his construction of a new self' (Carter 1999: 121). But, as we

have seen, Boswell also has an 'outlaw' self, which he identifies specifically with Macheath. This alternative, blackguard persona, allows him his excursions into the eighteenth-century underworld, and allows him, too, an alternative model of masculinity – the lawless, lustful, libidinous male sexual predator. Does Boswell, then, 'identify' with Macheath? On one level, certainly. Boswell's use of Macheath seems to fall into precisely that mode of naïve identification which the moralistic commentators of the 1720s most feared.

The point, however, is that Boswell's identification is not naïve at all. What is striking about the story is the way in which Boswell is quite self-consciously *performing* gender. Furnished with the romantic Captain as a fantasy model, to counterbalance the man of civility to which he elsewhere aspires, Boswell allows himself to play the part of the outlaw masculine in order to afford his licentious self some kind of holiday from the man of sense and responsibility which he wishes to present to the world ('I have discovered that we may be, in some degree, whatever character we choose'). He is acting the part of Macheath, but he knows he is acting it, he watches himself acting it, and even applauds himself in the role. All of which fits in, too, with Boswell's own theories about stage acting. He records a debate at the house of Thomas Sheridan concerning the centuries-old theatrical conundrum, as to whether actors should immerse themselves in their part completely, or whether the actor should retain some critical distance and control over the emotions they seem to express:

> *Tuesday 28 December.* I should have mentioned, on Sunday last that I drank tea at Sheridan's, where was a Captain Maud of the Blues, with whom he [i.e. Thomas Sheridan] disputed on the propriety of theatrical action. He said that an actor ought to forget himself and the audience entirely, and be quite the real character; and that for his part he was so much so that he remembered nothing at all but the character. This Mr Maud opposed as wrong; because an actor in that case would not play so well, as he would not be enough master of himself. I think he was right.
>
> (Pottle 1950: 119)

The pronouns are frustratingly imprecise, but the logic of the diary entry seems to suggest that the 'he' in the final sentence refers to Maud: that is to say that Boswell agrees with Maud that an actor should not lose himself in his part, that he should remain 'master of himself', and keep, as it were, a distance from his part. In the same way, Boswell himself performs his social roles, whether of man of civility or of blackguard, while simultaneously appearing to be the spectator of his own performance.

The split between the man of civility and the outlaw masculine may be an index of the fragmented eighteenth-century masculine psyche, yet the blackguard persona and the man of civility are deeply interconnected in Boswell's sense of himself. Like Mrs Peachum's youth in the cart with the air of a lord, Boswell's self-image as Macheath is predicated not only on his libidinous roguery but simultaneously on his sense of style: the 'high debauchery' which he enjoys is debauchery accompanied by high ceremonial, and he parts with his ladies 'politely'. The Macheath role is one among many which are open to him – and its meaning for him is integrally connected with the whole web of meanings which *The Beggar's Opera* seems to have held for Boswell. Perhaps most importantly, however, the Macheath fantasy which Boswell plays out on 19 May needs to be seen in the light of another nexus of meanings which appear to have obsessed Boswell.

'It is a curious turn,' he tells us, 'but I never can resist seeing executions' (Brady and Pottle 1957: 150). In this, of course, Boswell was hardly alone: the street theatre of the public execution was a major dramatic attraction in the eighteenth century, attended by thousands. Boswell, too, is not unaware of the ironic parallels between these two kinds of fictional and actual dramas. On 24 February 1768 he attended the execution of one of his criminal clients, John Raybould the forger. That night, to 'relieve [his] gloom' he attended the theatre – a performance of *The Beggar's Opera*. 'It was curious,' he remarks, 'that after seeing a real hanging I should meet with two mock ones on the stage' (Brady and Pottle 1957: 141). Moreover, Boswell is self-aware enough to analyse his own response to the spectacle of the scaffold – which involved a form of imaginative projection, placing himself in the position of the condemned: 'I always use to compare the conduct of malefactors with what I suppose my conduct may be … I never saw a man hanged but I thought I could behave better than he did' (Brady and Pottle 1957: 150). Boswell imagines himself both being there, in the position of the prisoner, and also watching himself 'behave' in a seemly fashion.

While Boswell's regular attendance at public executions, both in London and in Edinburgh, gave him the opportunity for one form of imaginative engagement with this outlaw masculine, the references in his journal to Macheath suggest that the fictional character became a focus for his imaginings of various kinds. The two come together again in a journal entry which takes place only a couple of weeks before his encounter on 19 May (in his Macheath persona) with the prostitutes. On 3 May Boswell visited Newgate out of idle curiosity as a sightseer. Among the prisoners he viewed was the young Paul Lewis, a condemned robber. Boswell notes that 'Paul, who had been in the sea-service and was called Captain, was a genteel, spirited young fellow. He was just a Macheath. He was dressed in a white coat and blue silk vest and silver, with his hair neatly queued and a silver-laced hat, smartly cocked' (Pottle 1950: 251). Translating the fictional character into the real-life criminal affected Boswell with a deep depression which he attempted to confront the next day:

> In my younger years I had read in the *Lives of the Convicts* so much about Tyburn that I had a sort of horrid eagerness to be there. I also wished to see the last behaviour of Paul Lewis, the handsome fellow whom I had seen the day before. Accordingly I took Captain Temple with me, and he and I got upon a scaffold very near the fatal tree, so that we could clearly see all the dismal scene. There was a most prodigious crowd of spectators. I was most terribly shocked, and thrown into a very deep melancholy.
>
> (Pottle 1950: 252)

Another of the prisoners whom Boswell had seen the previous day, Hannah Diego (or Dagoe), was hanged at the same time (Linebaugh 1991: 303). Boswell, though, is interested only in the gallant Macheath-like figure of Lewis.

In Gay's opera, the dashing Macheath is saved at the last moment by a *deus ex machina*. But no such fortune awaited this real-life highway-man whom Boswell had the day before identified as 'just a Macheath'. The very deep melancholy which Boswell feels after Lewis's execution lasted several days – until 9 May, in fact. Its source may well have been the disparity between the fantasy character and the reality of dying, the materiality of the death of the prime actor which proves once and for all that the discourse of the scaffold and the discourse of the theatrical performance are *not* identical. If this is the case, then Lewis-as-Macheath, and libidinous-Boswell-as-Macheath, taken together, suggest something more than naïve identification. They suggest an interplay between the outlaw masculine as internalized gender construct and an awareness of its limitations. The Macheath fantasy derives in part from Boswell's realization of the performative nature of social identity, dating from his discovery on his arrival in London 'that we may be, in some degree, whatever character we choose'. It derives too, from his fascination with the theatre in general, not only as a place of continual erotic excitement, whether as spectacle, or as a hunting ground for his amours amongst the London actresses, but also as a model for his own self-fashioning. But contemplating the doomed Lewis, Eros gives way to Thanatos; the fantasy principle comes up, eventually, against the reality principle.

5.4 'An open, generous manliness of Temper': mercantile masculinity in *The London Merchant* (1731)

> Last Tuesday ... *George Barnwell* was perform'd ... with great Applause, to a crowded Audience, there being present most of the eminent Merchants of the City of London; they appear'd greatly pleased with the Play and Performance.
>
> *Daily Post,* 22 July 1731

The reality principle is never far away in George Lillo's *The London Merchant or The History of George Barnwell*, a play whose dramaturgy seems expressly designed to prevent any romantic identification with the outlaw masculine. The *Beggar's Opera* had attained popularity on the eighteenth-century stage by being – albeit in a rather safe way – somewhat scandalous, and by poking fun at the rich and respectable. In doing so it dramatized and glamourized, in the figure of Macheath, a romantic form of outlaw masculinity which seems to have appealed to the subversive fantasies of many in its audience. *The London Merchant*, on the other hand, appears to play directly to the interests, tastes and values of the respectable citizens who are satirized by Gay's ballad opera. In most respects, indeed, it appears (at first sight at least) to position itself culturally as the very opposite of *The Beggar's Opera*. In this section I shall be exploring ways in which this affects the play's treatment of masculinity.

The London Merchant opened at Drury Lane – the rival house to *The Beggar's Opera*'s Lincoln's Inn Fields – on 22 June 1731. Within the month, if the brief notice in the *Daily Post* is to be taken at face value, word appears to have reached 'most of the eminent Merchants of the City of London' (not always the theatre's greatest supporters), who turned up in strength and were 'greatly pleased' with the dramatic representation of their own class and interests which they saw enacted. Like *The Beggar's Opera*, Lillo's play contains prison and gallows settings, scenes of robbery and violence, and young men on the run betrayed to the law by faithless prostitutes. Unlike the Newgate pastoral, however, *The London Merchant* couches its tale of theft, prostitution, murder and betrayal within a didactic moral framework which continually asserts the values of mercantilism, Englishness and nonconformist Christianity. No wonder the eminent merchants were greatly pleased.

The play is, effectively, a theatrical response to some of the questions of aesthetics, social morality and, indeed, gender which had been raised by *The Beggar's Opera*. It was the second such response, in fact, on Lillo's part. His first had been a ballad-opera of his own entitled

Silvia or The Country Burial (1730). This was one of the plethora of imitations which the success of *The Beggar's Opera* had engendered; between 1728 and 1730, 25 of these ballad-operas had appeared and by 1734 the number was nearer 75 (Lillo 1993: 1). *Silvia* was staged with an experienced and talented cast, many of whom, indeed, had appeared in the original *Beggar's Opera*. Thomas Davies, one of Lillo's eighteenth-century editors and biographers, describes *Silvia* as

> one of the best dramatic pieces which had then appeared, written in imita-tion of the celebrated *Beggar's Opera* ... But what will still more recommend it to the judicious, this Pastoral Burlesque Serio-Comic opera was written with a view to inculcate the love of truth and virtue, and a hatred of vice and falshood.
>
> (Davies 1775: xii)

But, despite its earnest recommendation of 'the love of truth and virtue and a hatred of vice and falsehood', *Silvia* was a failure. The genre of the ballad-opera was not Lillo's natural milieu, and he neither mastered the form as Gay had originally conceived it, nor did he make it uniquely his own. The latter was not for want of trying: in *Silvia* Lillo located the action in the country rather than the town; he lost the low-life elements of Gay's play; substituted sentimentality for satire; and he reversed Gay's strategy of continually lowering the tone of his source tunes for a cheap laugh. As a result the play received only three full performances at Lincoln's Inn Fields.

Having failed to engage with *The Beggar's Opera* at one level, however, Lillo returned to it the following year, approaching it this time in a different way. Using the ballad form not as a musical vehicle so much as a narrative structure, he exploited as the major source for his next play the well-known 'Ballad of George Barnwell'. In the process he also did to eighteenth-century tragic form what Gay had done to the form of Italian opera: he revitalized it and gave it new meanings by juxtaposing it with the content of London lowlife. In *The London Merchant* Lillo took the genre, emotions and language of high tragedy and applied them to a Tyburn narrative, written in prose and peopled by merchants, apprentices and whores. As its Prologue states:

> A London Prentice ruin'd is our Theme
> Drawn from the fam'd old Song that bears his Name.
> We hope your Taste is not so high to scorn
> A moral Tale ...
>
> (*London Merchant* Prologue 21–4)

And a 'moral Tale' it is indeed, employing recognizable social and moral stereotypes, and rarely straying far from the predictable ethical and narrative structures which are announced early on the proceedings. The eponymous 'London Merchant' is Thorowgood, a character who, as his name suggests, is presented as an archetypal figure of the thoroughly good merchant. Honest, generous, benevolent and fatherly, he represents all the bourgeois virtues which Lillo seeks to endorse. As a father, he worries about his teenage daughter (but would not dream of forcing her into any marriage, however advantageous to him, against her will); as a man of business he is scrupulous in paying his tradesmen's bills promptly; and as a master he is not only a fair and generous employer, but also a moral guardian to his young apprentices. Thorowgood, in fact, represents the acceptable, not to say idealized, face of eighteenth-century mercantile capitalism. His world-view unites in a coherent and harmonious whole all the values of that world: nationalism, religion, science and commerce are all brought together into a single vision of virtue. As he explains eagerly to one of his apprentices,

> Methinks I wou'd not have you only learn the Method of Merchandize, and practise it hereafter, merely as a Means of getting Wealth. – 'Twill be well worth your Pains to study it as a Science. – See how it is founded in Reason and the Nature of Things. – How it promotes Humanity, as it has opened and yet keeps up an Intercourse between Nations ... promoting Arts, Industry, Peace and Plenty; by mutual benefits diffusing mutual Love from Pole to Pole.
>
> (*London Merchant* III.i.1–7)

Thorowgood goes on to explain how the Merchant's calling is to bring goods from around the world 'to enrich his native Country', while Trueman, the archetypal 'good apprentice', solemnly agrees how beneficial this will be to those savages whose 'useless Superfluities' are thereby being taken from them! (III.i.13).

Thorowgood's all-encompassing vision of mercantile capitalism as the driving motor of a providential Christian world, founded in Reason and the Nature of things, promoting Humanity and 'diffusing mutual Love from Pole to Pole' may seem comically naïve and impossibly disingenuous. But while a modern reader finds it hard to read these speeches without irony, Lillo is clearly presenting his merchant as an exemplary figure, an epitome of manliness in that eighteenth-century sense of the word which can be glossed as 'desirable and emulative male behaviour' (Carter 2001: 4). Behaviour which is desirable and emulative, of course, varies from society to society and from subgroup to subgroup within that society. The manliness which Thorowgood represents is founded in Lillo's wider beliefs about the shape of society, and the central position of the bourgeoisie in general and merchants in particular within that society. Thus the play becomes a parable of hegemonic masculinity – a masculinity which, in terms of the theatre for which Lillo was writing in the 1730s, was taking on a distinctly mercantile aspect. Thorowgood is a figure who has achieved, in social, material and financial terms, that secure masculine identity to which his young apprentices are supposed to aspire. He is the 'man of civility' – a civility which, as the play continually insists, should now be identified with the rising mercantile classes. The play's function, on one level, is to endorse the hegemonic values which Thorowgood represents. Like the gallows ballad from which it derives, it entreats young men and apprentices to follow the path of virtue by showing the pitfalls on the way to achieving the secure identity which embodies those values.

Thorowgood, then, is the unshakeable moral centre of Lillo's narrative. Its main protagonist, however, is his 18-year-old apprentice George Barnwell. At the start of the play Barnwell is a seemingly perfect example of a successful and young apprentice, described by his friend Trueman as follows:

> Never had Youth a higher Sense of Virtue – Justly he thought, and as he thought he practised; never was Life more regular than his; an Understanding uncommon at his Years; an open, generous manliness of Temper; his Manners, easy, unaffected and engaging.
>
> (*London Merchant* III.ii.16–20)

But George Barnwell, this apparent epitome of 'open, generous manliness', is seduced and entrapped by the wiles of an amoral prostitute: the lovely but fallen Sarah Millwood. Barnwell becomes a Hogarthian figure – the fallen apprentice, led from virtue into vice by the wiles of a harlot, and the play charts his inevitable progress down the slippery slope which leads him from lust to robbery and then to murder. Like Hogarth's portraits and etchings, the world which Lillo creates is one in which we are always aware how short the distance is between the comfortable respectability of the well-off citizen's life and the crime, squalor and 'wickedness' of the recently created urban underclass. In Boswell's responses to *The Beggar's Opera* we have seen one kind of interplay between these two worlds, as Boswell identifies himself with Macheath in order to fuel his own erotic fantasies, and contemplates and imaginatively projects himself into the figure of the condemned man on the gallows. In *The London Merchant* there is no such romantic identification: Barnwell does not fancy himself as a heroic outlaw, even if, on one level, that is what he becomes. Rather, Lillo's bourgeois fable is about a young man at a crucial stage in his development. Sexually mature without being morally mature enough to cope with the desires this engenders, he is led astray, and slips from one world into the other. To maintain Millwood he steals, with increasing regularity, from Thorowgood. When his embezzlement is discovered, he runs from his master to his mistress, who then urges him to compound his misdeeds by murdering and robbing his benefactor and guardian, his own uncle.

Lillo does everything in his power to enlist the audience's sympathy for Barnwell, who is portrayed as young, naïve, easily manipulated by the knowing and sexually experienced Millwood, and constantly racked with self-doubt. Eventually, however, Barnwell does commit the horrid deed: masked and armed, he tries to draw back at the last moment, but his uncle discovers him, and in the ensuing struggle Barnwell stabs him almost by accident. When he returns, full of remorse and self-loathing, to Millwood she recognizes that 'in his Madness he will discover all' (IV.x.40) and, to clear herself, immediately has him arrested and accused. Like Macheath, Barnwell finds that the false woman is all too ready to betray him when it suits her. However, Millwood in her turn is also betrayed: her own servants, finally appalled by the level of wickedness and cruelty to which she has sunk, inform on her to Thorowgood, at whose suit she is arrested, tried, and hanged along with young Barnwell. Unlike the meta-theatrically comic structure of *The Beggar's Opera*, the tragedy of George Barnwell allows for no last-minute rescue from the gallows. If one of the fears expressed by critics of Gay's play was that it might encourage young men to turn to crime, Lillo addresses the problem directly by showing in stark terms the fate of any young man so foolish as to do so.

The London Merchant was breaking new theatrical ground by showing a tragic story which dealt with mundane contemporary figures such as merchants and apprentices – and, what is more, by doing it in prose! There had been some domestic tragedies in the Elizabethan theatre that had used similar subject-matter, but in 1730 plays such as *Arden of Feversham* were more or less unknown to Lillo's contemporaries (despite Lillo's own best attempts: he wrote an adaptation of *Arden of Feversham*, but it was not staged until 1759, 20 years after his death). While stage comedies had been exploiting the 'everyday' nature of their London or provincial English settings since the 1660s, tragic form of the time had generally relied on classical or oriental settings to provide a note of cultural seriousness. In the theatre of the day the word 'tragedy' did not necessarily refer primarily to a particular narrative structure – such as a story that ends with the hero's death. Rather it was used to denote a play of a certain level of high moral seriousness. The play's first producer, Theophilus Cibber, clearly saw *The London Merchant*'s experimental form as a risky venture, describing it as 'almost a new species of tragedy, wrote on a very uncommon subject' (Cibber 1753: 339). Thomas Davies, too, writing long after the event, gives a sense of the theatrical daring of Lillo's enterprise:

> The author's friends, though they were well acquainted with the merit of BARNWELL, could not be without their fears for the success of a play, which was formed on a new plan – a history of manners deduced from an old ballad; and which the witlings of the time called a Newgate Tragedy.
>
> It is true some of our best dramatic poets, in their most affecting pieces, had lowered the buskin, and fitted it to characters in life inferior to Kings and Heroes; yet no writer had adventured to descend so low as to introduce the character of a merchant, or his apprentice, into a tragedy.
>
> (Davies 1775: xii)

In order to address this problem of the relationship between form and content, Lillo gestures towards a technique of historical distancing. Since the 'Ballad of George Barnwell' was believed to date from Elizabethan times, Lillo sets his play in that period – thereby simultaneously imbuing it with connotations of the high tragedy of Shakespeare and his contemporaries. In fact, the Elizabethan setting of the play amounts to little more than a few early references to the Spanish Armada, Walsingham and 'our gracious queen' (I.i.38), after which any historical specificity fades from the writing. In performance, of course, the Elizabethan setting might well have been kept before the audience's eye by means of representative costumes. But the play is very much about the London of Lillo's own era. The everyday socio-economic details of prostitution and apprenticeship which the play articulates are those of mid-eighteenth-century London, and the token historical distance that Lillo's Elizabethan references provide tend to emphasize the contemporary nature of the play rather than disguise it. Nonetheless, the very nature of that historical distance is significant and there is something fitting about the choice of period which Lillo employs. The Elizabethan age, the first major phase of a nascent English preindustrial mercantilism which was coming to its peak in Lillo's time, turns out to be an appropriate and effective mirror for the bourgeois London society of the early eighteenth century, to whose inhabitants Lillo was addressing his narrative.

Therefore, it is important to note that while a merchant may be described as 'low' in terms of this tragic decorum, this should not be confused with judgements about his real-life social status. On the contrary, the early years of the eighteenth century had already seen a key transition 'when the focus of English culture moved from the Court to the City' (Brewer 1997: 98). Now the middle years of the century saw a continued growth in the economic, social and ideological importance of that sector of society which Thorowgood represents and to which Barnwell and Truman aspire. Eighteenth-century England was a culture which sometimes made sense of its own social structures by reference to a time-honoured, inflexible and all-encompassing hierarchy of social ranks, and sometimes by reference to a simple polarity between rich and poor. However, a third model was also available, which saw a three-part model of society in which the 'middling sort' held a kind of balance of power between the 'poorest rank' and 'the great', and were the true preservers of that society's freedoms. The definition of this 'middling sort' could, of course, be drawn as narrowly or as broadly as the occasion required – encompassing on occasion bankers and financiers, merchants and businessmen, manufacturers and entrepreneurs, lawyers and scholars, as well as shopkeepers, yeomen, the agrarian gentry and the Whig landowners who still represented a major social and economic force in the country (see Canadine 2000: 24–6). While the court and courtiers continued to wield power, one consequence of the urbanization of eighteenth-century life was the emergence of a polite society which was predominantly metropolitan and non-aristocratic in character, and which gave a cultural identity and voice to the 'middling sort'. First defined in the periodicals of the early eighteenth century such as Addison and Steele's *Spectator,* it combined a rejection of court values as false, superficial, servile and frequently immoral with a new insistence on the 'polite' values of the new urban middle classes. Politeness in this eighteenth-century sense of the term connotes far more than its present-day meanings of courtesy, etiquette and conventional good manners.

> It was at once a philosophy, a way of life to which one committed oneself, and the means to understand oneself and one's place in the world. Embracing every aspect of manners and morals, it was a complete system of conduct ... The aim of politeness was to reach an accommodation with the complexities of modern life and to replace political zeal and religious bigotry with mutual tolerance and understanding ... It involved both learning a technique of self-discipline and adopting the values of a refined, moderate sociability.

> (Brewer 1997: 101–2)

'Tolerance', 'understanding', 'self-discipline', 'moderate sociability': it could be Thorowgood speaking. The world-view which *The London Merchant* espouses and articulates is completely congruent with the ethos of politeness. Moreover, the values of this emergent polite society gave rise to new notions of manliness, encouraging

> new styles of refined manhood distinguishable from existing images of the early modern courtier and the country gentleman. In place of these figures, reformers proposed the 'polite town gentleman' as the embodiment of more relaxed and genuine forms of sociability located in a series of professional and leisured urban venues. Central to the refined gentleman's genuine sociability was his synthesis of external manners with an inner virtue based on a Christian morality ...
>
> (Carter 2001: 10)

But, more than this, 'manliness' became a positive moral term within a structure in which social values were both gendered and polarized. The opposite of manliness was 'effeminacy' – a term which was used in different contexts to mean different things, and which was variously associated with ideas of luxurious living, economic superfluity, display, vanity and self-indulgence on both the material and moral level. Its central force, however, was

> the surrender to private desire and passion, whether this took the form of vanity, concupiscence, cupidity or avarice. Human feeling and desire, they believed should either be controlled or be shaped so as to act for the public good. A failure to do so was 'effeminate' ... [And] the issue of effeminacy was very much an issue for men.
>
> (Brewer 1997: 80)

And according to such criteria, clearly, George Barnwell acts effeminately: he leaves the path of duty and that mercantile calling which so clearly (according to Lillo) operates for the public good. His death on the gallows alongside Millwood is an effect of his lack of 'manliness'.

Thus, the gender formation which I am calling 'mercantile masculinity' is closely implicated with the emergence of the polite society. It differs slightly from the phrase which R. W. Connell, taking a slightly different tack, has used to characterize this phase of masculine history: 'gentry masculinity' (Connell 1995: 190). Connell's emphasis on the notion of gentry is valuable, but I wish here to point to something slightly different. Mercantile and gentry masculinities inevitably overlap, and are closely related to each other. But I am invoking the epithet 'mercantile' in order to place emphasis on the town rather than the country and on a masculinity which finds meaning in a trade-based rather than a land-based economy.

We have seen earlier in this chapter the self-confident belief which Thorowgood's speeches show in the centrality of the merchant to the nation's health and well-being. In the play's first scene, too, he insists that 'As the Name of Merchant never degrades the Gentleman, so by no means does it exclude him' (I.i.21–2). Thorowgood's daughter Maria is being wooed by 'noble Lords' and 'Courtiers' (I.ii.12, 40) – and one of the moral ironies which the play stresses is the fact that Barnwell, who ends on the gallows because of the wiles of a woman, spurns in the process Maria, who adores him in silence, preferring him to the 'Men of the greatest Rank and Merit' (I.ii.31–2) who are courting her. The path had been open, it is implied, for Barnwell to follow one of the classic paths to preferment: to marry his master's daughter and to join Thorowgood amongst the ranks of the highest in the land, as a master in his own right. His failing is partly one of sexual choice: Millwood represents an undisciplined sexuality, while the repressed Maria is clearly the 'right' choice for the properly restrained and patient apprentice to make.

According to a long-standing tradition, the eminently rational Thorowgood was Lillo's own self-portrait. Lillo was himself an eminent London merchant – a rich businessman in the gold and jewellery trade. Thomas Davies, researching his biography for his 1775 edition of the plays, interviewed a retired colleague of Lillo's, who reported that 'in his moral conduct, and in the candour, generosity and openness of his temper he resembled the character of Thorowgood in his own BARN-WELL' (Davies 1775: xlvi). If further proof were needed of the seriousness with which Lillo himself took the values that Thorowgood articulates in the play, it can be found in Lillo's dedication of the play to John Eyles. Eyles had been Lord Mayor of London and was at the time of the play's composition a Sub-Governor of the South Sea Company, and thus himself one of the most eminent of London merchants.

Like *The Beggar's Opera*, the play was a highly popular item in the eighteenth-century theatre company's repertoire, and its popularity continued into the next century. The precise extent of, and the reasons for, the popularity of *The London Merchant* are a matter for debate, but James L. Steffensen's cautious estimate that '*The London Merchant* was one of the five most popular non-Shakespearean tragedies acted in London' (Lillo 1993: 124) during the period 1731–76, is a reasonable reflection of the play's importance in eighteenth-century theatre. Steffensen's analysis of theatre records also shows, as might be expected, that this popularity was by no means uniform, and that the pattern was one of 'highly successful revivals alternating with years in which *The London Merchant* virtually disappeared from the stage' (Lillo 1993: 124). Even such a qualified success, however, is no mean feat, although one tradition in eighteenth-century theatre history seems to give a rather wry explanation for the phenomenon. Writing in 1965, the editor of the Regent's Restoration Drama edition, William McBurney, repeats and endorses a legend which dates back to Theophilus Cibber's *The Lives of the Poets of Great Britain and Ireland* (1753) that:

> By the middle of the century it had become the traditional offering for Christmas and Easter holidays, since it was 'judged a proper entertainment for the apprentices &c as being a more instructive, moral and cautionary drama, than many pieces that had usually been exhibited on those days with little but farce and ribaldry to recommend them.' It was also usually given on Lord Mayor's Day in November, presumably for the same reason. Ernest Bernbaum may be correct in speculating that 'the frequent performance of *George Barnwell* was encouraged by influential citizens, not because they themselves enjoyed it, but because they thought young people should.
>
> (Lillo 1965: xiii)

Now this is an extremely suggestive notion in the context of a debate about the staging of masculinities. The implication is that the play was popular because the real-life merchants of Lillo's London believed that the moral structure of the tale, combined with Lillo's own intensely moralistic dialogue, made it a suitable moral vehicle for instructing the young apprentice in the 'right' way to behave. We saw in the *Daily Post* notices which was quoted at the beginning of this section, that 'most of the eminent merchants of the City of London' had been well pleased with what they saw in 1731. But it seems to have been taken a step further. These eminent merchants and influential citizens, according to tradition, sponsored repeated performances of the play, to be staged at the apprentices' holiday times, and thus co-opted the London play-house to function as an apparatus of ideological control, and to provide an authoritative modelling of social and gender identity.

This takes us back, of course, to the identification theory of specta-torship, which demands moral exemplars such as Thorowgood and Trueman, against whom the evil of Millwood and the folly of Barnwell may be securely judged. Lillo is happy to oblige, and, as he puts it in his Dedication to *The London Merchant*, 'the more extensively useful the Moral of any Tragedy is, the more excellent that piece must be of its kind. ... Such Plays are the best Answers to them who deny the

Lawfulness of the Stage' (Lillo 1993: 151–2). Moreover, Theophilus
Cibber, who originated the story that the play was 'judged a proper
entertainment for the apprentices &c as being a[n] ... instructive,
moral and cautionary drama' (Cibber 1753: V, 339), is a pretty reliable
first-hand source: he was the play's first producer, managing the
summer company at Drury Lane when *The London Merchant* opened
there in 1731, and he played George Barnwell in the play's opening
run.

Cibber's suggestion that the play was co-opted and sponsored by the
London guilds makes sense, too, in the light of the very real fears that
haunted the masters of London apprentices in the eighteenth century.
The relationship between apprentice and master in this society was a
complex and often troubled one. At best, it offered a mutually
beneficial scheme whereby the young man received protection, food,
clothing, lodging and education from a master on whom he was meant
to model himself, and whom he was to grow up to emulate; at worst, it
was rife with the possibilities of exploitation. It was the product of a
changing economic structure, in which the poor were increasingly distanced from the means of production, and in which urbanization both
created and exploited a culture of poverty. A vicious circle led to 'the
poor' being increasingly identified with the 'the criminal classes', while
the legal contract into which the typical apprentice entered ensured
that he would indeed remain poor (and effectively without legal or
sexual rights) until at least his twenty-first birthday. It had aspects both
of the commercial contract and the patriarchal family, for the apprentice paid financially for his upkeep and his education and then paid
again with his living labour. Little wonder, then, that one of the frequently expressed fears amongst the mercantile classes was that of the
apprentice 'going to the bad', and running away from, or robbing or
even murdering, his master or benefactor. Nor was this unjustified.
According to historian Peter Linebaugh, 'Two-fifths of those hanged at
Tyburn in the eighteenth century had started an apprenticeship'
(Linebaugh 1991: 62) and stealing from one's master was one of the
commonest of punishable offences. George Barnwell's story was by no
means an untypical one.

This question of the extent to which the play's success was due to the
financial and moral sponsorship of those whose interests lay in the
direction of public morality and social control, touches at the heart of
the gender questions of *The London Merchant*. The traditional account
portrays Lillo as essentially a rather prim moralist. His dissenting background, and his own known trade associations, the ease with which he
can be 'mapped' onto Thorowgood, all mean that he fits the bill as a

propagandist for a masculinity which was based on a Protestant work ethic, telling stories designed to frighten young men into virtue, to scare them away from loose women, and to keep them subservient to their masters' authority. The additional implication that it was only because of sponsorship from his fellow-merchants that Lillo's play succeeded as it did, adds weight to an account which portrays *The London Merchant* as the epitome of the theatre whose function is to police social and gender ideology and to act as a means of control.

It is true that recent work on the production history of *The London Merchant* suggests that the play's commercial dependency on the backing of eminent merchants might have been less marked than is often supposed, and that the play was genuinely popular in its own terms, and not simply as a co-opted sermon. Early performances of the play were indeed, as Cibber puts it, 'bespoke by some eminent merchants and citizens who much approved its moral tendency' (Cibber 1753: V, 339). However, this sponsorship of the play seems not to have lasted much beyond 1734, and James Steffenson, the play's most recent editor, has argued that 'The theatrical record for the years after 1735 provides virtually no support for this explanation of the play's extended if sporadic history of successful performances' (Lillo 1993: 127). This, though, remains debatable. The holiday performances continued to be staged, while as late as 4 June 1771 the playbill announces that the production is being mounted 'at the particular desire of several Eminent Merchants in the City of London' (Scouten 1968: 919). As Steffenson points out, however, it is not clear whether this 'particular desire' was accompanied by any financial incentive.

The debate about the merchants' sponsorship of the play reflects an argument as to whether Lillo was effectively a spokesman for a certain influential class of patrons, or whether, as one of his defenders argues, he 'was attached to the stage for its own sake, and not because of its potential as a medium of propaganda' (Burgess 1968: 7). The dichotomy is a false one. Theatre, as was suggested earlier, works on a number of levels, and often simultaneously. The eminent merchants may well have believed that what they saw was the theatrical equivalent of a conduct-book, teaching the manly virtues of honest industry and obedience to both divine and earthly laws. But there is more to it than that – as can be seen when we look at the way in which the play actually works in the theatre. On one level it certainly works in a calculatedly programmatic and didactic way: the overall narrative structure of the play works to enhance precisely the sort of moral message which Lillo promises in his dedication. Yet there is also a continual sense of meanings slipping away from this overt sermonizing. Most of these are concerned with the character of Millwood, the prostitute who leads Barnwell astray. This is a brilliant starring role, a great woman's part – on one level she is a low-life Lady Macbeth, inciting Barnwell to murder. But Millwood is also powerful in her contrary analysis of masculinity.

Millwood is extraordinary in that a huge proportion of her lines – including many of those by which she seduces Barnwell – are meditations on eighteenth-century gender roles. One of her first speeches is to her maid Lucy: 'We are but slaves to Men ... Slaves have no property; no, not even in themselves. – All is the Victor's' (I.iii.15, 17). This early statement of the social and economic basis of eighteenth-century gender relations underpins all her actions. When she disingenuously tells the naïve Barnwell that 'I hate my Sex, my self! Had I been a Man, I might, perhaps, have been ... happy in your Friendship ...' (I.v.40–1), she is being duplicitous – and yet there is a truth to what she says. Not only does she point to her own exclusion from male homosociality, but she expresses a sense – repeated elsewhere in the play – that all her villainy is part of a life-long attempt to equalize the disadvantages which she has always felt as a woman. At the end of the play, when she is finally unmasked and arrested, she turns on her captors with unexpected ferocity.

> Fool, Hypocrite, Villain, – Man! Thou canst not call me that ... Well may I curse your barbarous Sex, who robbed me of [innocence and beauty] ere I know their Worth, then left me, too late, to count their Value by their Loss. Another and another Spoiler came, and all my gain was Poverty and Reproach ... Men of all Degrees and Professions I have known, yet found no Difference but in their several Capacities; all were alike wicked to the utmost of their Power ... I know you and I hate you all; I expect no Mercy and I ask for none; I follow'd my Inclinations, and that the best of you does evry Day ... Thus you go on, deceiving and being deceiv'd, harassing, plaguing and destroying one another; but Women are your universal Prey.
>
> (*London Merchant* IV.xiii.2, 10–13, 19–21, 33–4, 51–3)

Starting from the point that 'Man!' is the worst of all insults, this is an extraordinary speech. Far too long to quote in full here, it goes on for nearly two pages, and is a catalogue of men's crimes against women, a completely convincing account of abuse and oppression. The abuse which Millwood has suffered at the hands of men, she has elevated to a universal principle in which Religion and Laws are completely implicated. Describing herself as 'Not Fool enough to be an Atheist' (IV.xviii.39) she sees instead a Universe ruled by a (male-identified)

God whose religion has 'turn[ed] the present World into Hell' (IV.xviii.44) and who – like all the father-figures and lovers in her life before – 'will Destroy [her]' (V.xi.28). Thorowgood tries to stand up to her, but her world-view is even more coherent and passionately held than his: where he sees a benevolently ordered universe with the merchant as its epitome of Virtue, Millwood sees a universe in which men, like beasts 'devour, or are devour'd' (IV.xviii.35–6) and 'Women are [their] universal Prey' (IV.xviii.53).

The radicalism of Millwood's speeches, especially in her climactic moments of arrest and execution, are testament to an energy which is far in excess of the play's apparently straightforward didactic structure. In addressing the gender roles of his society, Lillo has come up against something uncontrolled and uncontrollable – a vision in which poverty and crime, the destructive power of organized religion, the injustice of the legal system are all laid at the door of male oppression of women, in a sequence of vibrant speeches which make Thorowgood's praise for 'pure Religion, Liberty, and Laws' (I.i.2) seem bland indeed.

Most of the play's fifth act is set in the prison where Barnwell and Millwood are held before their execution, and is concerned with questions of Christian redemption, forgiveness and repentance. It should, in theory, fulfil the same function as the last stanza of the Tyburn ballad, warning the youth to 'take warning by me'. Barnwell himself, in fact, enacts this in an address to the audience about justice in which he warns the youths in the audience to heed his example, so that he will not die in vain. So Barnwell dies penitent, and praying earnestly for salvation, while Millwood goes to her execution in a state between despair and defiance.

Yet however hard Lillo works to prevent it and to achieve a conventional moralistic closure, the presence of Millwood disrupts it. Lillo even suppressed, in early editions and performances, the climactic gallows scene, in which Millwood's despair and defiance take on a positively heroic aspect. But no matter how the play's ending is staged, its lingering final image is not of Barnwell but of Millwood. Her death is clearly meant to provide an image of unregenerate evil *in extremis*, and thereby to reinforce the providential moral vision by which we are to make sense of Barnwell's death. Somehow, though, it threatens instead to undercut it, and takes the audience back imaginatively to Millwood's great arrest scene and the very different – and completely believable – perspective on the gender relations which have led her to her fate. On the gallows she tells Barnwell that 'Mercy's beyond my Hope, almost beyond my Wish. I can't repent, nor ask to be forgiven'(V.xi.25–6). Taken at face value, Millwood dies in a state of damnation. Yet her refusal to repent also leaves the dichotomy between her world-view and Thorowgood's unresolved on any but the most superficial level.

Thus *The London Merchant* works in a way which, paradoxically, both resembles and differs from, *The Beggar's Opera*. Both dramatize the contradictions of eighteenth-century masculinity. The sophisticated comedy of *The Beggar's Opera* invites the audience to read the play ironically, implicating Macheath's outlaw masculinity in a satire that is both social and political; yet simultaneously the erotics of Macheath's performance position him as an object of subversive desire. In *The London Merchant*, Lillo does everything he can to discredit this romantic lawlessness, to show it as a failure of masculinity rather than as an attractively successful form in its own right, and to dramatize in its place the positive values of a mercantile masculinity. But here, too, theatrical meanings exceed authorial intentions. Even as the values of a hegemonic mercantile masculinity – polite, civilized and socialized – are identified and propounded, the opposite vision rises to the surface, the vision of a world in which men, even respectable men like Thorowgood, 'devour, or are devour'd' and 'Women are [their] universal Prey'. The play's most telling statements about the mercantile masculinity of eighteenth-century England belong, after all, to Millwood.

6

Doll's Houses and Wendy Houses: Masculinities on Nineteenth- and Early Twentieth-Century Stages

6.1 Doors that slam: naturalism and masculinity

In his 'Preface to *Miss Julie*', one of the seminal documents of dramatic naturalism, Strindberg inveighs against stage doors that 'are made of canvas and flap at the slightest touch [and] … will not even allow an angry father to express his fury by … slamming the door "so that the whole house shakes" ' (Strindberg 1976: 101). Above all, the scenography which Strindberg and his naturalist contemporaries wanted (and eventually got) was one which would give the impression of solidity. It was an important demand: a theatre which wanted to address the middle classes of nineteenth-century Europe needed to insist on its own solidity, for 'solid' was one of the cardinal bourgeois virtues, a term of praise for both people and objects. A solid man was one of probity, integrity and conscientious application. The solid buildings and monuments, the town halls, churches and statues which the Victorian age erected to commemorate the builders of its wealth are still there to be seen. Inside the home, the heavy material solidity of the period's tables, chairs, wardrobes, cupboards and pianos, and of the smaller objects and ornaments with which the drawing-rooms and parlours were crammed – all these are testaments to a society in which one of the finest compliments was that something was 'built to last'. The middle-class Victorian home was designed to embody attributes to which its inhabitants aspired: not just a place in which to live, but also a symbolic structure, which articulated the meanings that governed their lives (see Hobsbawm 1975: 270–1).

The naturalist theatre which arose in order to address this culture expressed the importance of such domestic materiality. The setting of most of its plays is the home – and the nineteenth-century middle-class home is an environment with already inscribed gender meanings. Specifically, it is a space which, in theory, at least, is the domain of the woman rather than of the man. Nineteenth-century social theory frequently articulated the concept of 'separate spheres': the man's domain of influence and importance was his workplace, or the world of public affairs. The domestic sphere, on the other hand, was presumed to belong to the woman of the house (see Davidoff, in Corr and Jamieson: 1990). The self-fashioning of the bourgeois male demanded the competitive arena which was provided by the world of work, that world outside the family. In this highly industrialized and technological society, the successful achievement of a bourgeois manhood becomes, increasingly, defined in terms of success within this male sphere of industry and commerce. And if the public sphere was identified as the domain of the masculine, with its concomitant exclusion of women from most key areas of public life, the domestic sphere was, as a corollary, identified with the feminine. The Victorian home was, broadly speaking, a feminine space, though some of its rooms, such as the kitchen or nursery, were more definitely feminine spaces than others.

Ruskin described it lyrically in *Sesame and Lilies*, enthusing that '[Man] is eminently the doer, the creator, the discoverer, the defender … By [woman's] office and place, she is protected from all danger and temptation. The man, in his rough work in the open world, must encounter all peril and trial' (cited in Templeton 1997: 138). More recent gender theorists have analysed it in terms of exclusion and defence of privilege:

> The height of the private form [of patriarchy] was to be found in the mid-nineteenth century in the middle classes. Many scholars have argued that there was an intensification in the domestic ideology and the extent to which middle-class women were confined to the private sphere of the home … There were extremely strong sanctions against non-marital sexuality for such women. They did not work in public, only in their own households, and were excluded from the public sphere of the state, lacking citizenship rights such as suffrage and, if married, ability to own property.
>
> (Walby 1990: 179)

As the century progressed, it saw what Lawrence Stone has described as 'the Victorian revival of patriarchy' (Stone 1977: 665), as masculine and feminine gender roles and identities became increasingly polarized. The masculine and feminine spheres might have been separate, but they were by no means symmetrical. On the contrary, the doctrine of separate spheres was 'an ideological construct that masked inequality and forced segregation on the basis of sex' (Templeton 1997: 138). For most women this meant that they were effectively excluded from influence in, or participation in, public life. Nor was the woman's ownership of the domestic realm secure – predicated as it was on her financial dependence on her husband.

But for men, too, the doctrine of separate spheres led to a classic double-bind, since successful bourgeois masculinity was defined not only in terms of success in the world of affairs, but also 'in relation to the domestic sphere within criteria that value the role of the breadwinner for a domestic establishment and that situate affectionate as well as sexual life within marriage' (Sussman 1995: 5). Success in the domestic 'feminine' sphere was the expected corollary of success in the masculine sphere of work. The man laboured in the outside world in order to maintain the idealized home, which was in theory the woman's domain, but of which he, as paterfamilias, was overlord.

The nineteenth-century naturalist theatre, then, tells stories of this revived patriarchy which are largely set within the middle-class home: a realm which patriarchy itself has designated – but problematically – as 'feminine'. A further complexity is added, however, by one of the paradoxes of naturalist theatre itself. As Michael Booth has suggested, 'the Victorian materialism that created a stage art faithful to the surface of things also liked to see the inner workings of that materialism' (Booth 1980: 38). But in looking at these inner workings, nineteenth-century playwrights soon began to exploit a contradiction between the scenography of naturalism and its narratology. The scenography assures the audience of the tangibility of reality: plays are set time after time in solid-looking, middle-class drawing-rooms, the private, intimate spaces of the audience's own lives, in which people hold conversations in everyday language about everyday things. The theatre of naturalism does not stage the doings of gods and heroes, or monarchs and armies; it does not show the pageant of history, nor melodramatic heroes and villains striking impossible postures. It offers, in all its solid detail, the material world of everyday life. But the theme of naturalist plays, time after time, is that in this solid material world all is not as it seems. The happy marriage is a sham, the prosperous family business is on the verge of crisis, the respectable reputation is a mask for weakness, maliciousness, dishonesty. For naturalistic theatre always looked to go beyond surface realism: to use the solidity of its surfaces to show what lay beneath the surface.

Thus the essential strategy of the naturalist theatre is first to convince the audience of the solidity of what they are seeing: everything, including set, dialogue etc. conspires to this effect. *Then* the solid edifice is dismantled, and the audience sees how its values are effectively built on sand. If Strindberg and Zola are the key theorists of this naturalism, it was Ibsen who most powerfully represented its practice in the minds of nineteenth-century theatre-goers. The basic plot of naturalism is also Ibsen's basic plot, and he returns to it continually. In *A Doll's House* the solid edifice which is dismantled in the course of the play is that of the dominant gender ideology.

Ibsen repeatedly disclaimed having any interest in women's rights. As he told the Norwegian Society for Women's Rights in 1898 (somewhat ungraciously since he was guest of honour at their banquet at the time):

> I ... must disclaim the honour of having consciously worked for women's rights. I am not even quite sure what women's rights really are. To me it has been a question of human rights. And if you read my books carefully you will realize that. Of course it is desirable to solve the problem of women; but that has not been my whole object. My task has been the portrayal of human beings.
>
> (cited in Meyer 1992: 817)

Critics anxious to 'rescue [Ibsen] from the contamination of feminism' (Templeton 1997: xv) have tended to leap joyfully onto these conservative and condescending remarks. It is difficult to take Ibsen entirely at his word, however: in *A Doll's House* Ibsen certainly 'portrays human beings' – but he also deals directly with precisely those issues of the rights of women (legal and financial, as well as moral) which he disavows in his after-dinner address to these early feminists. Perhaps, though, there is some truth in what Ibsen says about himself. It makes some kind of sense, at least, if we consider that what Ibsen dramatized so powerfully in his plays was not so much 'the problem of women' as a nineteenth-century crisis of masculinity.

In *A Doll's House*, Ibsen once more plays a variation on his regular theme of the underlying fissures that threaten the apparent stability of bourgeois family life. The seemingly happy marriage of Nora and Torvald Helmer is actually more fragile than either of its participants understand, and their financial security and standing in respectable society is less assured than they suspect. The bourgeois home is not only the backdrop for the play but also its subject.

Before the play begins, we discover, Nora Helmer had borrowed money in order to take her husband, who was critically ill, south for his health. She did it without his knowledge – for, as she explains to her friend Mrs Linde in Act I, Torvald's masculine pride and self-reliance would have been affronted if he had known that he owed anything to his wife. But to secure the loan (which is she is trying secretly to repay, earning small sums by working – 'almost like being a man!' (Ibsen 1991: 16)) Nora had forged her dying father's signature. Now, however, the clerk from whom she had borrowed the money, Krogstadt, has been given notice of dismissal by the newly-promoted Torvald, and threatens Nora with exposure unless she convinces her husband to retain him. Nora attempts to prevent the scandal from coming to light, convinced that Torvald will sacrifice himself for her if it does. When he *does* find out, however, Torvald's reaction is the opposite of what Nora expected. The viciousness of his response only subsides when he learns that Krogstadt is not, after all, going to cause a public scandal. Realizing finally how little she understands about her husband, herself, or the world she lives in, Nora leaves.

In *A Doll's House* the masculine and feminine spheres appear to be clearly and separately delineated. Torvald goes out to work in his bank, while Nora looks after the Christmas decorations and does the shopping. The couple appear to be quite comfortable inhabiting their separate realms; but it is the subversion of this which the play undertakes. Nora comes to understand that her separate sphere of domesticity is a prison as well as a playroom, and that it is her acceptance of the masculine doctrine of separation which has kept her so dangerously ignorant of the world. The exchanges at the end of the play involve a complete dismantling not only of Torvald's masculine authority within the home, but also of the ideological structures which underpin it. Torvald fires these at Nora like ammunition:

> First and foremost you are a wife and mother ... Surely you are clear about your position in your own home? ... Haven't you an infallible guide in questions like these? Haven't you your religion? ... I suppose you do have some moral sense? ...
>
> You understand nothing about the society you live in. ...You don't love me any more.
>
> (Ibsen 1991: 82–3)

As Torvald's lines make clear, feelings and ideas such as maternal instincts, religion, morality, and love may all be pressed into service by the bourgeois male in defence of a patriarchal masculinity that is both oppressive and exploitative.

In *The Doll's House* this masculinity is represented by a gallery of failed stereotypes, all of whom let Nora down or threaten her in some way. Her father, dead before the play begins, is an ambiguous figure. He is depicted memorably by Nora herself, who pictures him as the dominant patriarch, and as Torvald's predecessor, accomplice and perhaps even role model in an unbroken line of oppression:

> At home Daddy used to tell me what he thought, then I thought the same. And if I thought differently I kept quiet about it, because he wouldn't have liked it ... I passed out of Daddy's hands into yours. You arranged every-thing to your tastes, and I acquired the same tastes ... I lived by doing tricks for you, Torvald. But that's the way you wanted it. You and Daddy did me a great wrong. It's your fault that I've never made anything of my life ... our house has never been anything but a playroom. I have been your doll wife, just as at home I was Daddy's doll-child.
>
> (Ibsen 1991: 80)

Yet looked at more closely, the father is a much more contradictory character. In the home Nora perpetuates the myth that he provided the money which saved Torvald's life, but this was not the case: Nora had managed to find that for herself in the shape of Krogstad's loan. As a man of affairs, moreover, Nora's father had a dubious reputation:

> NORA: You remember all the nasty insinuations those wicked people put in the papers about Daddy? I honestly think they would have had him dismissed if the Ministry hadn't sent you down to investigate, and you hadn't been so kind and helpful.
>
> HELMER: My dear little Nora, there is a considerable difference between your father and me. Your father's professional conduct was not entirely above suspicion. Mine is.
>
> (Ibsen 1991: 42)

Daddy, is not, after all, a model of successful and comfortable bour-geois paternalism but a corrupt businessman who gets away with his crooked dealings by the skin of his teeth. And Torvald himself, for all his posturing about being above suspicion, appears to have been impli-cated in this corruption when he was sent to investigate his father-in-law's improprieties and had proved 'so kind and helpful'. This hint is elaborated on towards the end of the play. When Torvald learns about Krogstad's blackmail, he turns on Nora, and throws heredity in her face:

> I should have seen it coming. All your father's irresponsible ways. ... Quiet! All your father's irresponsible ways are coming out in you. No reli-gion, no morals, no sense of duty. ... Oh, this is my punishment for turning a blind eye to him. It was for your sake I did it, and this is what I get for it.
>
> (Ibsen 1991: 76)

It happens at a moment when our attention is elsewhere, and it is easy to miss, but Torvald is sketching in the back-story in a way which changes its meaning. Far from exemplifying the ideals of bourgeois hegemonic masculinity, Nora's father turns out to have had 'no religion, no morals, no sense of duty'. And Torvald's outburst now confirms the earlier suspicion that he himself clearly *was* complicit in the father's corruption, if only to the extent of turning a blind eye to it. And so the picture changes: the paternalism which has structured Nora's life is itself deeply flawed.

The theme of corrupted masculinity is repeated in the figure of Dr Rank. Here, though, we are dealing with a physical corruption. Once more there is a father involved – a precursor of Captain Alving in *Ghosts*, who has passed on his diseases to his son, whose 'poor innocent spine must do penance for my father's gay subaltern life' (Ibsen 1991: 46). For while Rank and Nora talk euphemistically and nonsensically of his disease as a tuberculosis of the spine caused by his father's excessive fondness for asparagus and *pâté de foie gras*, it is actually syphilis to which Ibsen refers. Thus, if Nora's father is financially corrupt, so Rank is sexually diseased – the 'natural' masculine sexual appetites of his father contained within them the seeds of destruction. His status as a Doctor emphasizes the irony of the situation: like Torvald, he holds a respectable social role in an exclusively masculine profession – the very one, in fact, which might have been able to save him. Yet it cannot. In Dr Rank we see masculine power both corrupted and circumscribed. Nor is Rank merely the passive victim of his father's past promiscuity. His own illicit desire for Nora, his best friend's wife, goes some way towards repeating the pattern of sexual transgression in the present. It has the effect, too, of making it impossible for her to accept (or even to ask for!) a loan from him: her feminine sense of honour proves far more robust than Torvald's masculine one.

Krogstadt is another complicated figure, one of the casualties of bourgeois ideology, at the beginning of the play at least. For the nineteenth-century bourgeois, a successful masculine identity was defined in both moral and social terms. The moral aspect involves notions of 'manliness' (moral probity, courage, decency etc.); the social aspect relates to ways in which masculinity is defined in terms of both the domestic sphere and the world of paid employment. Krogstadt lost his manly good name when he was 'mixed up in a bit of trouble ... It never got to the courts; but immediately it was as if all paths were barred to me' (Ibsen 1991: 24). He is, in fact a mirror both of Nora's father and of Nora herself, whose crime of forgery he shares. As a result he had been unable to find respectable work – hence his recourse to loan-sharking. His more recent attempts to regain some worldly position have met with a little success, but now his very ability to hold down respectable paid employment in the bank is threatened by Torvald's decision. His position as paterfamilias, too, has been compromised. At the time of his disgrace he appears to have been married, but now he clearly is not. But while his wife has disappeared, his sons are still with him and are now growing up. He is now struggling to reconstruct something of his former identity, to regain his respectable position in society – not for himself but for his sons: as they approach manhood, he is attempting to prevent them from being compromised by their relationship with him. He is only too aware of how these various roles interrelate, and he understands the extent to which his ability to fulfil something of his role as father depends upon his being accepted again as an employable worker. 'This job in the Bank was like the first step on the ladder for me', he tells Nora (Ibsen 1991: 26).

Torvald, meanwhile, sees Krogstadt-as-father in a different light:

> Many a man might be able to redeem himself, if he honestly confessed his guilt and took his punishment ... But that wasn't the way Krogstadt chose. He dodged what was due to him by a cunning trick. And that's what's been the cause of his corruption ... Just think how a man with a thing like that on his conscience will always be having to lie and cheat and dissemble; he can never drop the mask, not even with his own wife and children... A fog of lies like that in a household, and it spreads disease and infection to every part of it. Every breath the children take in that kind of house is reeking with evil germs.
>
> (Ibsen 1991: 32–3)

Krogstadt's first real crime, according to Torvald, was not the initial act of dishonesty, but his failure to own up to it and take his punishment 'like a man'. The result is his contagious moral corruption which Torvald portrays as spreading inevitably to the children. The obvious parallel between this moral corruption and the physical corruption which Dr Rank caught from his father is emphasized by Torvald's use of disease imagery.

One of the recurrent myths of bourgeois masculinity is that of rugged individualism, but another is of the need for completion: completion by challenging employment 'in the open world', completion through paternity, completion through the love of a good woman. Krogstadt stands on the brink of losing all of these, but Ibsen contrives a sentimental ending by which all are restored to him, and he and Mrs Linde are left to redeem each other. It is a redemption which might be possible, the play suggests, because both start from the point of an awareness of their own weaknesses, rather than from an attachment to dominant ideologies about what a man and women *should* be.

Most of the play's analysis of masculinity devolves on the unlovely character of Torvald, who not only represents the workings and effects of bourgeois gender ideology, but also articulates its precepts. He knows what true 'manliness' should entail, as he makes clear through his condemnation of Nora's father and of Krogstadt – even if in doing so he reveals his own limitations in living up to those ideals. Elsewhere he lectures Nora about what it is to be 'a real man'. After discovering that Krogstadt no longer intends to persecute them, he snaps back immediately into his accustomed role of protector:

> No, no, you just lean on me, I shall give you all the advice and guidance you need. I wouldn't be a proper man if I didn't find a woman doubly attractive for being so obviously helpless … Have a good long sleep; you know you are safe and sound under my wing … You don't really imagine me ever thinking of turning you out, or even of reproaching you? Oh, a real man isn't made that way, you know, Nora. For a man, there's something indescribably moving and very satisfying in knowing that he has forgiven his wife – forgiven her, completely and genuinely, from the depths of his heart. It's as though it made her his property in a double sense: he has, as it were, given her a new life, and she becomes in a way both his wife and, at the same time, his child.
>
> (Ibsen 1991: 78)

The 'proper man' takes pleasure in his wife's helplessness, for it ensures his own role as protector. The 'real man' takes an almost religious pleasure in forgiveness because it makes his wife 'his property in a double sense'. There is something deeply chilling about Torvald's joyful reassurances. Why does Nora leave Torvald? Because he fails to live up to the masculine ideals which he professes? Or because if he were to live up to them it would be even more terrible?

Nora tells him that it is because 'I realized you weren't the man I thought you were' (Ibsen 1991: 84). The flesh-and-blood male fails live up to the model of masculinity which he has constructed for himself and which his wife has projected onto him. But the play undermines Torvald, and masculine ideology, at a deeper level than this. His masculine gender role was dismantled much earlier in the play. Nora's naïve persona, that of the flighty, scatterbrained spendthrift wife, has blinded him to the fact that actually *he* is the doll in the doll's house every bit as much as she is. When the crisis is over, he acts quickly to attempt to restore the status quo, but the oppressive paternalism to which he lays claim is no longer available to him: his mean-spiritedness saw to that. Not only that, but their symbiotic role-playing had blinded him to a larger truth: that within the doll's house the gender roles had actually been reversed all along. His scatterbrained, unworldly, delicate wife had been the true provider and the rescuer from the start – literally so, since she saved his life. She had played the chivalric role of self-sacrificing protector which he could not emulate. He, on the other hand, stands in constant need of protection. His friend Dr Rank protects him from the knowledge that he, Rank, is dying even while he talks about his impending death to Nora. He tells her that Torvald, after all, 'is a sensitive soul; he loathes anything that's ugly. I don't want him visiting me' (Ibsen 1991: 45). In the same way, Nora had protected Torvald from knowing the full extent of his own nearly-fatal illness ('it was me the doctors came and told', she tells Mrs Linde (Ibsen 1991: 14)), just as she had also been 'sav[ing] her own father from worry and anxiety on his deathbed' (Ibsen 1991: 29). The gender ideology by which Torvald lives is an illusion: it is not just that a single moment of weakness brings it crashing down about his ears. Rather it is that the masculine authority in which he believes is one which he never possessed in the first place.

At the end of the play he can no longer even lay claim to the illusion of this authority. Nor does he have, as Nora sees, the ability to change in order to adjust to the new perceptions. The fissure is too big for that. Underpinning the ending of the play is a classic liberal feminist proposition: that patriarchy damages men as well as women. The doll-house marriage has impoverished Torvald as well as (though not nearly as much as) Nora. Well though it worked for him on a number of levels, it has also cut him off from all those aspects of Nora which are most valuable and alive. And if the disease affects them both, so does the cure. When Torvald, beginning to understand the fixity of Nora's purpose, pleads 'I still have it in me to change', Nora replies, 'Perhaps ... if you have your doll taken away' (Ibsen 1991: 85). It is merely a hint, and there is little suggestion that it will be taken up; nonetheless, in Nora's departure Torvald is being given, not punishment, but the possibility of healing some of the wounds of patriarchal masculinity.

Strindberg, then, demanded sets with doors which could slam – but it turned out to be his great rival, Ibsen, who wrote the most famous door-slamming in Western drama. Ironically, it happens off-stage. At the end of *A Doll's House* Nora ...

> *... goes out through the hall door.*]
>
> HELMER: [*sinks down on a chair near the door, and covers his face with his hands*]. Nora! Nora! [*He rises and looks round.*] Empty! She's gone! [*With sudden hope.*] The miracle of miracles ...?
> [*The heavy sound of a door being slammed is heard from below*]
>
> (Ibsen 1991: 86)

With that slamming of the door Nora Helmer walks out of her domestic sphere and away from her dual roles of mother and wife. The controversy which that ending caused when the play was first published and staged in 1879 is well documented: the quarrels as audiences left the playhouses, the famous requests on dinner invitations in Stockholm not to discuss *A Doll's House* (Ibsen 1991: viii), and Shaw's pronouncement that 'the slam of the door behind [Nora] is more momentous than the cannon of Waterloo or Sedan' (Shaw 1948: III, 131), all testify to the importance of the play – and that sound-effect – as a defining moment in the gender debates of nineteenth-century middle-class culture.

6.2 Doors that don't: responses to *A Doll's House*

But, in fact, this door did not always actually slam at all, and some of the most bitter arguments about the play and the issues which it raised took place, not over Stockholm dinner-tables, but in the theatre itself. Both in Europe and America, productions of the play were staged which incorporated changes designed to negate its critique of dominant gender ideology. The first American production of the play, for example, was in Milwaukee in 1883, 'a very free version entitled *The Child Wife*, with a "happy ending"', (Meyer 1985: 34). German theatre managements were equally cautious: when the German actress Hedwig Niemann-Raabe agreed to play the part of Nora on tour in that country, she did so only on condition that the ending was rewritten. Rather than allow the play to be butchered by others, Ibsen himself reluctantly wrote an alternative ending in which Torvald shows Nora the sleeping children, and her maternal instincts rise up to prevent her from leaving: 'This is a sin against myself,' she declares, 'but I cannot leave them' (Ibsen 1991: 88). Paradoxically, what Ibsen himself called the 'barbaric outrage' (Ibsen 1991: 88) of his own rewritten ending has a bleakly radical truth to it which Niemann-Raabe may not have envisaged. Patriarchy, after all, may not be as easy to walk away from as Ibsen's original suggests! But the point of the German rewrite is to reassure the audience, not to disturb it. The bourgeois family may come under stress, it implies, but it *will* survive, thanks to the conditioning power of 'maternal instincts'.

In England, Ibsen attracted enthusiastic supporters, but also some powerful detractors. Henry Irving and Ellen Terry would have no truck with him, and refused to stage his works at the influential and fashionable Lyceum, while Beerbohm Tree declared magisterially that Ibsen's only use to the English theatre was as a 'manure for the future, a dunghill from which many a fair flower of the drama may bloom' (cited in Powell 1990: 75). Quite what flowers he had in mind is not clear: possibly those which comprised the minor dramatic and literary genre which arose in England, consisting of parodies of Ibsen. For Nora's famous exit generated a whole line of parodies, sequels, espousals and ripostes in both dramatic and prose form, and these responses to *A Doll's House* constitute one of the sites in late nineteenth-century English culture where gender meanings were contested.

The translation into English of *A Doll's House* is a complicated story. The first translation appeared in Copenhagen in 1879, the same year that the play was published in Scandinavia. This was by a man called Weber, a Danish schoolteacher with a rather rudimentary grasp of English; the translation made no impact at all. Slightly more influential was Henrietta Frances Lord's translation of the play, published in 1882, which received a single amateur production in 1885 under the title of *Nora*. *The Doll's House*, though, did not receive a full professional British production until 1889, when Janet Achurch played the lead in a production of William Archer's faithful translation of the play at the Novelty Theatre. Before this production sparked off the inevitable Ibsenite gender debates, however, another production of a play 'founded on Ibsen's *Nora*' had run for a month on the London stage in 1884: this was Henry Arthur Jones's and Henry Herman's *Breaking a Butterfly*.

In later life, it is true, Jones had the good grace to be rather ashamed of his travesty of Ibsen's play. It was not published among his own collected works, and the printed copy in the British Library proclaims clearly that this was 'printed for Private Use Only: NOT Published ... This Play is NOT on the List of the Dramatic Authors' Society and cannot be played ANYWHERE without the special written permission of the Authors' (Jones and Herman 1884). *Breaking a Butterfly* is a direct riposte to the analysis of bourgeois masculinity which is offered in *A Doll's House* – although as far as the British theatre-going public was concerned, Jones and Herman were getting their retaliation in first. As such, it does a good deal of work for us by showing exactly where the Norwegian dramatist was hitting hardest.

Thus the Helmers become Humphrey and Flora Goddard. Like Torvald, Humphrey is a newly promoted bank manager. The Goddards' home life, though, is even more closely tied in to the husband's professional identity than was the case with the Helmers, for Humphrey lives above (or rather beside) the shop, with one door from their living-room leading directly to 'the Manager's room at the Bank' (Jones and Herman 1884: 7). And as if this diagrammatic intertwining of home and hearth and commerce and finance were not enough, the Goddards' living-room is also 'backed by a cloth representing the Cathedral Close of Saint-Mary's, and the Cathedral' (ibid.: 7). The reassuring canvas backdrop of the Church guarantees the stability of traditional values – values which in a later scene are also symbolically represented by a Christmas tree. In *A Doll's House*, the Helmers' Christmas tree took on an increasingly ironic meaning, as the secure values of the comfortable family structure which it appeared to represent crumbled away. No such irony haunts *Breaking a Butterfly*, where the symbolism of the united home is continually reinforced, and the Christian values which the tree signifies are validated, not undercut, by the narrative.

The play reinstates just that uncomplicated moral diagram which Ibsen had deconstructed so carefully in his own play. The ending of *Breaking a Butterfly* works to reinforce rather than to disrupt the dominant gender structures, and to reassure its bourgeois audience about the values of their world rather than to question them. Similarly, the play's method of characterization reflects this reinstatement of certainties. There is a clear and unambiguous division between the good characters and the bad ones. In Ibsen's play, for example, the threat to Nora's happiness came from the complex Krogstadt, who was seen simultaneously as being himself a victim of the harsh rules of the capitalist financial world. He had enough basic decency in him to repent, and was eventually rewarded by the redeeming relationship with Mrs Linde. This comparatively complex character is split into two by Jones and Herman, who give the audience the villainous Dunkley on the one hand, and the gentle, decent, downtrodden Grittle on the other. Grittle is Flora's friend and eventually her rescuer, a trusting and trustworthy soul whom Humphrey treats kindly. Dunkley, in contrast, is 'a thorough-paced scoundrel who was at the bottom of that rotten mining affair – the Unity Tin Consoles' (Jones and Herman 1884: 19), a fraudulent business deal which had ruined hundreds (including the unfortunate Grittle, who sank into the deal all his savings for his retirement). This is no discreetly victimless crime like Krogstadt's forgery: it is a cold-hearted pension fund scandal of Maxwellian proportions, and its victims are visible to the audience.

Dunkley is also given additional psychological motivation for his villainy: he desires Flora and his hatred towards Humphrey contains a large degree of sexual jealousy. More, this desire and his villainy are seen as interrelated:

> DUNK: I have known her all her life. We lived next door to one another. I
>   watched her grow up from a child. I saw her getting prettier and
>   prettier every day. She used to blow me a kiss as she went to
>   school. I came to love her ... I was not perhaps what you would
>   call a good man. (HUMPHREY *laughs*) But the thought of one day
>   making her my wife seemed to purify me. I worked hard – in my
>   little way I succeeded. I became the head clerk of Churchill
>   Habershon's, respected by all who knew me. She would have been
>   my good angel –
> HUM: (*scornfully*) Pah!
>
> (Jones and Herman 1884: 60–1)

Humphrey's scornful 'Pah!' is the response of the idealized Victorian bourgeois in full and confident control of his masculinity. For while Dunkley is articulating one kind of masculine gender identity, Humphrey embodies another. His self-discipline stands in contrast to Dunkley, who embodies the formless masculine energy which Victorian gender ideology pictured as the dark side of masculine identity. This energy, uncontrolled by woman-as-good-angel, will run riot, become corrupt and cause destruction. Just as Krogstadt needed to be completed by Mrs Linde, so Dunkley needed to be completed by the good angel which he once imagined Flora to be. Failing this, he paradoxically attains a form of that completeness by being paired with his shadow-image Grittle. Like Jekyll and Hyde (whose story was published two years later) Grittle and Dunkley are opposite sides of a single entity. They live in the same house; they are both clerks in the bank – where, in fact, one is about to take the other's place. As one enters the stage the other leaves it; and eventually, just as Krogstadt's Good Nature triumphs over his Bad, so the Good Clerk triumphs over the Bad Clerk by destroying the evidence of forgery by which he was blackmailing Nora. Grittle is good, Dunkley is bad: but neither of them by himself is a whole man.

Elsewhere , Ibsen's brooding, dying Dr Rank becomes jolly Dan Birdseye, who is, fortuitously, in love with Humphrey's sister Agnes rather than his wife Flora. Thus when *he* makes the offer, indirectly, to Agnes, that he should repay Flora's loan, it causes no moral crisis of the kind faced by Nora in the face of Dr Rank's offer. (On the contrary, Agnes cheerfully offers to marry him as a reward for his generosity!) And since Dan Birdseye is such a decent, uncomplicated chap, he and Humphrey talk over Flora's problem in a man-to-man way, and try to work out how to get out of the fix which Humphrey's flighty little wife has got them – or rather Humphrey – into. Dan Birdseye's uncomplicated and rugged masculinity is the perfect complement of Humphrey's. Dan is the rough diamond and the independent outsider, a traveller and adventurer whose instinctive frontiersman's response to the villainous Dunkley is to give him a good thrashing. The urbane Humphrey, on the other hand, is the fully socialized male: he has successfully conquered both the private and the public sphere, and established a harmony between the two. 'In business I am harsh and severe' (Jones and Herman 1884: 8), he claims; but in the household, of which he is the undisputed master, he is also sensitive and solicitous for his wife's well-being. He suspects, for example, something of the trouble that Flora is in before he is ever told, and being in a position of honour and trust himself, he is fully aware of the consequences of Dunkley's blackmail threat. And so, facing up to Dunkley directly, Humphrey takes all the blame for Flora's indiscretion upon himself.

HUM:	(*very calmly*) You make one mistake, Mr. Dunkley! My wife did not forge that note.
DUNK:	Not? Then who did?
HUM:	I did!
DUNK:	You?!
HUM:	Yes – I! Now do your worst to me. You shall not touch a hair of her head.

(*FLORA rushes forward from door with a shriek, and falls at HUMPHREY's feet*)

CURTAIN

(Jones and Herman 1884: 61–2)

Humphrey's solid masculinity is supported by the other women in the play. His sister and his mother, in fact, are in the play largely in order to support his values. In *A Doll's House*, Ibsen structures his narrative to bring about the audience's gradual realization that it is Torvald rather than Nora who is protected by the doll's house environment. *Breaking a Butterfly*, on the other hand, is structured so as to ignore the palpable fact that Humphrey is even more cosseted than Torvald. Torvald has his doll-wife to entertain, support and (unbeknown to him) provide for and protect him. Humphrey not only has Flora (whose equally life-saving efforts he appears to ignore), but also his sister *and* his mother, who are both there to meet his needs and to minister to him. His entire environment is structured upon the principle of his comfort and maintenance, but the play asks the audience to accept this, without question, as the natural order of things.

As well as supporting Humphrey, his sister and mother represent a 'sensible' style of femininity which is extremely critical of 'Flossie's' girlish flightiness. In *A Doll's House* Nora was the first character we encountered; the play started with her opening a door and ended with her closing one. It was the workings of her mind that the audience got to know in most detail: she was the subject and the subjectivity of the play. Our response to Flora, on the other hand, has been fully 'framed' before we ever meet her, by the comments of her sister and her mother-in-law:

AGNES: ...I often wish Flora were more of a real helpmate to him, more staid and serious. However, she is but young ...
MRS. G: ...she has not as much common sense and prudence as a girl of ten ... .
AGNES: ...She is more like a bird than a woman ...

                                                    (Jones and Herman 1884: 7)

The effect of this framing is to displace Flora from the centre of the play. The audience is positioned in such a way as to see the events, problems and issues of the play primarily through the eyes of Humphrey rather than those of his wife: Flora is relegated to the role of a supporting character, while Humphrey's point of view dominates. This is exacerbated by the fact that Flora makes little attempt to deal with her problems alone, and so she continually seeks help from other characters, thus weakening any empathic bond that develops between herself and the audience. And while she does have her moment of nobility (she threatens suicide, momentarily unsettling Dunkley), it is the men in her life who attempt to find practical solutions to her dilemma. Feminine agency is ineffectual: it is up to the men to save the day.

The easy division of characters into the categories of hero and villain is a technique that allows the larger ideological assumptions to remain unquestioned. In Ibsen's play, for example, the similarity between Krogstadt's earlier crime and Nora's had been structurally important. It served as an illustration of just how fragile the apparently robust dividing line between the successful bourgeois and the marginalized or outlawed outsider actually was. In *Breaking a Butterfly*, as we have seen,

Jones and Herman make the two crimes as different as possible. There is no confusion here; Flora may be silly but Dunkley is downright wicked. Both of them flout the kind of authority which Humphrey represents, but in totally different ways. It is this structuring of character which clears the way for Humphrey to take on the role of the straightforwardly admirable example of the successful Victorian paterfamilias. The melodramatic apparatus allows him to be this without incongruity – his noble gesture at the end of Act II is generically quite coherent. There is no surprise in finding that Humphrey's authority is strong enough to be able to withstand and eventually contain any such challenge – in a way that Torvald's had not been.

Jones and Herman, of course, are telling a completely different story within what seems like a similar narrative framework. Both plays contain the notion of an immature woman growing up: indeed *Breaking a Butterfly* ends with the line: 'Flossie was a child yesterday: today she is a woman' (Jones and Herman 1884: 76). However, the terms in which this growing-up is conceived shows the difference between Ibsen's attitudes towards conventional masculine authority and that of Jones and Herman. Nora learned that what little she already knew of the world had ill prepared her to understand it or live in it and that consequently she needed to develop a greater independence. 'Flossie', on the other hand, learns that to act independently of masculine authority is to be 'a child', while to submit to it is to become a woman.

To analyse in detail a play which, while moderately commercially successful in its own time, has left little imprint on stage history, and which its own authors seemed later to disown – this in itself might look somewhat like breaking a butterfly upon a wheel. Yet it is in Jones' and Herman's response to the Ibsen original that we see most clearly the extent to which *A Doll's House* generated masculine anxieties, and the terms in which those anxieties needed to be allayed. The English play amounts to far more than just the weak ending which Ibsen wrote for the German tour. It dismantles the whole dramatic mechanism which Ibsen had used to explore the nineteenth-century bourgeois gender system. When Humphrey Goddard performs the very miracle which Nora Helmer had hoped for from Torvald, he lives up to and affirms the chivalrous ideal, as Torvald did not. Torvald's failure had opened up the gap between masculine self-image and the actuality of bourgeois gender relationships, and had thrown into question bourgeois paternalism itself. Humphrey's noble act of self-sacrifice, on the contrary, stands as Jones' and Herman's ringing affirmation of the existing gender order – a gender order which, he is anxious to reassure his audience, is guaranteed by the unimpugned strength of masculinity itself.

6.3 'The dolls are not all female': *Candida* (1897)

The most famous dialogue between Ibsen and British culture involved Ibsen's illustrious supporter George Bernard Shaw. When Karl Marx's daughter Eleanor staged a private reading of *A Doll's House*, two years after the production of *Breaking a Butterfly*, in a Great Russell Street lodging house opposite the British Museum, a slightly bemused Shaw played Krogstadt to Eleanor's Nora. As Ibsen's work grew more well known in England, however, Shaw recognized the congruence between Ibsen's dramaturgical practice and the tenets of his own Fabian socialism, and he explored this in detail in *The Quintessence of Ibsenism*. Elsewhere he defended Ibsen, and in particular *A Doll's House*, from the attacks of critics such as Robert Buchanan, whose letter in the *Pall Mall Gazette* entitled 'Is Ibsen "a Zola with a Wooden Leg"?' drew from Shaw the answering polemic 'Is Mr. Buchanan a Critic with a Wooden Head?' Again, when Walter Besant parodied Ibsen's play in his short story 'The Doll's House – and After', Shaw parried within a month with his own fiction, 'Still After the Doll's House'. In this, Shaw stages a confrontation, many years after, between Nora and Krogstadt, in which Nora tells her old antagonist that

> it is not always the woman who is sacrificed. Twenty years ago, when I walked out of the doll's house, I saw only my own side of the question ... Now I have had my eyes open for twenty years, during which I have peeped into a great many doll's houses; and I have found that the dolls are not all female
>
> (cited in Ackerman 1987: 62)

Candida was Shaw's dramatic exploration of this idea. The play, briefly, is about an admirably energetic middle-aged Christian Socialist clergyman, James Morell, who is challenged by a young poet, Eugene Marchbanks, for the love of Morell's wife Candida. This primary conflict is between two kinds of social vision, but also between two styles of masculinity. Marchbanks is an unworldly and socially inept adolescent, a 'strange, shy youth of eighteen, slight, effeminate, with a delicate childish voice ' (Shaw 1960: 190). Morell had originally taken him under his wing, having 'found him sleeping on the Embankment' (Shaw 1960: 189) in a state of temporary destitution. He is also aristocratic – the nephew of an earl – and 'so entirely uncommon as to be almost unearthly' (Shaw 1960: 190). His bid for Candida's love is initially implausible, but gathers strength as the play develops, to the point where Candida is forced to choose between the two men. The action takes place in another ambivalently domestic space: Morell's parsonage is both home and workplace, and the contest between the poet and the clergyman impinges on the masculine values associated with both these worlds. Issues of gender and power are complex in the play: on the one hand, the men put all the power of choice into Candida's hands, while on the other, she herself plays the game according to their rules, and allows them to make her the prize of their contest. The play's climactic final scene shows Candida not only making her choice between the two men, but also explaining the reasons behind that choice.

Shaw stated explicitly on more than one occasion that 'the play is a counterblast to Ibsen's *Doll's House,* showing that in the real typical doll's house it is the man who is the doll', and that 'Morell is nothing but Helmer getting fair play' (cited in Wisenthal 1979: 60–1). The tone of these remarks, coming from another British writer of the period, might lead one to expect a butterfly-breaking rebuttal of Ibsen's gender politics. Shaw, however, is more concerned to expand and explore Ibsen's insights than he is to refute them. In performance, the intertextuality of *Candida* and *The Doll's House* was emphasized by the casting of Janet Achurch, who was already effectively identified in the mind of British theatre-goers with the role of Nora, in the title role of Candida Morell.

The play is often described as ambivalent, or even confused (see Gordon 1990: 92 and Eric Bentley's Foreword to Shaw 1960: xxii). Much of this ambivalence or confusion derives from the title character, Candida herself, who is a strangely drawn figure. She is clearly meant to be assertive, attractive, psychologically rounded and very contemporary. She is in many respects a New Woman, and *Candida* is a 'New Woman play'. Yet as a central figure Candida remains oddly shadowy and incomplete, compared to the men who fight over her. Part of this is due to Shaw's own ambivalence towards her. As Eric Bentley puts it: 'though Shaw's intellect is against Candida, his emotions are for her ... he would like to reject this kind of woman, but actually he dotes on her' (Foreword to Shaw 1960: xxii). But the ambivalence is also due to the fact that in *Candida* Shaw is playing with conventions: offering the audience a debate play in the guise of psychological realism. The realism of the play's setting is deliberately contrasted with the self-aware and even sometimes self-conscious artifice of Shavian dialogue, and the play continuously teases the audience as to its generic allegiances. Many of the characters, for example, have names which contain their own character-notes: Morell is indeed a moral man, Burgess is the representative bourgeois, and Candida speaks candidly at the end of the play.

A good debate play needs to have strong characters on both sides of its argument, and Shaw allows himself no such easy bourgeois targets as Ibsen did with the deeply conventional Helmer. This paterfamilias, the 'unconventional' Morell, has a radical social agenda, while the industrial bourgeoisie is represented by the openly exploitative Burgess, Candida's father. Throughout the early part of the play Morell and he are engaged in debates and in each of these Burgess continually acts as a butt for Morell's energetic and muscular Christian Socialism. In Morell we do not have a character who represents comfortable middle-class British society, but one who represents a vigorous critique of it. He has already seen through the bourgeois hypocrisy and self-serving which Burgess represents:

> [Y]ou paid worse wages than any other employer – starvation wages – aye, worse than starvation wages – to the women who made the clothing. Your wages would have driven them to the streets to keep body and soul together. [*Getting angrier and angrier.*] Those women were my parishioners. I shamed the Guardians out of accepting your tender: I shamed the ratepayers out of letting them do it: I shamed everybody but you.
>
> (Shaw 1960: 185)

In fact Morell's Christian Socialism places him as a progressive in terms of gender politics: like Shaw himself, he is agitating for more equal pay for women in the workplace. It also locates him at the centre of late Victorian debates about masculinity; for 'manliness' was very much part of the programme of that popular nineteenth-century form of Christianity. In a deliberate attempt to counter the notion that Christianity was somehow weak and effeminate, many Christian preachers, writers and Christian activists had set out deliberately to construct a model of manly Christianity. One of the outcomes of this was the foundation of the Boys' Brigade in 1883 by William Alexander Smith. 'There is undoubtedly among Boys an impression that to be a Christian means to be a "molly-coddle",' Smith asserted, 'and in order to disabuse their minds of this idea we sought to construct our organisation on a model which would appeal to all their sentiments of manliness and honour.' One of the early promotional pamphlets put the programme succinctly: 'All a boy's aspirations are towards *manliness* ... We must show them the *manliness* of Christianity' (cited in Mangan and Walvin 1987: 55).

Morell's Christian Socialism, then, gives him a masculine identity which is located societally in this tradition, and which is located dramatically in contrast to that of Burgess. It appears to be between these two that Candida's choice has initially been made: she has progressed from the energetically self-centred Burgess to the energetically altruistic Morell. In fact, though, Burgess is a red herring. It is not he but Marchbanks who is Morell's primary antagonist, and the real debate is not between the moral man and the cynical industrialist, but between the manly man and the effeminate aesthete.

At first Morell laughs off Marchbanks's announcement that he is in love with Candida, but when the younger man finally gets under his skin he explodes with the threat of physical violence:

MORELL: [*wrathfully*] Leave my house. Do you hear? [*He advances on him threateningly*]

MARCHBANKS: [*shrinking back against the couch*] Let me alone. Don't touch me. [*Morell grabs him powerfully by the lapel of his coat: he cowers down on the sofa and screams passionately.*] Stop, Morell, if you strike me, I'll kill myself: I won't bear it. [*Almost in hysterics*] Let me go. Take your hand away.

MORELL: [*with slow emphatic scorn*] You little snivelling cowardly whelp.

(Shaw 1960: 197)

The scene is calculated to align the audience, for the moment, with Morell – or at least to alienate them from Marchbanks. His recourse to the traditionally masculine tactic of physical domination of the rival ends in an apparent victory. Having briefly revelled in the role of romantic outsider, Marchbanks now seems indeed to be reduced to the role of the 'snivelling cowardly whelp' which Morell accuses him of being. His 'true nature' stands revealed.

But, once more, Shaw involves us in a genre shift: 'revealing the true nature' of his characters is not what this play is about. On the contrary, having early on established, and asked the audience to accept, the binary opposition of Morell, the manly man versus Marchbanks, the fragile aesthete, Shaw then goes on to ask, 'so what?' And the answer that he comes up with is that the apparent structure of domination can be reversed.

MARCHBANKS: [*on the sofa, gasping, but relieved by the withdrawal of Morell's hand*] I'm not afraid of you: it's you who are afraid of me ... You think that because I shrink from being brutally handled – because [*with tears in his voice*] I can do nothing but cry with rage when met with violence

> – because I can't lift a heavy trunk down from the top of
> a cab like you – because I can't fight for your wife as a
> navvy would: all that makes you think I'm afraid of you.
> But you're wrong. If I haven't got what you call British
> pluck, I haven't British cowardice either: I'm not afraid
> of a clergyman's ideas. I'll fight your ideas.
>
> (Shaw 1960: 197–8)

Not only does Marchbanks here deny the masculine superiority of
Morell; he goes on to base his claim to Candida on precisely the opposite grounds from the traditional romantic lover's. He deserves
Candida, and she him, he asserts, because of his own weakness and
neediness. The final moment of choice is presented to Candida: the
choice between two versions of masculinity: the one with all the mature
claims of hegemony, the other with the childlike claims of egotistic
need:

MORELL:	[*with proud humility*] I have nothing to offer you but my strength for your defence, my honesty of purpose for your surety, my ability and industry for your livelihood, and my authority and position for your dignity. That is all it becomes a man to offer to a woman.
CANDIDA:	[*quite quietly*] And you, Eugene? What do you offer?
MARCHBANKS:	My weakness! my desolation! my heart's need!
CANDIDA:	[*impressed*] That's a good bid, Eugene. Now I know how to make my choice… [*significantly*] I give myself to the weaker of the two.

> (Shaw 1960: 232)

Strength, honesty of purpose, ability, industry, authority and position: it appears that the radical Morell's own gender values are not so
far removed from the solid bourgeois ones after all. They are contrasted with Marchbanks's weakness, desolation and neediness. And
the possible resolution with which Shaw teases the audience is that the
dominant gender paradigms might indeed be reversed: that, paradoxically, Marchbanks's weakness may give him the stronger claim to
Candida's love. Shaw's intention seems to be that, as the audience
waits for Candida to make her choice, the men in the audience should
be thinking 'have we got it wrong all this time? Are the masculine
values on which we were brought up, now out of date?' And when she
announces that she gives herself to the weaker of the two, she appears
to be answering 'yes' to both questions.

Shaw, however, is not a playwright who will settle for one ironic
inversion when he can have two. The rest of the play is devoted to

Candida's explanation that her choice of the 'weaker' of the two candidates refers to Morell, not to Marchbanks: that, like Torvald, Morell's apparent strength is actually weakness, and that his masculine authority and position are actually expressions of dependence. Unlike Nora, she can articulate what the construction of Morell's masculinity has cost the women in his life; unlike Nora, too, she has always known it and has accepted it. She tells Marchbanks:

> You know how strong he is (I hope he didn't hurt you) – how clever he is – how happy! [*With deepening gravity*] Ask James's mother and his three sisters what it cost to save James the trouble of doing anything but be strong and clever and happy. Ask me what it cost to be James's mother and three sisters and wife and mother to his children all in one. I build a castle of comfort and indulgence and love for him, and stand sentinel always to keep little vulgar cares out. I make him master here, though he does not know it ...
>
> (Shaw 1960: 233)

Thus the 'Manly man' wins the battle for Candida's affection – but, paradoxically, he wins only because of the actual fragility of that manliness. Morell's model of masculinity is, as Candida says, the weaker of the two, and utterly dependent on the women in Morell's life for its construction and maintenance.

In its placing and its dramatic effect, Candida's speech parallels Katherine's in *The Taming of the Shrew*: after all the wooing games, the fights and the courtship rituals, the woman steps forward and states what gender relationships should really be like. The 'message' of Candida's analysis of marriage is very different from Katherine's, of course: at least, on the surface. The insights which she expresses are incisive and enlightening. They arise from a progressive political standpoint, and articulate some of the insights of first-wave feminism regarding the hidden costs to women of Victorian gender relationships, which is summed up in Candida's line about how she builds 'a castle of comfort and indulgence and love for him, and stand[s] sentinel always to keep little vulgar cares out'. If Candida Morell's marriage speech can be compared on one level to Katherine Minola's, her phrasing is more reminiscent of Nora from the early scenes of *A Doll's House*. It would be interesting, though, to know just *how* Achurch delivered it. With tender adoration? Or was there just a hint of steel, of irony, in the way she spoke that line? Was it given enough toughness to remind the audience that they were *not* looking at a romantic, but at a realist who has sized up her place in society and understands not only what her function is in servicing the masculine image, but also the extent to which (in normal circumstances) this is to be kept hidden from its main beneficiary, her husband?

Shaw himself was a feminist: he campaigned actively in favour of women's suffrage and wrote vigorously in favour of equality within marriage, and of equality of opportunity in employment. *Candida,* though, is not a 'feminist' play, or at least not one which seems to push strongly in the direction of the societal changes demanded by first-wave feminism. Candida's own apparent willingness to be the prize in the contest between Morell and Marchbanks (a contest, essentially, about two different styles of masculinity) indicates her compliance with the 'traffic' in women on which the Victorian gender system depended. She provides a trenchant analysis of the role women play in substantiating and supporting the masculine idea of the self – and then, with apparent contentment, she continues to play that role. Candida's speech about the cost of keeping Morrell strong, clever and happy, is followed by this exchange:

MORELL:	[*quite overcome, kneeling beside her chair and embracing her with boyish ingenuousness*] It's all true, every word. What I am you have made me with the labour of your hands and the love of your heart! You are my wife, my mother, my sisters: you are the sum of all loving care to me.
CANDIDA:	[*in his arms, smiling, to Eugene*] Am I your mother and sisters to you, Eugene?
MARCHBANKS:	[*rising with a fierce gesture of disgust*] Ah, never. Out, then, into the night with me!
CANDIDA:	[*rising quickly and intercepting him*] You are not going like that, Eugene?
MARCHBANKS:	[*with the ring of a man's voice – no longer a boy's – in the words*] I know the hour when it strikes. I am patient to do what must be done.

(Shaw 1960: 234)

Eric Bentley, who was in no doubt about the bleakness of the play's ending, argued that at the end of the play 'Morell finally loses the image of his wife, and of himself' (Foreword, Shaw 1960: xxxv), but this is hardly the case. On the contrary, at the end of the play Morell is, if anything, more firmly in possession of those images than ever. Candida has taken them out of their hiding place and has shown them to him, but the vision has not shattered him (as it might have done with an Ibsen hero). At the end of *Candida*, Morell may be chastened and even enlightened, but there is no need for him to change – indeed part of the logical demand of the play's conclusion is that he should *not* change. He happily agrees with his wife's analysis, and, by agreeing, continues to benefit from it. In fact, he even pursues its logic further, acknowledging that Candida for him is wife, mother and sisters rolled into one. Morell had solved one of the key problems of nineteenth-century masculinity, that of separation from the mother and from the home, by *not* solving it; he had, on the contrary, embraced it, as he now embraces Candida, 'with boyish ingenuousness'. What so confused and horrified Strindberg's Captain in *The Father* – that his wife might want to relate to him more as mother than as lover – comes as a pleasurable realization to Morell.

What is now made explicit should come as no surprise to the audience: it has been implicit throughout the play. Whereas Torvald Helmer had attempted to fulfil the dual role of father and husband, Candida Morell has always been a wife-mother, or rather, as Shaw wrote to William Archer, 'a mother first, a wife twenty-seventh, and nothing else' (Shaw 1972: 137). We never see her two actual children, but we do see the motherly way she acts and speaks towards the two adult males, both of whom she continually infantilizes, referring to them as 'good boy', 'little boy', 'silly boy' and so on (Shaw 1960: 189, 190, 199, 210 and *passim*). In a letter to Ellen Terry in 1896 Shaw exclaimed triumphantly, 'I have written THE Mother Play ... and Candida, between you and me, is the Virgin Mother and nobody else' (Shaw 1932: 29). Not just mother, then, but 'Virgin Mother': spiritual-ized, desexualized, holy. Above the fireplace in the Morells' drawing-room hangs 'a large autotype of the chief figure in Titian's Virgin of the Assumption' (Shaw 1960: 178), and Shaw makes clear in the stage directions the emblematic importance of this in terms of Candida's own character:

> *A wisehearted observer, looking at her, would at once guess that whoever had placed the Virgin of the Assumption over her hearth did so because he fancied some spiritual resemblance between them, and yet would not suspect either her husband or herself of any such idea, or indeed of any concern with the art of Titian.*

> (Shaw 1960: 189)

Shaw's lengthy 'stage directions' are notoriously problematic in theatrical terms. Aimed as much at a reading public as at any potential staging practice, they frequently operate in parallel to the performative text. Sometimes they operate in order to clarify questions of tone and meaning (often complex in Shaw's dramaturgy), while equally frequently they problematize the dramatic moment. In fact, this is less difficult than most: the link between the picture and the character is an easy one to make in visual terms. It is important that it *is* made, because a few moments later the audience discovers that the mysterious 'person who placed [the picture] over her hearth' is actually Eugene Marchbanks, who had bought the picture as a gift for the Morells – or perhaps more precisely for Candida Morell, offering her an artistic image of his idealized picture of her as Virgin Mother.

Paradoxically, however, it is Eugene who outgrows this mother-fixation at the end of the play. While Morell continues to cling to his mother/wife with 'boyish ingenuousness', Marchbanks, as we have seen, rejects the idea 'with a fierce gesture of disgust' and bids her farewell 'with the ring of a man's voice – no longer a boy's – in the words'. For Marchbanks, the failure of his bid for the love of Candida has become a rite of passage to manhood. For the play is both a romantic and a familial triangle, and presents a variation on a classically Oedipal plot: the youth on the verge of adulthood (Eugene is 18) has unsuccessfully challenged the father, the paterfamilias, for the love of the mother/wife, and in the ensuing realization that he can never possess the mother *as* wife lies his potential for growth into an adult masculine identity. Eugene's final exit, as he leaves without Candida and without happiness, but 'with a better secret ... in my heart' (Shaw 1960: 234) is melodramatic, but it is also dignified and enigmatic. The audience is left with the definite impression that something has been gained by him – even if it would be hard pressed to say quite what. Morell, on the other hand, wins the Oedipal contest, but at the cost of losing any potential for growth or change: it is the father who, paradoxically, is left stranded in his maternal fixation.

The complex of attitudes which Marchbanks and Morell between them express towards Candida as mother/wife may have had their roots in Shaw's own well-documented 'deep ambivalence towards ... [and] lifelong emotional involvement with his own mother' (Silver 1982: 102). Arnold Silver has pointed out the correspondences which exist between the name Candida itself, and the name of Shaw's mother: Lucinda. The two names resemble each other phonetically, syllabically and orthographically. Their semantic connotations are also very close to each other: 'lucid' and 'candid' both suggest clarity and openness, and both have etymological roots which derive from Latin words referring to light ('lucere', to shine and 'candere' to gleam). While Shaw insisted that he had no models for Candida (Mander and Mitchenson 1955: 43), it is not at all far-fetched to suggest, as Silver does, that, on a subconscious level at least, a writer dealing so prominently with a mother figure might well draw on the feelings associated with the foremost mother in his life (Silver 1982: 102–3).

But the question of motherhood also has a wider resonance in terms of late Victorian masculinities. The rigidifying of gender roles, the

Victorian revival of patriarchy, and the increasing pressure in England to create a new kind of masculinity for a successfully imperialist nation, was coupled with an increasing distrust, even fear, of domesticity in the generations of males who grew up in the late nineteenth century. The Victorian mother was culturally inscribed as ambivalent from the start. She was simultaneously idealized as the symbolic centre of the Victorian bourgeois concept of the family, and demonized as the engulfing presence who is 'incapable of nurturing her young son into independence' but who, on the contrary 'becomes the potential gorgon, who will deny men their potency and autonomy and turn them to blocks of stone' (Rutherford 1997: 22). As a defence against this, the Victorian pattern of manhood involves a rejection of the feminine, a glorification of independence, toughness and asceticism and the consequent suppression of all external signs of emotion. No wonder, then, that 'the gendered order of the Victorian middle-class family produced an intense ambivalence in the masculinity of its sons. A boy's unresolved need for his mother continually threatened to undermine his tenuous identifications with his emotionally distant, often absent father' (Rutherford 1997: 22). Which brings us to *Peter Pan.*

6.4 'No man in him at all': J. M. Barrie's lost boys

In France and Germany, Expressionism and Symbolism were the dominant forms of reaction against naturalism. In England reactions against the naturalist theatre took a variety of forms, and, as we have seen, one of them was the spate of delighted parodies of Ibsen. One of these was written by J. M. Barrie, who later recalled in some embarrassment, the

> little piece, produced by Mr. Toole. It was called *Ibsen's Ghost*, and was a parody of the mightiest craftsman that ever wrote for our kind friends in front. To save the management the cost of typing I wrote out the 'parts', after being told what parts were, and I can still recall my first words, spoken so plaintively by a now famous actress, – 'To run away from my second husband just as I ran away from my first, it feels quite like old times.' On the first night a man in the pit found *Ibsen's Ghost* so diverting that he had to be removed in hysterics. After that no-one seems to have thought of it at all.
> (Barrie 1948: 5)

Barrie progressed from parodying Ibsen to trying to imitate him: his 1899 play *The Wedding Guest* was itself a 'problem play' in the Ibsen mould, but it turned out to be a critical and commercial failure –

attracting praise, significantly, only from the Ibsenite critic William
Archer, who hailed Barrie as 'our new dramatist' (Birkin 1979: 72). But
it is not as the author of bourgeois tragedies that he is best known
today, but as the author of *Peter Pan or The Boy Who Wouldn't Grow
Up*, his children's fantasy play which was first performed in 1904. *Peter
Pan* is perhaps one of the most important anti-naturalistic dramas of
the period: certainly it is one of the few twentieth-century British plays
which has attained the status of a cultural myth. Its author, James
Barrie, had recently been described by one of his friends as 'part
mother, part hero-worshipping maiden, part grandfather, and part
pixie with no man in him at all' (quoted in Kelley-Lainé 1997: 152).

Peter, is, correspondingly, the boy who refuses manhood. He is the
magical face at the window who appears one night and whisks the
Darling children, John, Michael and Wendy, off to the Never Land,
the timeless island which is intertextually constructed from the stock
motifs of nineteenth-century boys' adventure fiction. Barrie's literary
hero was his fellow Scot and the author of *Treasure Island*, Robert
Louis Stevenson. Stevenson returned the admiration, and their mutual
regard is evident in the letters and correspondence which passed
between the two (Birkin 1979: 18). The influence of Stevenson's own
taste for fantasy and adventure is palpable, not only in *Peter Pan* but
also in Barrie's earliest experiments with the novel. The genre of boys'
adventure fiction was clearly important to Barrie's own imaginative
life. Stevenson was to some extent an 'art' writer and a respected literary stylist, but from his youth Barrie had also been a great fan of R. M.
Ballantyne, a writer whose work was very definitely at the popular end
of the market. In his notebooks, written at Edinburgh University
*c.*1880, Barrie records: 'Want to stop everybody in street and ask if
they've read *The Coral Island*. Feel sorry for if not' (Birkin 1979: 12).
Ballantyne's books, of which *The Coral Island* is a typical example, told
stories of heroic and plucky young British lads whose adventures,
usually in exotic settings amongst natives and pirates, always ended
with their triumph over the 'other' which these represent. These were
books aimed fairly and squarely at inculcating and celebrating the
values of British manhood in a context which is always implicitly, if
rarely explicitly, imperialist: *The Coral Island* was the book parodied in
Lord of the Flies by William Golding, whose theme was the savagery
that he saw lying at the heart of those apparently civilized boys on the
island.

Barrie does something rather different with the Ballantyne/
Stevenson island setting. If Golding turned it into a dystopia, Barrie
makes of it a fantasy playground in which several fictional and psycho-

logical worlds collide. The Never Land is an autonomous boys' paradise, a place inhabited by pirates, wild animals, and 'redskins'. These redskins themselves appear to be a composite of various aboriginal peoples: African 'Piccaninnies' (as they are sometimes referred to), native North Americans, and even Asians (the name Tiger Lily has oriental connotations). This is the colonialist Briton's view of the 'savage', in which all are alike, and blend into an undifferentiated 'other', but it also reinforces the sense of the Never Land as the place where alternative geographies, narratives and times all exist simultaneously. The Never Land is also home to Peter's companions and playmates, the Lost Boys, the rejected, motherless children who, like Peter, will never reach adulthood. It is a locus for fights and escapes and captures and rescues. But it is also, in direct contrast to this, a locus for domesticity: after the arrival of the Darling children, the house in which Peter and the Lost Boys live takes on more and more of the characteristics of a Victorian family home, and the economy of this magical bourgeois household is given as much attention as the adventures with Indians and Pirates. Lurking somewhere behind the creation of the Never Land, perhaps, is that far more pragmatic desert island story of the *Swiss Family Robinson*. And finally, the Never Land is the setting for the confrontation between father and son, between Peter the eternal child and Hook the adult, the father-figure (who is traditionally doubled by the actor playing Mr Darling) whom the child has to kill.

The circumstances of the writing of *Peter Pan* are worth recounting briefly. Walking with his wife in Kensington Gardens in 1897, Barrie met and fell into conversation with two small boys. Soon afterwards, and quite coincidentally, he met their parents, Arthur and Sylvia Llewelyn Davies at a dinner party. Barrie appears to have fallen in love both with the boys, George and Jack, and with their mother. From that moment on he attached himself to their family (his own marriage already beginning to fail), and became a surrogate father to the boys – much to the irritation of their actual father, who found it hard to get rid of this unwelcome but generous guest. He was also a constant companion to the mother. Sylvia Llewelyn Davies was described by Barrie in his diary as a 'glorious woman ... whom one can trust. No question of sex!' (Kelley-Lainé 1997: 133).

'No question of sex!' – and this asexuality extends to both the mother and the boys: in no account of the relationships between Barrie and the Davies family is there any suggestion of sexual impropriety. Many contemporaries, indeed, stress the opposite. (See, for example, Nico Davies's rebuttal of any suspicion of homosexuality or paedophilia on Barrie's part, cited in Birkin 1979: 130.) Nico did, however, accept that

Barrie was 'in love' with both the boys and the mother.) Yet it is a relationship which is clearly characterized by desire: desire for the boys,
not as the objects of genital sexuality, but as the eternal children with
whom the child in Barrie could play; and desire for the mother as the
idealized mother/wife. 'No question of sex!', for it was as mother to the
boys into whom he projected himself that Sylvia Llewelyn Davies most
attracted Barrie. Like Shaw's Candida, it was the woman as mother
that was desirable rather than the woman as wife – although in Barrie's
life, as in the Shaw play, the confusion between the two desires is palpable. Many years later, on the day of Sylvia's death, he claimed, to
the anger of her surviving sons, that she had promised to marry him.

It was as the surrogate father/uncle to the Davies boys that Barrie
began to tell the tales which eventually became *Peter Pan*. These were
initially told to the two eldest boys, George and Jack, as the adventures
of their baby brother Peter, who was still in his pram ... but who in the
fantasy could fly. Gradually, as Peter Davies grew into childhood, his
literary namesake turned into Peter Pan (whose surname, cognate with
Bacchus and Dionysos, is already charged with theatrical resonances).
Traces of the stories which Barrie told the brothers found their way
into a privately produced volume of pictures and fragments called *The
Boy Castaways of Black Lake Island* – actually not much more than a
photograph album bound, printed and with a cover to resemble an R.
M. Ballantyne story. This was a memento of a summer holiday which
Barrie took with the Davies boys at Black Lake in Surrey, where he
told them tales of pirates and shipwrecks, and where they played out
Ballantynesque adventures, with Barrie himself as the piratical Captain
Swarthy (Birkin 1979: 84). The character of Peter Pan began to obsess
Barrie, who introduced him, in a long digression, into chapters
XIII–XVIII of his adult novel *The Little White Bird, or Adventures in
Kensington Gardens* (1902), where the story-telling between Barrie and
the Davies boys is recoded for an adult audience. In 1904 Peter found
his stage form in a three-act play entitled *Peter Pan or the Boy Who
Would Not Grow Up*. This was a significantly different Peter from the
one in *The Little White Bird* – which Barrie then rewrote and adapted
for children as *Peter Pan in Kensington Gardens*. He also rewrote the
play – not once, but continually, until 1928, when it was included in the
'definitive' volume of his Complete Plays. Among his many rewrites
was a short sequel to the play, entitled 'When Wendy Grew Up: An
Afterthought', written in 1907 and performed only once, in 1908,
although it did appear again as the final chapter of what was one of the
twentieth-century's first 'novelizations', Barrie's children's novel *Peter
and Wendy* (1911), which he based on the play.

Thus the play had its genesis as a private fantasy, encoded both as story-telling and as play-acting and role-playing, and shared between the adult male and the boys who were the site of his projections and the objects ('No question of sex!') of his desire. The private nature of the fiction continued even as it became public: the play contains a wealth of private references meant for the enjoyment of the family only, and public and private meanings continually intertwine within it. For example, Barrie changed the names of characters (including Michael Darling) in order to incorporate those of the family's children; the clothes of the Darling children and the Lost Boys were based on those of the Davies boys, and the costume for the nurse-dog Nana was copied from the coat of Barrie's own Newfoundland dog Luath, with whom the boys played. When, in 1906, five-year-old Michael Davies was too ill to come to London for the revival of *Peter Pan*, Barrie took the play to him, complete with some of the scenery and actors from the London cast.

It is a masterpiece of repression and sublimation. Within its winsome and lyrical texture it encodes, among other things, a good deal of Barrie's own personal pain concerning his memories of his brother David, another boy who never grew up because he died in a skating accident at the age of 13. This, which happened when he (James) was six, had deeply affected Barrie's relationship with his own mother. She abandoned him – not literally, but emotionally – and he 'lost' her, as Peter and the Lost Boys had lost their mothers, to the memory of the dead child. Barrie continued to live in the shadow of his dead brother, continually trying to comfort his mother and to regain her love and attention, and haunted by a sense that David, not he, was her 'real' son (Kelley-Lainé 1997: 92–125). On more than one level, Barrie, like Peter, was stuck in a childhood prison of ambivalent masculinity, which was one of his life's most public themes. It is an ambivalence which is evident in Barrie's obsession with Sylvia Llewelyn Davies and her sons, and one which haunted the public persona of the physically diminutive Barrie. Max Beerbohm's enthusiastic review of *Peter Pan* included the following backhanded compliment:

> Mr Barrie is not that rare creature, a man of genius. He is something even more rare – a child who, by some divine grace, can express through an artistic medium the childishness that is in him ... Mr Barrie has never grown up. He is still a child, absolutely. But some fairy once waved a wand over him, and changed him from a dear little boy into a dear little girl.
>
> (Cited in Birkin 1979: 118)

Barrie's artistic triumph, according to Beerbohm, is inseparable from the ambivalence concerning his masculinity.

Just as the Peter Pan narrative itself is multiform – the result of Barrie's continual rewrites – so, too are its codes, signs and structures of signification. In terms of a study of masculinities we might do well to approach them a layer at a time. The first and easiest is the way in which, in terms of contemporary popular psychology and gender theory, the play, and its central figure, has taken on an iconic significance. In books such as Dan Kiley's *The Peter Pan Syndrome* (1984), Peter Pan is used as a signifier for the kind of man who refuses to become fully 'masculine'. At its most basic this means the immature male, the 'man behaving badly', who simply refuses to grow up and assume the responsibilities of adult masculinity, but attempts to cling to – and to live out – the myth of an eternal boyhood.

The second layer is, once more, an overtly Freudian narrative. (It was in the period 1897–1900, halfway between *Candida* and *Peter Pan*, that Freud developed and published his theories of the Oedipus complex.) The play stages a conflict with the father on two levels, both in the persona of Mr Darling and, more dramatically, in that of Hook. It seems to beg for an Oedipal reading. According to the psychoanalytic account, the boy comes into conflict with the father over claims to the mother. He fears the father's castrating power, and has to kill him (symbolically) in order to negotiate that conflict and bring himself to adulthood. Similarly, Peter the child is in conflict with Hook over – among other things – possession of Wendy, the mother-wife whose total attention Peter demands. The fight is to the death and it is Peter who wins: the phallic battle between Hook's great cutlass and his own small dagger ends with Hook's death in the symbolically gaping jaws of the crocodile. But the pattern in *Peter Pan* deviates significantly from the classical Freudian one. I am not referring here to the details of the narrative: in a literary reworking of the Oedipal conflict, it is not so important that, say, Hook is not literally Peter's father. Imaginatively he is, or as near as makes no difference. Peter aligns himself with the Darling children (at the end of the play Mr and Mrs Darling offer to adopt him); while Hook, traditionally doubled by the actor who also plays Mr Darling, represents the Father as the punishing adult male. But it is Peter who has already symbolically castrated Hook: the amputated arm and the iron prosthesis from which the pirate derives his name are evidence of that. And the conflict takes place, not in order that Peter can resolve the psychic block and proceed to a mature adulthood, but so that he can validate and guarantee his own eternal childhood. This is what in fact happens – yet even this is not allowed to take place unproblematically. At one point Barrie gestures towards the very maturing process which the play denies: after the fight in which Peter finally defeats Hook

> *The curtain rises to show* PETER *a very Napoleon on his ship. It must not rise again lest we see him on the poop in* HOOK's *hat and cigars, and with a small iron claw.*

(Barrie 1948: 568)

What Barrie teases the reader with, the play in performance is unable to show: the authorial choice *not* to follow the route which leads the child to take the place of the father.

Only on the imaginatively much less urgent level of the Darling boys does the Oedipal conflict find any form of resolution: within the bourgeois family Michael and John are left to grow up after their adventures in the Never Land. But it is Peter's narrative, not theirs, that commands attention, and within this, the refusal of adulthood is absolute and repeated. In an early version of the Peter Pan story, the reader is confronted with the casual detail that when any one of the Lost Boys appears to be about to grow up, Peter kills him. Paradoxically, however, the idea of the bourgeois nuclear family haunts Peter. It is what he has lost in his transformation into the god-child (poignantly, he remembers peering back in through his own nursery window at the child in the cot with whom his parents had replaced him) and as such it continually encroaches in the patterns of life which Wendy and Peter adopt in their Wendy-house as head of their fantasy family.

In the gendered topography of the Victorian household, the nursery was clearly defined as a feminine space. Like the kitchen, it was marked off as being devoted to a specifically female activity, and in it mothers or paid employees got on with the role of nurturing. On a metaphorical level, it was the woman's domain from which the young Victorian boy needed to escape in order to proceed towards manhood. In *Peter Pan,* the nursery is itself a surreal place, where the mother has been displaced by a large dog, who is herself later displaced in the doghouse by Mr Darling. Nonetheless, it is figured as a place of safety and apparent protection, whose opposite is the dangerous and attractive adventure-playground which is the Never Land. The overt structure of the story is that of the classic children's fiction:

> the perfect adventure story ... A little boy breaks into a nursery, and takes the children away to an island of redskins and pirates, where they act out

the adventures which they normally read in books, before safely returning home.

(Rose 1992: 33)

But the two spaces, the nursery and the island, only *appear* to be the mutually exclusive opposite of each other. The fantasy island has domesticity imported into it, in the shape of Wendy – whose metaphorical task as a young Victorian female is to leave the nursery as a child in order to return to it in later life as a mother. She starts her work a little early, however, and the 'Wendy-house' (the child's play-house was named after the house in the play) is placed at the centre of the action.

And so the fantasy remains under the dominion of the parents/nurse, and the lost boys desire Wendy as a mother ('No question of sex!'). Wendy, in fact, inverts the usual relationships of mother/child tale-telling, for she tells stories *about* the nursery to the inhabitants of the fantasy island, telling the Lost Boys about domesticity and about growing up. Peter himself is more ambiguous in his attitude to the nursery, precisely because to accept it also means eventually to leave it. He is both attracted to the idea, and repelled by it, for domesticity is something which Peter can only engage with by breaking in, like a burglar. The feminizing nursery is a place from which Peter has escaped, but only by being shut out of it. And in his exile from the nursery he has also lost his chance of passing through it and growing up. Wendy's account of English domesticity threatens Peter *because* it appeals so strongly to the rest of the Lost Boys: it threatens to break up the island community when the Lost Boys want to follow her back home. The Never Land is a place both of escape from the maternal and of desire for the maternal, and it is not so much adulthood as motherhood which threatens the community of boys. At the end of the play, Peter does go back, temporarily, to the nursery, in order to return Wendy, John and Michael to their home. When Mrs Darling invites him to stay, he is briefly tempted by the offer, but rejects it, aware of the consequences. The painful process of re-entering the temporal world and maturing with it is alien to Peter: he is willing only to play at mothers and fathers on the island with Wendy.

A confusion about masculine roles, and in particular about how these relate to male–female relationships, is one of the repeated themes of the play. Thus in the ambiguous triangular relationship between Peter, Wendy and the Lost Boys on the island, Peter himself is uncertain quite what his role should be. Significantly, he settles for playing at being the father to the Lost Boys while emotionally identifying himself as Wendy's son:

WENDY: ... What is wrong, Peter?
PETER: (*scared*) It is only pretend, isn't it, that I am their father?
WENDY: (*drooping*) Oh yes
           (*His sigh of relief is without consideration for her feelings*)
           But they are ours, Peter. Yours and mine.
PETER: (*determined to get at facts, the only things that puzzle him*) But not really?
WENDY: Not if you don't wish it.
PETER: I don't.
WENDY: (*knowing she ought not to probe, but driven to it by something within*) What are your exact feelings for me, Peter?
PETER: (*in the classroom*) Those of a devoted son, Wendy.
WENDY: (*turning away*) I thought so
PETER: You are so puzzling. Tiger Lily is just the same. There is something or other she wants to be to me, but she says it is not my mother.

(Barrie 1948: 550)

Both Wendy and Tiger Lily offer the possibility of a male–female relationship based on something other than a parental configuration, and both are rejected. With Tiger Lily, Peter had earlier enacted a classic hero pattern, rescuing the damsel in distress, but then refusing (or ignoring) the conventional reward of marriage to her. If Peter had grown up, he would probably have become a 'Muscular' Christian minister in a poor area of London!

When Barrie first offered his play for production to the Broadway producer Charles Frohman, the manuscript he showed him was entitled *The Great White Father*. There is something accurate about the imperialist overtones of the title, but there is no doubt that Frohman was quite right in changing the title back to *Peter Pan*. The 'Great White Father' is actually what Peter wants *not* to be: he can cope with the role only in play. And fathers, as a whole, get rather a poor press in *Peter Pan*. The weak, pompous and rather ridiculous Mr Darling is presented with an amused condescension; he is the clownish *reductio ad absurdum* of those representations of masculine failure that inhabit Ibsen's dramas. Like Hjalmar Ekdal in *The Wild Duck*, his attempts to present an authoritative figure at home contrast with his anonymity in the outside world. Barrie describes him in the stage directions as follows:

> *He is really a good man as breadwinners go ... In the city where he sits on a stool all day, as fixed as a postage stamp, he is so like all the others on stools that*

you recognize him not by his face but by his stool, but at home the way to gratify
him is to say that he has a distinct personality ... It is with regret, therefore, that
we introduce him as a tornado, rushing into the nursery in evening dress, but
without his coat, and brandishing in his hand a recalcitrant white tie ...

MR. DARLING: I warn you, Mary, that unless this tie is round my neck, we
don't go out to dinner to-night, and if I don't go out to dinner to-night I
never go to the office again, and if I don't go to the office again you and I
starve, and our children will be thrown into the streets.

(Barrie 1948: 507)

Mr Darling (whose name so clearly contains him within his familial
role), is yet another figure who positions himself both as husband and
as son in relation to his wife. Their first appearance on stage together
sees Mrs Darling helping her husband to dress himself. He later
declines in status to the level of the family pet, as his ineffectuality is
symbolized by his eventual and literal self-banishment to the doghouse.
But if Mr Darling represents an inadequate masculinity, his alter ego,
Captain James Hook, represents a destructive one.

The doubling of the parts of Hook and Mr Darling is an inherent
part of the play's meaning, and dates back to the first production of
the play, where Gerald du Maurier played both parts. This is another
point at which the stage play and the relationship with the Davies
boys which inspired it intertwine; for Gerald du Maurier was the
boys' real-life uncle, the brother of Sylvia Llewelyn Davies. And
while in real life Arthur Llewelyn Davies, the boys' father, was 'in no
sense the typical Edwardian father of the Mr. Darling variety'
(Birkin 1979: 122), du Maurier caricatured several of his manner-
isms as a basis for his portrayal of Mr Darling. Thus the boys saw
their uncle play a role which was, in part at least, a parody of their
own father, and then turn from that into its demonic obverse in
Hook. Daphne du Maurier later described the character which her
father created on stage as

a tragic and rather ghastly creation who knew no peace and whose soul was
in torment; a dark shadow, a sinister dream, a bogey of fear who lives per-
petually in the grey recesses of every small boy's mind. All boys had their
Hooks, as Barrie knew; he was the phantom who came by night and stole his
way into their murky dreams. He was the spirit of Stevenson and of Dumas,
and he was Father-but-for-the-grace-of-God.

(Dunbar 1970: 140–1)

Hook was the spirit of Stevenson, of Dumas, and of a generation of
boys' adventure stories. He was a darker, funnier and more terrifying
character than Captain Swarthy of *The Boy Castaways of Black Lake*.

As we have seen, one of the inspirations behind the *Peter Pan* stories which Barrie told to the Davies boys was the adventure fiction of R. M. Ballantyne. Ballantyne's books were themselves one manifestation of the larger cultural effort to create 'the imaginary Englishman with his stiff upper lip and masterly control over world affairs' (Rutherford 1997: 12). They stood alongside boys' journals such as *The Union Jack* and the more famous *Boys' Own Paper*, designed to popularize the public-school virtues of the English ruling classes amongst boys of the middle and lower-middle classes, in order to encourage a form of masculine character development based upon an imagined ideal of Englishness. They were an important element in the development and support of English colonialism, and Barrie, writing just after the end of the Victorian age in the years before and after the First World War, sometimes treats their values ironically. He did not share, for example, the earlier narratives' apparently unqualified admiration for public-school values. Public schools, in fact, are a matter for wry humour in the play: one of the pirates, 'Gentleman Starkey', was once an usher at an English public school, while Hook himself was, according to most versions of the text, an alumnus of Eton (Barrie 1948: 526–7). On the whole, however, Barrie continues the Victorian imperial theme, importing the values of the boys' adventure story along with their characters and narrative structures. Indeed there was quite a rich and complex relationship between Barrie and *Peter Pan* and other cultural myths of British heroism. For example, Baden-Powell, founder of the Boy Scouts, named his own son Peter after Peter Pan, as did Captain Robert Falcon Scott, of the ill-fated Antarctic expedition. Barrie became godfather to the young Peter Scott, and after Robert Scott's death Barrie came to regard the explorer as embodying a noble and heroic variation on the Peter Pan theme, as he and his companions 'emerge out of the white immensities, always young' (Barrie 1922: 32).

The importance of the adventure narrative, then, operates at several levels, and at many of these, including the political, it is complicated by the theme of the desire for the mother. This is attributed to nearly all the male characters in the play, including Hook and the pirates. The climax of the play's adventure comes when the pirates finally capture Wendy, John, Michael and the Lost Boys. Offered the chance to save themselves by turning pirate themselves, the Lost Boys refuse because, as Tootles puts it, 'I don't think my mother would like me to be a pirate' (Barrie 1948: 561). John and Michael, on the other hand, are tempted, until John says:

JOHN: Stop, should we still be respectful subjects of King George?
HOOK: You would have to swear 'Down with King George.'

JOHN: (*Grandly*) Then I refuse!
MICHAEL: And I refuse.

(Barrie 1948: 561)

Moments later, Wendy tells the Lost Boys that she is sure their mothers would "'hope our sons would die like English gentlemen'", and the 'brave children' show their defiance of the pirates by singing the National Anthem. The pirates are resisted, and the boys' moral fibre vindicated, in the name of both motherhood and country. The scene embodies the rich interplay between masculinity, motherhood and ideas of nationalism and imperialism which is characteristic of late nineteenth- and early twentieth-century English culture.

The importance of the mother within the ideology of the Victorian and Edwardian family was itself shot through with contradictions: both demonized and idealized, wielding great domestic and emotional power which she was simultaneously encouraged to disavow, the mother was figured both as that which the male child needed, and that from which he most needed to be protected. Something of this cultural sense of reassuring yet terrifying maternal power comes through in one of Barrie's jokes about Mrs Darling. According to the stage directions, she

> *does not often go out to dinner, preferring when the children are in bed to sit beside them tidying up their minds, just as if they were drawers. If WENDY and the boys could keep awake, they might see her re-packing into their proper places the many articles of the mind that have strayed during the day, lingering humorously over some of their contents ...*

(Barrie 1948: 505)

Cultural anxiety about excessive mothering led to a patriarchal insistence that the young male child be weaned away from his mother's influence, often before the child was old enough to cope with the separation. That, combined with a normative code of male emotional distance which made difficult any identification between the young boy and his father, led to an ambivalence in masculinity which was only partially compensated for in 'the imperial fantasy of manly racial supremacy' (Rutherford 1997: 25) in which *Peter Pan*, like its Victorian antecedents, was implicated.

However, the relationship between *Peter Pan* and this ambivalence in masculinity was more complex than that of its *Boys' Own Paper*-style forebears. They tended to suppress it – along with any narrative reference to the world of domesticity, of motherhood, or of emotional need. *Peter Pan*, on the contrary, not only made these things a part of its own narrative, but did so in terms of a theatrical code which foregrounded ambivalence. The casting of a young woman as Peter was strictly the decision of Charles Frohman, the American producer, and it seems to have run counter to Barrie's original intentions. Barrie cannot have been too surprised, however: child protection laws would have made it impossible for the part to be played by a child; there were clear objections to having a post-adolescent male playing the part; and female-to-male cross-dressing was a well-established theatrical convention to deal with the problem of staging boys. Rarely, though, had the cross-cast actress had anything other than a bit part to play. Here Peter, and Nina Boucicault and Maude Adams, who played him in England and America respectively, were the stars of the show. And the eternal boy, the problematic masculine, was played by a girl. 'Peter Pan was the first of the pre-teen heroes: girls wanted to mother him, boys wanted to fight by his side, while the ambiguity of his sex stimulated a confusion of emotional responses' (Birkin 1979: 118). Not only Peter: Michael, Tootles, Nibs, Curly and both Twins were also played by young women. Only John and Slightly were cast to gender.

Peter Pan is one of the most complex texts of the period as regards the staging of masculinity. It brings together so many of the period's gender themes and anxieties: motherhood, growing up, the inadequate father-figure, adventure stories, heroism, the colonial imagination, Oedipal conflicts and the subconscious, the nature of a man's desire for young boys, together with questions of fantasy and theatrical representation. The play's own dream-like logic, the ironic voice of Barrie as author, the intertwining of public and private levels of meaning, and the continual rewriting and restaging to which the play was subject, all conspire to present a shifting, unstable kaleidoscope of these themes, to which Barrie himself clearly relates differently at different times in his career. In his rewritings, he seems to be continually attempting to rework the difficult material which he first unearthed, almost naïvely, in his story-telling to the boys. Simultaneously, Barrie clings onto the story, but also questions his own claim to the authorship of it. The exuberance of his early drafts contrasts poignantly with the sombre and nostalgic tones of his Dedication to the 1928 version, He dedicates the play to all five boys, adding:

> I suppose I always knew that I made Peter by rubbing the five of you together as savages with two sticks produce a flame. That is all he is, the spark I got from you. We had good sport of him before we clipped him small to make him fit the boards. ... This brings me to my most uncomfortable admission, that I have no recollection of writing the play of *Peter Pan*. ... I talk of dedicating the play to you, but how can I prove it is mine? How ought I to

act if some other hand, who could also have made a copy, thinks it worth while to contest the cold rights? Cold they are to me now as that laughter of yours in which Peter came into being long before he was caught and written down. There is Peter still, but to me he lies sunk in the gay Black Lake.

(Barrie 1948: 489, 490, 491)

It was written at a time when Sylvia and Arthur Llewelyn Davies had both died, when George, the eldest of the boys, had been killed in the First World War, and Michael, Barrie's favourite, had drowned – accidentally or as suicide – at Oxford. The deaths of these two are poignantly symbolic. Michael's death repeats the tragedy of James Barrie's brother David, the tragedy to which Barrie alludes in the most famous line in the play, spoken by Peter Pan as he, too, sits waiting to drown in the Mermaids' Lagoon: 'To die will be an awfully big adventure' (Barrie 1948: 545). In the boyhood fantasies of Never Land, even death's sting is removed by being re-presented as 'an awfully big adventure'. But if it was Michael's death which Barrie felt most keenly on a personal level, it was George's which is perhaps the more significant. He died in the conflict that threw such a pall over those fantasies of masculine adventure, which Barrie had so loved, which had spoken so thrillingly to generations of Victorian and Edwardian boys, and which had prepared them so inadequately for the realities of the fields of Flanders.

7

Contemporary Masculinities

7.1 Messages men hear

In his study of contemporary masculine gender identity, *Messages Men Hear: Constructing Masculinities* (1995), sociologist Ian M. Harris illustrates both the characteristics of hegemonic masculinity, and also some of the problems which they raise. Harris conducts an empirical survey which draws on a sample of over 500 men from a variety of ages, ethnic groups and class backgrounds. He structures this in terms of their varying responses to a list of 24 gender-role messages, which he suggests set the standards for appropriate male behaviour over the past 50 or so. These are the representative messages which define masculine gender norms, and which men in modern technological societies 'hear', from the media, from church and community, from school and peers, from other men and (importantly) from women. The list is worth reproducing in full:

C   *Adventurer*:   Men take risks and have adventures. They are brave and courageous.
    Be Like Your Father: Dad is your role model. Males express feelings in ways similar to their fathers.
C   *Be the Best You Can*:   Do your best. Don't accept being second. 'I can't' is unacceptable.
C   *Breadwinner*:   Men provide for and protect family members. Fathering means bringing home the bacon, not necessarily nurturing.
C   *Control*:   Men are in control of their relationships, emotions, and job.
    Faithful Husband: Men give up their freedom when they get married.
    Good Samaritan: Do good deeds and acts. Put others' needs first. Set a good example.

C   *Hurdles:*   To be a man is to pass a series of tests. Accomplishment is
        central to the male style.
C   *Money:*   A man is judged by how much money he makes and the
        status of his job.
        Nature Lover: Love of outdoors. Respectful treatment of plants
        and animals. Harmony with nature.
        Nurturer: Among other things men are gentle, supportive, warm,
        sensitive, and concerned about others' feelings.
C   *Playboy:*   Men should be sexually aggressive, attractive and
        muscular.
C   *President:*   Men pursue power and success. They strive for success.
        Rebel: Defy authority and be a non-conformist. Question and
        rebel against the system.
        Scholar: Be knowledgeable. Go to college. Value book learning.
        Read and study
C   *Self-reliant:*   Asking for help is a sign of weakness. Go it alone. Be
        self-sufficient and don't depend on others.
C   *Sportsman:*   Men enjoy playing sports, where they learn the thrill of
        victory and how to compete.
C   *Stoic:*   Ignore pain in your body. Achieve even though it hurts. Don't
        admit weakness.
C   *Superman:*   Men are supposed to be perfect. They don't admit
        mistakes.
        Technician: Men relate to, understand and maintain
        machines. They fix and repair things around the house.
        The Law: Do right and obey. Don't question authority.
C.   *Tough guy:*   Men don't touch, show emotions or cry. They don't let
        others push them around.
C   *Warrior:*   Men take death-defying risks to prove themselves and
        identify with war heroes.
C   *Work ethic:*   Men are supposed to work for a living and not take
        handouts.

(Harris 1995: 12–13)

The messages that Harris marks with a 'C' are those which the
earlier gender theorist, Clyde Franklin, labelled 'the classical man', and
which have been around for a long time. The remaining nine are messages which Harris describes as being specifically 'modern expectations
on men [which] transcend classical standards for male behaviour'
(Harris 1995: 13). Taken together, these masculine messages make up
a rough diagram of the values which comprise the dominant social constructions of desirable masculinity.

Although it is hard to substantiate its validity in any absolute way, it
is a diagram which probably feels instinctively 'right' to many men, who
could confirm memories of such messages from their own experiences

in childhood, adolescence and manhood. However, Harris's list also highlights certain contradictions – both within the dominant ideology of contemporary masculinity itself, and within attempts to describe the nature and workings of that ideology.

First of all, there is the ambivalent effect which any normative gender scheme such as this will have upon the individual, to whom it may be simultaneously reassuring and anxiety-provoking. To the extent that the individual can recognize his conformity to gender requirements, it offers reassurance. To the extent that he sees his shortcomings, it is a source of unease. The very existence of this unspoken and largely unconscious 'shopping list' of gender requirements gives rise to the 'anxiety' which is so much a commonplace of modern discussions of masculinity.

Secondly, the list seems to contradict itself at several points. For example, it pinpoints the contradictory messages that a man should be both a 'Faithful Husband' and a 'Playboy'. Clearly, it is virtually impossible to fulfil both roles at the same time: how, then, can these contradictions be negotiated? By choosing the one and ignoring the other? Or by understanding the two as successive: the man sows his wild oats early in life, then settles down? Or as part of an evolutionary development from an old-fashioned model of masculinity, which is being superseded by a more modern (and domesticated) one? Some men will successfully negotiate the contradictions within the gender scheme, for others the existence of apparently contradictory messages will be a source of long-standing confusion. Perhaps the most important aspects of gender ideology are less to do with the messages themselves, than with what men do with them once they have 'heard' them.

Problems arise, too, from Harris's own opposition of classical and non-classical categories of gender messages. It is not entirely clear, for example, what relationship is being posited between those items marked with a 'C' and those that are not. If the unmarked nine are more 'modern', it is not made explicit what determines their modernity. (The category 'technician', for example, would seem to have been as applicable to masculine gender identity in the 1930s as it is in the 1990s.) And does this modernity mean that these messages are therefore more urgent and pressing because they are somehow more 'immediate'? Or less so because they are more ephemeral?

A list such as this, then, may provoke more questions than it answers. Even if it is true that these are indeed the 'messages men hear', and that Harris's list of 24 does indeed constitute the messages of contemporary hegemonic masculinity, we are still faced with the questions which might be asked of any ideological construct. In what ways is it propagated? How effectively does it fulfil its normative function? How does it work in the individual? How coherent or contradictory is it? What competing ideological constructs contextualize it? What – if any – strategies of opposition and resistance are available?

Moreover, as Harris concedes, these are not the *only* messages men hear: ideology is more complex than that, and messages whose subject is gender identity and gender formation compete for attention amidst a cacophony of other cultural messages relating to race, age, class, status and so on. Conversely, there are some messages on Harris's list that are not in themselves particularly gender-specific. For example, the injunction relating to '*The Law*', to 'Do right and obey. Don't question authority', is surely relayed every bit as loudly and clearly to women as it is to men.

To the first few of these questions Harris himself provides a sweeping answer: although the list is generated from research carried out in the United States, Harris asserts confidently that 'it has universal application. Because of the power of the US media, these messages are hegemonic, heard around the world' (Harris 1995: 12). It is a very big claim, and one which is of considerable importance to this present study. 'The media' is a broad term, and presumably in Harris's argument it should be taken to include more than just the film and television industries; nonetheless these (together with the popular music industry) are the elements of that powerful 'US media' which travel most easily between countries and which have most influence in the formation and dissemination of ideological structures. One implication of Harris's assertion, then, is the possibility that the universal hegemonic masculinity which he posits is a product of its own screen dramatization.

The claim of universality needs to be treated with a certain scepticism. It is true that the messages which Harris highlights could be illustrated easily enough from the cultural representations of masculinity within mainstream film and television. Even so, the US media may not have quite the universal reach which Harris ascribes to it: Hollywood is a powerful ideological tool, but it is not necessarily a totalizing one. At the very least there will be regional and national variations of emphasis: some of these messages resonate more loudly in one culture than in another, while, even within a single nation state (such as the US itself, or the UK) class or racial differences will affect *how* various messages are heard.

Yet it is hard to ignore the force of Harris's claim that 'because of the power of the US media, these messages are hegemonic, heard around the world'. Certainly contemporary culture contains an increasingly multinational dimension (with all that that implies, both positively and negatively). While not ignoring the importance of national differences, it is clear that the mechanisms of production and distribution of films, television programmes and pop music have created a powerful sense of a shared culture between various Western nations, and particularly between English-speaking nations. And, as the continuous two-way traffic between Broadway and the West End demonstrates, theatrical culture is not immune from this. In terms of contemporary constructions of masculinity, however, it is the influence of Hollywood films which has been most hotly discussed for much of the latter part of the century. At the popular level, there are the repeated debates as to whether the glorification of masculine violence in movies and on television leads to violence in young males; at a more sophisticated level, there have been many recent studies of the role of the 'male myths and icons' drawn from the screen in the cultural construction of gender identity (Horrocks 1995).

This has implications in terms of the staging of masculinity in the theatre, for if there has been a crisis in masculinity, there has also been a crisis in theatricality. One of the key problems which the theatre has had to deal with in the last half-century has been its relation to popular culture in general, and to film and television in particular. Never before has any culture been so thoroughly 'dramatized' as is twentieth-century Western society. It sees its own stories about itself, its dreams, its realities, its fantasies, its memories acted out continually in comedies, thrillers, drama-documentaries, soap operas, blockbusters, action movies, costume dramas and so on. And of course most of this proliferation of dramatic narrative takes place on screen, through the broadcast and recorded media (Williams 1975: 3–4). This has left the live theatre with the continual question of where it now fits in. This interface between stage and screen has been a continual question for the theatre, which has struggled to find strategies to negotiate the twin perils of being either totally subsumed or completely marginalized. The former would mean that it would seem to have nothing to offer that was not available better (or more cheaply) on television, video or film. The latter would mean that it was addressing itself to an increasingly elite minority audience. The theatre has continued to make claims over the past half-century for its own cultural centrality; they are claims, however, which have had to be made more and more loudly, often in the face of polite disbelief.

The question of live theatre's position in (or relation to?) popular culture is a general problem for theatrical culture. However, it is a particularly urgent one in terms of the staging of masculinities – especially if, as Harris suggests, it is through 'the power of the media' that the messages of contemporary masculinity are heard. In the next section I want to explore an aspect of this problem with reference to a film text which itself juxtaposes constructions of masculinity from, on the one hand, mainstream Hollywood movies and, on the other, from the 'classical' theatre. My aim is not so much to analyse Hollywood's construction of masculinity for its own sake (there are many books which already do this well), but to point to one way in which masculinity becomes defined in terms of a relationship between theatre and film.

7.2 'Just DO it!': film, theatre and masculinity

In an early scene from John McTiernan's 1993 movie *The Last Action Hero*, we see a Shakespeare class in an American high school. An elderly, and rather refined, woman teacher is desperately attempting to instil some kind of interest in Shakespeare into a bored collection of pre-adolescents, whose own immediate cultural referents are Wile E. Coyote, Sylvester Stallone and Arnold Schwarzenegger. 'Murder, incest, treachery', she offers them desperately, as she prepares to show a section from Olivier's *Hamlet,* 'and in the end everyone dies. Yes, Shakespeare's Hamlet really *is* the First Action Hero'. The ploy fails, of course. Rather than convincing her audience of the continuity between the popular culture of the Elizabethan era and that of the 1990s, the teacher's juxtaposition of the two simply highlights the difference.

There is a gender mix within the high school class who view (amidst some giggling) the Shakespeare extract, but the significant spectator is a young male member of the class: Danny Madigan, the 13-year-old protagonist of the movie. Danny, as we have seen in an earlier sequence, is obsessed with Jack Slater, a Hollywood Action Hero played by Schwarzenegger. As he watches Hamlet fail in his attempt to kill the praying Claudius, he snorts in disgust, 'Don't talk ... just DO it!' The Olivier sequence just doesn't live up to his genre expectations: it is not really a *movie* at all. It is (as has often been commented on) too theatre-bound. Convinced of the utter uselessness of Olivier's – and Shakespeare's – hero, Danny then fantasizes a hilarious black-and-white sequence of his own: the trailer for an imaginary Schwarzenegger

Hamlet, in which 'There's something rotten in the state of Denmark – and Prince Hamlet's here to take out the trash!' Gloriously, Danny's fantasy Schwarzenegger/Hamlet goes on to avenge his father's memory with machine-gun and howitzer and no introspection whatsoever. His trail of destruction culminates in the action movie's traditional finale: a massive explosion which reduces Elsinore to rubble.

The sequence is both funny and complicated. While playing largely on the lowest common denominators of Shakespeare-as-cultural-referent ('To be or not to be' is the talismanic signifier which ensures that we're all 'in' on the humour) it also contains several in-jokes for film and Shakespeare *cognoscenti*. For example, the elderly teacher who sighs sadly that possibly the class may recognize Laurence Olivier from TV advertisements or from his appearance in (the embarrassingly awful) *Clash of the Titans*, is played by Olivier's widow Joan Plowright. The sequence also takes a gleeful side-swipe at one of Schwarzenegger's own real-life Hollywood competitors for the 'Action Hero' crown, Mel Gibson, who had starred in Franco Zeffirelli's remarkably straight and unexpectedly well-reviewed 1990 film version of *Hamlet*. It also stages a variety of oppositions, of which the most obvious is that between high culture and popular culture. In popular American films and TV programmes it is Shakespeare, above all, who stands metonymically for high culture; and if Gibson's success as Hamlet had claimed that high culture and popular culture can easily be reconciled, the more conservative satire of *The Last Action Hero* replies that there is something inherently ludicrous about the idea.

Underlying all of this is a deeper level of opposition: a gendered one. It is no surprise to discover a little later in the narrative that Danny is being brought up by his mother alone, that his father died a few years ago, and that what he is (by implication) seeking in his cinematic obsession with Jack Slater is a masculine role model. Film criticism has had a lot to say about the gender issues and gender politics inherent in Hollywood movies, and recent work has been particularly interesting on the issue of masculinities. A good example is Steven Cohan and Ina Rae Hark's collection of critical and theoretical essays, *Screening the Male: Exploring Masculinities in Hollywood Cinema* (Cohan and Hark 1993), which contains, among other things, an interesting chapter on Schwarzenegger by Susan Jeffords. Hollywood, however, is fast on its feet, and is adept both at responding to its critics and at incorporating their critiques within its own fictions. *The Last Action Hero* came out in the same year as Cohan and Hark's volume, and it deals with many of the issues ('Masculinity as Fathering', 'Masculinity as Individualism') which Jeffords raises in her essay. The values of the action movie as a significant fantasy experience for the pre-adolescent male are both knowingly satirized and also reaffirmed.

All of this is fairly straightforward: in the figure of Jack Slater, Danny sees represented many of the characteristics of hegemonic masculinity that Harris outlines (e.g. *Adventurer, Be the Best You Can, Control, Good Samaritan, Hurdles, Self-Reliant, Stoic, Superman, Technician, The Law, Tough Guy, Warrior*). What is specifically interesting for our current purposes, in the sequence which I have examined from *The Last Action Hero*, is the way in which the action movie's configuration of masculinity is contrasted with the implied 'irrelevance' of Shakespeare and classical theatre. In the context of the film's knowingness about its own gender agenda, movies and popular culture are presented in opposition to theatre and minority, or elitist, culture. It is significant that the teacher who attempts to offer Shakespeare and high culture to Danny is not only culturally 'refined' but also female. For although she attempts to present Olivier's *Hamlet* as a precursor of the action movie, the gesture succeeds only in suggesting how limited an understanding she has of the pleasures which that genre offers, or the psychological functions which it performs, for the pre-adolescent male. By aligning her with the implied values of Shakespeare and the Olivier film (thought, words, emotional reflection, self-knowledge, scruples – even pity and mercy) the film encodes those values as essentially feminine – and, indeed, English, as opposed to the stereotypical all-American masculinity which Jack Slater and Schwarzenegger represent.

Thus the source of the humour in the opening sequences of *The Last Action Hero* lies in the binary opposition which it constructs between two sets of values:

Film	Theatre
Popular culture	Elite culture
Street	Classroom
Action	Words
Getting things done	Introspection
Present	Past
Relevant	Irrelevant
American	English
Youth	Age
Masculine	Feminine

And so the elitist and irrelevant theatre is mobilized as the opposite of the action movie, which carries the values of a particular kind of masculinity with which the growing boy can identify. The rest of *The Last Action Hero* continues in the vein of knowing self-reference which the 'Hamlet' routine implies: on one level an action movie in its own right, it also functions simultaneously as an ironic essay on Hollywood's use of action heroes as male spectacle and adolescent fantasy-figures. This irony, it is true, is limited in its range and force; the film as a whole broadly affirms the values of the action movie. Even so, the fact of that irony is important. It points towards an underlying self-consciousness, even a sense of embarrassment, about the figure of the action hero, and towards an anxiety which is familiar, at least in contemporary gender theory.

This scene from a movie offers a definition of masculinity at the interface between film and theatre, where the former is culturally coded as masculine and the latter as feminine – or, at the very least, as unmasculine. Over the last 20 or so years, the theatrical staging of masculinities, too, has made frequent reference to the paradigms of masculinity that are available on the screen. In doing so, however, it has been forced to take account of this bipolar gender coding of screen and stage – a coding which is itself part of larger cultural questions about the relative social function of theatre, film and television. As I have already suggested, an important aspect of the history of the theatre in the twentieth century has concerned its need to carve out a space for itself in a world of screen and broadcast media, and to reinvent the experience of live theatre in a way which distinguished it from that of film and television . Simultaneously, however, television and film offered to the theatre new opportunities. Audiences became familiar with a wide range of screen codes, of narrative genres and archetypes – all of which the theatre quickly adopted, plundered, parodied or developed. Meanwhile, as actors, writers and directors learned to flourish in both the live and the recorded media, all sorts of cross-fertilizations ensued. Stage plays were turned into movies; movies turned into plays. Movies were made about the theatre, plays written about movie making. Television started to stage theatrical scripts and then developed a dramatic language of its own. The theatre produced plays stimulated by popular television series – and so on.

To illustrate the importance of this, we can turn briefly to the reception history of *Look Back in Anger* – a play whose iconic position in British theatre history has ensured that it is usually thought of in purely theatrical terms. It is (according to the now rather shop-worn textbook account) the play which is generally credited with blowing away the genteel cobwebs of postwar English dramas of the Rattigan generation, and generally being the harbinger of a revolution in British theatre. Ironically, however, this iconic 1950s stage play owed much of its theatrical success to the television. During its first run at the Royal Court in 1956, a 20-minute fragment of the play was broadcast on BBC television, to an estimated audience of five million, and, according to Richard Eyre and Nicholas Wright, 'only with the showing of [the] twenty-minute excerpt of the play on BBC TV was its success at the Royal Court established' (Eyre and Wright 2000: 243). Within two years audiences had no need to go to the theatre at all to see the 'play': Tony Richardson, its director at the Court, had turned it into a movie. Thus the notion of the 'angry young man', circulating by way of theatre, film and television, became a widely available cultural artefact, and the protest masculinity which the play stages became common cultural currency. Ironically, in the film version of *Look Back in Anger* – which was one of the seminal works of the gritty, urban and essentially masculine British cinematic New Wave of the 1950s and 1960s – there is a scene, not in the original stage piece, in which its (now filmic) angry young hero ridicules the falseness and effeteness of the British theatre (see Rebellato 1999: 213).

Thus the relationship which developed in the twentieth century between film, television and theatre has led to a complex intertextual circulation of meanings. In the following section of this chapter I shall be looking at two British plays from the mid-1980s which configure the relationship between theatre and popular culture – especially film culture – in very different ways.

7.2.1   *Cartoons and cinematic techniques:* Up 'n' Under *(1984)*

John Godber's 1984 stage hit *Up 'n' Under* draws on popular culture – of a very male kind – in several respects. It is about the very masculine world of Rugby League football: his characters are members of an amateur team, playing in the pub leagues of East Yorkshire. Sport, of course, is an important symbolic arena of gender ideologies, and the sporting environment has become a classic topic for studies of masculinity – studies both by academic historians and sociologists, and also by novelists, playwrights and film makers. Rugby football generally is seen as a 'masculine ritual' (Schacht 1996: 553–7), while Rugby League in particular, with its origins in working-class history, is already loaded with certain kinds of class connotations.

One writer, David Storey, had already made it his own fictional territory, drawing on his own experiences as a professional player in order to portray the tensions within this often brutal world, both in novel and in play form. His novel *This Sporting Life* was turned into a successful film in 1963 (one of the British New Wave films mentioned above), directed by Lindsay Anderson, who went on to direct *The Changing Room*, Storey's play on a similar theme at the Royal Court Theatre in 1971. Storey was clearly an early influence on Godber. They were both Yorkshire working-class writers, and Godber's MA thesis at Leeds University, on Storey and John Arden, explored this fact. Significantly, however, the text which most directly informs Godber's Rugby League play is not one of Storey's, but a popular mainstream Hollywood movie. 'At the time of writing,' said Godber, 'the most popular videos available on the mass market are the *Rocky* videos. This is an attempt to stage *Rocky* ... and where else? In Yorkshire, of course' (Godber 1989: 111).

Rocky is a 'man's movie' – almost parodically so. It fetishizes the manly muscularity of its hero, and the accompanying masculine virtues of strength, sporting prowess, courage and determination. Its story is that of the no-hoper who gets a crack at the big-time. Failing boxer Rocky Balboa is matched in what is supposed to be a show-bout against the world-beater Apollo Creed, whom he takes on, and very nearly beats. Part of the commercial success of *Rocky* lay in the fact that its tale of a struggle against seemingly impossible odds was applicable to its writer and lead actor as well: at the time, Sylvester Stallone was an underemployed and unknown bit-part actor who persuaded two producers to back his script, with him in the main part. Stallone's success became part of the mythology of the movie itself.

Up 'n' Under is one of many plays by Godber which 'deal with aspects of working-class life and, to a greater or lesser extent, working-class leisure time' (Godber 1989: vii). Unlike Storey's professionals, the men of The Wheatsheaf team play Rugby League as a hobby, not to earn a living, and the rituals of male comradeship which it stages – both of the game itself and of the pub social life which surrounds the training and playing – are those of leisure rather than of the workplace. The story is simple: for a bet, an idealistic coach tries to turn a bunch of pathetically bad rugby players into a champion-beating side. As in *Rocky*, the plucky lads from The Wheatsheaf only *nearly* beat their rich, powerful and prestigious rivals, losing with the last kick of the match. That, though, is one of the key plots of the masculine mythology: it's not necessarily about winning, it's about going the distance, proving you have the heart. Like *Rocky*, the play ends on a note that promises – and delivers – a (disappointing) sequel: *Up 'n' Under 2,* with its rematch between the teams, had its premier the following year.

The play bristles with references to other cultural forms, and particularly to popular culture. There is a parody of the prologue to *Romeo and Juliet,* and a knowing wink towards Steven Berkoff, but the majority of the play's references are to popular films, TV programmes, pop music and comics. *Rocky* itself is invoked several times, of course, but characters also refer to (among others) *Zulu, Flesh-Eating Zombies, Kes, Top of the Pops, Opportunity Knocks,* 'Alf Tupper, the Tough of the Track', and the current pop hit 'Relax'. These references are an essential part of the dramatic language of *Up 'n' Under.* Through its web of intertextuality, the play both indulges in and is also gently ironic about those male fantasies of sporting glory upon which *Rocky* is based. For example, one of the characters, Phil, is an English teacher, and just before the game he narrates his surreal dream of playing at Wembley against Featherstone Rovers. Earlier in the play, however, he has been shown briefly in front of a class, to whom he's teaching the text *A Kestrel for a Knave,* Barry Hines's boy's-coming-of-age story. The film of this book, *Kes,* had had a great influence on Godber; when he saw it as a teenager it was 'something of a revelation: "I thought, God, you can make films about growing up in Yorkshire"' (Bennett 2001: 130), *Kes* features a famous and very funny sequence in which a thuggish PE master acts out his own fantasies of masculine sporting glory in a games lesson, which his egoistic imagination transforms into a Wembley Cup Final. When Phil tells us about *his* Wembley fantasy, the echoes of the *Kes* sequence surround his narrative. The middle-aged man's dreams of glory are both touching and ludicrous.

But Godber's plays from this period do not just quote popular culture: in so far as it is possible for theatre texts to do so, they attempt to position themselves *as* popular culture. The much-quoted statistic from *Plays and Players* in 1993 that Godber is 'the third most per-formed playwright in the United Kingdom, after William Shakespeare and Alan Ayckbourn' (Bennett 2001: 129), should be read in connec-tion with Godber's own stated aim as a theatre writer. He defines himself as an out-and-out populist, in clear opposition to the 'minority' Royal Court tradition:

> Why aren't I writing plays that would go on at the Royal Court? Well
> there's a number of reasons, one is because I want my work to be done a lot,
> for financial reasons, because it is my living, you know, I don't have any
> other means of keeping the electric on. Secondly, I don't want to shut the-

atres, I want to keep as many people coming to the theatre as possible ... I think, over the last twelve years, I've done as much as anybody in British theatre to try and break down or de-mystify the barriers between those who go to the theatre and those who don't, ... Now, that was my initial kind of purge, motivation, to get people from my sort of background, a working-class, mining background, to go to the theatre.

(Godber 1996: 10)

In the 1970s and early 1980s, the atmosphere of British Labourite working-class politics with which Godber had grown up tended to be very male-dominated and male-oriented (see Wainwright 1987: 162–205) and Godber's work, especially his early work, shows the traces of this. The populist aim of breaking down the barriers between those that go to the theatre and those that don't, inevitably involved certain choices of subject-matter – choices which frequently appear to have gender implications. The stories that have most successfully got 'people from my sort of background ... to go to the theatre' seem to have been those about masculine subjects such as night-club bouncers and rugby players. (Even when Godber puts a woman at the centre of a play, as in *Blood, Sweat and Tears*, she is playing boys' games.) In terms of theatrical style, too, Godber consciously reacted against the realist tradition. 'Directors of [*Bouncers*] should never think of Chekhov,' he warned, 'rather they should think of cartoons and cinematic techniques' (Godber 1989: 3). His dislike of 'box-sets, big red curtains and tedious actors' (Godber 1989: 3) led him, in the 1970s and 1980s, towards a very physical form of theatre. *Up 'n' Under*, in particular, is 'an attempt to create a popular piece of drama that is all action' (Godber 1989: 111). Its theatrical climax involves a match between two seven-a-side teams, played by a total of six actors and some clever staging. Physical theatre in itself is not necessarily a more 'masculine' form of theatre than the realism and postrealism of the Royal Court's tradition. Nonetheless, Godber repeatedly uses the technique, in what he calls his '[r]unning about plays', of staging a sporting event or contest as part of a play. The rugby match in *Up 'n' Under*, the cricket match in *Everyday Heroes* (1990), the judo competition in *Blood, Sweat and Tears* (1986), skiing in *On the Piste* (1990) and – by extension – street fighting in *Bouncers* (1984) do suggest that at some level Godber sees the (primarily) male pleasures of sports spectatorship as a key tactic in his campaign to break down the barriers.

The description of *Up 'n' Under* so far might suggest that there is little to its consideration of masculinity beyond a populist appeal to an unreconstructed 'blokeishness'. Certainly, there are moments in the play which bear this out, as when the team members break into that epitome of masculine homosocial ritual, the rugby song:

> She was poor but she was honest
> Victim of a rich man's whim
> First he fucked her then he left her
> And she had a child by him ...
>
> Once a boy was no good
> Took a girl into a wood
> Bye bye blackbird
> Laid her down upon the grass
> Pinched her tits and slapped her arse
> Bye bye blackbird.
>   (Godber 1989: 136–7)

These boasting tales of male sexual aggression, parodying popular songs of various eras, are presented in a totally unproblematized way. Yet the sexist stereotype is balanced by other elements. There is also lyricism in the singing of the men, as the sexist chants give way to a straight rendition of the pop hit of the time, The Flying Pickets' a cappella version of 'When You're Young and In Love'. Moreover, this masculine world of Rugby League is able to accommodate the presence of a woman. Unlike *The Changing Room, Up 'n' Under* is *not* a male-cast play: it also includes the 'girl-in-a-boys'-gang' in the figure of Hazel, who represents, in a none-too-subtle way, Godber's recognition of the claims of sexual equality. Hazel, who owns a gymnasium, challenges the masculinity of the male team-members through her own sporting prowess, and by virtue of the fact that they discover her to be much fitter than they are. She is also granted a second-hand credibility in the eyes of the men by virtue of the fact that she is the ex-wife of an international scrum-half. At first Hazel's athletic ability is positioned as an acceptably 'feminine' form of physical fitness: her domain is the gymnasium rather than the playing-field. The separate spheres soon coalesce, however, and Hazel ends up playing for The Wheatsheaf team. She proves her worth, of course, as the genre demands. Not only does she play well in the climactic game against the Cobbler's Arms, but in the planned re-match between the teams (with the promise of which the play ends) she is due to take over the kicker's role, thus fully taking her place in the masculine world. Conversely, Arthur, the instigator and leader, shows his feminine side. At the end of the match he sits centre-stage crying, as his team-mates try clumsily to cheer him up with lines like: 'Rocky didn't cry, Arthur' (Godber 1989: 73). This is six years before the televised image of Paul Gascoigne, in tears at Italia '90, was beamed around the world, subsequently to be turned by the media tabloid press into an icon of a very 1990s style of masculinity – the 'new lad'.

In the end, *Up 'n' Under* isn't just *Rocky* in East Yorkshire: it is also all the aspirational movies of the 1970s and 1980s, many of them starring Goldie Hawn, whose thesis is that girls can be just as good at boys' activities as boys themselves. It is also a clear example of one way in which representations of masculinity in theatre of the late twentieth century are inevitably in dialogue with those on television and the movie screen. The stage experience does not simply annex the meanings of the screen: it inevitably takes up a position at a critical distance from them. 'To stage *Rocky* … in Yorkshire' is also to critique both Yorkshire and *Rocky*. If gender is, in one sense, performance, then like all performances it has an intertextual dimension: quoting, imitating, parodying, refashioning other pre-existing performances, performances which are no longer confined to the stage. Just as many actors, directors and writers move easily between one medium and another, and texts, characters, social stereotypes and narrative structures are adapted from one medium to another, so meanings circulate between the live and recorded forms of drama.

7.2.2   *Men that hate women:* Masterpieces *(1983)*

When *Up 'n' Under* opened in 1984, the writer-in-residence at the Royal Court – the theatre about which Godber was so dismissive – was Sarah Daniels. Her play *Masterpieces* had transferred to the Court the previous year, and moved into the main auditorium, where it enjoyed both success and notoriety, in January 1984. *Masterpieces* was one of the most uncompromising of the wave of feminist plays to be associated with the Court in the early 1980s, and the one whose image of masculinity is most negative. It is not just that it represents unpleasant men – although all the men in the play are oppressors and abusers of women. It also presents a damning analysis of masculinity. Once more, the analysis uses film as part of its argument – though in a totally different way from Godber's use of *Rocky*. In *Masterpieces*, theatre becomes not an extension of movie culture but a site of resistance to it – or at least to certain aspects which are implied in Daniels' feminist critique of it. Daniels uses theatre as a place of opposition – a necessary opposition, it is implied, since film culture and the wider culture which produced it are both sick.

In the play's prologue we hear three male monologues about the production, distribution and use of pornography. We then meet Rowena Jefferson-Stone – a somewhat stereotyped middle-class social worker whose privileged background has up till now protected her from the harsher realities of gender oppression, even within her own family. At a dinner party she laughs uncertainly at the sexist jokes of her father, husband and male acquaintance, and tentatively defends pornography against the attack of a feminist friend. In the next scene the audience sees Rowena on trial for the murder of a man. The rest of the play ties together these three initial images in a series of scenes, monologues and voice-overs which shift back and forward over a period of twelve months. Towards the end of the play we discover that the man had been a stranger to her, and that she had killed him by pushing him under an approaching Underground train when he approached her on a deserted Tube station platform.

As should be clear from this resumé, one thing which Daniels does share with Godber, albeit only tangentially, is a mistrust of conventional dramatic realism. Whereas Godber reacted against the (Chekhovian) realist tradition in the name of popular theatre, and adopted an alternative physical theatrical language, Daniels' feminist reaction was more deconstructive. Anticipating the claim of later feminist dramatic theorists that a realist drama reifies 'the dominant culture's traditional inscription of power relations' (Dolan 1988: 84), Daniels' dramaturgy, like Caryl Churchill's, embodies a resistance to any such inscription. Daniels, it is true, draws on a range of realist techniques, but subverts their illusionistic effect by devices such as a fragmented time sequence and a semiotically significant doubling plot. In such a way, Daniels makes the audience participate actively in constructing for themselves the meaning of Rowena's journey. There is, however, no final doubt as to what that meaning should be: just as the audience is being forced to construct meanings from the relationship between one scene and another, so the play insists on the audience making the connections between pornography, violence against women, and 'men who tell misogynist jokes' (Daniels 1984: 35). Robin Thornber's *Guardian* review of Annie Castledine's Leeds Playhouse production (staged later the same year) sums up the play's force:

> What Sarah Daniels sets out to do is to show how men are taught to see women as things rather than people, how this insidiously pervasive attitude connects obvious outrages like rape with apparently tolerable behaviour like misogynist jokes, how it diminishes men as much as it degrades women. And she demonstrates her point with irrefutable logic and devastating clarity through the story of one woman's progressive realisation of how awful it all is.

> Starting from conventionally tolerant clichés like 'looking at a picture never hurt anyone' and 'If women want to do it and men want to look at it, where's the harm?' she thoroughly catalogues exactly where the harm is.
>
> (Thornber 1984: 21)

The play's key image does not appear until comparatively late in the narrative. It is that of a snuff movie – that is to say, an illegally-made underground film in which women are literally and actually tortured and killed for the camera. Daniels refers, both in the narrative and in the acknowledgements in the published text of the play, to a specific actual movie, itself entitled *Snuff*, which was made in South America, and briefly distributed and then withdrawn in the UK in 1982. Rowena describes it as

> loosely based on the Charles Manson story. Then it changes, it becomes real. It's a film studio during a break in filming. The director is near a bed talking to a young woman ... He starts to cut into her shoulder, and the pain in her face ... It's real ... It is terrible ... I have watched a woman being cut up and she is alive ... And I kept forcing myself to pretend that it was only a movie.
>
> (Daniels 1984: 35)

Rowena's act of violence against the stranger was committed immediately after seeing this film *Snuff*. The film becomes the symbolic proof of the continuum between the apparently harmless activity of sexist joke-telling, the pornography industry, and violence against women. It is also – emotionally – the extenuating circumstances (which the court then ignores) of Rowena's case.

The dramatic technique of the trial inevitably pushes the audience towards judgement. The court condemns her but the audience is encouraged not to: in a world in which such violence towards women exists, Rowena should surely be exonerated. The final violence is presented ambiguously, however. Is the dead man in fact an innocent bystander, on whom Rowena has taken revenge for all the male violence towards women? This is the interpretation which Rowena herself suggests at one point.

PSYCHIATRIST: And you claim, Mrs. Jefferson-Stone, that looking at pornography was the turning-point?
ROWENA: Yes.
PSYCHIATRIST: Enough of a turning-point to make you try to kill a man?
ROWENA: Yes.

> (Daniels 1984: 35)

Yet the stage directions make it clear that the anonymous man's advance towards Rowena is to be staged in such a way as to represent him as a serious threat to her safety – even to her life. Whatever this character's 'actual' intentions might be, the staging certainly makes it look as if he is about to attack her. Consequently, what the audience actually *sees* is an act of self-defence on Rowena's part. Her subsequent conviction for murder – in circumstances where we feel no jury *should* convict – and her sentence of a long prison term clearly demonstrate the unfairness towards women of a patriarchal justice system which has been set up to safeguard the interests of men. Masculinity comes out of the play pretty badly however one reads it, but *Masterpieces* never quite solves the structural problem of Rowena's culminating act of violence. Is it a justified revenge killing for male violence towards women, or is it a straightforward act of self-defence? The two possible readings are not themselves mutually exclusive, yet in performance they muddy and confuse each other. The plea of 'self-defence' weakens that of 'justifiable homicide'.

More damaging to the play's long-term effect was the fact that the story of snuff movies – in real life – seems to have been an urban legend. Neither research nor the offer of financial rewards has ever turned out any evidence that a commercially made film has included footage of a person being murdered for the sake of the camera (Mikkelson 1999: 1–11). The on-screen death of the actress in *Snuff* was eventually exposed as a publicity stunt created and propagated by the film's makers as a marketing ploy. *Snuff* was 'nothing more' than an unpleasant and badly made 'sexploitation' film, whose 'reality' sequence, with its apparent shift from fiction into documentary, was actually a stitched-on fictional ending. On one level, of course, this changes little. 'Nothing more' is already bad enough. The fact that such a marketing ploy could be used at all, the fact that many people believed it to be true and were willing to pay good money to see it, the fact that the film still indulged in the imaginary torture of women – all these are themselves enough to make a case against the misogyny of the masculine culture which produced such an artefact. Moreover, the fact that research has uncovered no evidence of such practices to date does not necessarily mean that there are none in existence; while *Snuff* may not after all have literal blood on its hands, who knows what other films there may be – already in existence or yet to be made – which do? Besides, male violence towards women is so widespread that one film itself is of little consequence ... All of these are powerful arguments. Yet in the experience of *Masterpieces* it is the presumed *reality* of the snuff movie which is so rhetorically and emotionally important; it has the feel of documented fact. This 'feel' is all the more powerful because of its being presented in the context of a play whose fragmented theatricality guarantees the fictionality of the death which it portrays. The actor who plays the man killed by Rowena comes back for the curtain call.

Part of the importance of *Masterpieces* lies in the way in which it articulates a radical-feminist view of masculinity – and in the effect which this had on men. While liberal feminism argued that patriarchy was equally damaging to both women and men, radical feminism identified men as being its unequivocal beneficiaries, economically, sexually and psychologically. At its most extreme, it saw masculinity as inherently violent and men as intrinsically woman-hating. This is the picture of masculinity which *Masterpieces* paints with such force. To quote Robin Thornber's review of the Leeds production again: 'It is a long time since an evening in the theatre disturbed me so deeply … she doesn't just tell you or show you. She makes you feel it. I came out feeling not only threatened but muddled. The play made me angry and filled me with hate for men. But then I am one' (Thornber 1984: 21).

7.3 Into the 1990s: pleading for the defence

Robin Thornber's sense of confusion and self-hatred speaks for many pro-feminist men struggling to come to terms with the radical feminist analysis of hegemonic masculinity. The men's movement which came to prominence in the later part of the 1980s and the 1990s had many different strands and took many different positions *vis-à-vis* the feminist critiques of masculinity. In one way or another, however, the men's movement in all its manifestations is a product of feminism, a response to the various feminist analyses of traditional gender constructions. Within the men's movement there were many who agreed with feminist critiques of the oppressions of patriarchy, and worked to combat them. Not all, however: there were also those who saw it as their prime function to mount a defence of masculinity in the face of these attacks.

Typical, in many respects, of the way in which this backlash tendency developed during the 1990s is David Thomas's 1993 book *Not Guilty: In Defence of the Modern Man*. Thomas opens aggressively with the question, 'if men are so much better off than women, how come so many more of them kill themselves?' (Thomas 1993: 1), and starts from the position of male victimhood: 'Men certainly feel under attack ... increasingly men felt as if they stood accused. They felt as if they had been put in the wrong. And they didn't like it' (Thomas 1993: 3). He goes on to attempt to redress the moral balance in men's favour on issues such as equality in the workplace, sexual harassment and domestic violence. Thomas's book is not a subtle piece of argumentation. Nor, however, is it simply a knee-jerk misogynist's reaction to feminist critiques of masculinity; indeed many of the arguments which Thomas puts forward about masculinity and its discontents were themselves first voiced by feminists. Even so, his work is primarily driven by a sense of injustice – and anger – against

> those campaigners who accuse us of being bad by definition, those propa-
> gandists who maintain that all men are violent and all violence is male, and
> even those well-meaning young women who assume – as who would not
> after the sexual politics of the past twenty-five years? – that right is on their
> side, must come to terms with the fact that life is not that simple. Neither
> sex has the monopoly on virtue or vice. Men do not wear the black hats nor
> women the white. We are all of us fallible souls decked out in shades of
> grey. As a man I stand accused of violence, aggression, oppression and
> destructiveness. Members of the Jury, I plead ... not guilty.
>
> (Thomas 1993: 270–1)

In the rest of this chapter I shall be looking at two plays which also articulate this sense of men on the defensive. David Mamet's *Oleanna* and *Defending the Caveman* by Rob Becker and Mark Little are both plays which have been, in different ways, very successful (and, I would argue, in their own way very important) theatrical events in the UK. Together, they also represent something of the split between the main-stream/populist and minority/elitist theatrical cultures which was evident in the previous contrast between *Up 'n' Under* and *Masterpieces*. They both develop a theme suggested earlier in this chapter, of the increasing internationalism of the contemporary the-atrical scene and the importance of that in considering contemporary hegemonic masculinity: the first was written by an American playwright who is better known as a screenwriter and film director; the second, also originally written by an American, has been 'naturalized' for British audiences by way of an Australian actor familiar to British audi-ences from his television persona. Thus both, too, continue the theme, established earlier in the chapter, of the increasingly important rela-tionship between theatre, film and television. The two plays articulate very different responses to the sense of masculinity under attack, which is so central to Thomas's book.

7.3.1 *'I find that I am sexist':* Oleanna *(1992)*

I'm not one of those women who always had David Mamet down as a
misogynist. I loved both *Glengarry Glen Ross* and *American Buffalo*. But they
didn't have any women characters, so perhaps it was too early to call.

(Chunn in Anthony et al. 1993: 2)

In the dialectic between stage and screen, the general assumption is
that the latter is culturally more high-profile, and makes a greater
impression on a greater number of people – and usually that will
indeed be the case. But, as a corrective to any such generalizations,
there is David Mamet's *Oleanna*. *Oleanna* exists both as a play and as a
film, and there is little doubt that it was in its theatrical form that it had
the greater impact. Mamet directed the film himself, and did so with a
faithfulness to the original stage play which inevitably led to the film
being criticized as too stage-bound. Not untypical was *The Washington
Post*'s complaint that 'Like most plays transferred to screen, *Oleanna*
still bears traces of grease paint. Actually, all the cold cream in the
world wouldn't make this verbose material in the least cinematic'
(Kempley 1994: n.p.). The film created little stir and its time on the
major distribution circuits was very short-lived.

On stage, however, it was one of the cultural events of the early
1990s. *Oleanna* was brought to England in 1993 by the Royal Court
Theatre, where it was directed by Harold Pinter. This English production, like its American predecessor in Cambridge and New York the
previous year, generated a great amount of debate about what it has to
say about contemporary gender politics. The play appears, in the first
act, to be about theories of education and culture, rather than about
gender. A desperate female student, on the verge of failing her course,
comes to see her professor. She is characterized, in these first moments
of the play, as naïve, earnest and rather dull.

CAROL: I did what you told me. I did, I did everything that, I read your
           book, you told me to buy your book and read it. Everything you
           say I … I do… Ev… everything I'm told.

(Mamet 1993: 9)

On one level these two characters inhabit rather stereotypical roles:
John, the powerful, authoritative, career-minded and overbearing
male, is contrasted with insecure and (initially) submissive female
student. Mamet, however, complicates his stereotypes: John does not
fit comfortably into his professional world of academia; he himself was
an academic failure as a child, and the anti-oppressive theory of

pedagogy on which he is currently making his professional reputation is founded on his own early disaffection from school.

JOHN: I came late to teaching. And I found it Artificial. The notion of 'I know and you do not'; and I saw an exploitation in the education process. I told you. I hated school, I hated teachers. I hated everyone who was in the position of a 'boss' because I knew – I didn't think, mind you, I knew I was going to fail. Because I was a fuckup. I was just no damned good.

(Mamet 1993: 22)

John's own ideology is an avowedly anti-oppressive one; he is a radical educator in the tradition of educational theorists of the 1960s and 1970s such as Ivan Illich and John Holt, whose books *Deschooling Society* (1973) and *How Children Fail* (1969) criticize traditional education as oppressive and designed to instil failure into children.

JOHN: Look. The tests, you see, which you encounter, in school, in college, in life, were designed, in the most part, for idiots. By idiots. There is no need to fail at them. They are not a test of your worth. They are a test of your ability to retain and spout back misinformation. Of course you fail them. They're nonsense... They're garbage. They're a joke. Look at me. Look at me. The Tenure Committee. The Tenure Committee. Come to judge me. The Bad Tenure Committee.
          The 'Test'. Do you see? They put me to the test. Why, they had people voting on me I wouldn't employ to wax my car.

(Mamet 1993: 23)

Carol is the precisely the kind of student John seems to have been best suited to teach. She, too, carries around with her the burden of expected failure. 'I walk around', she says, 'From morning 'til night: with this one thought in my head: I'm stupid' (Mamet 1993: 12). The paradox, however, is that John's radical theories, and his scepticism about the educational system in which Carol is trying to succeed, confuse her even more. At one point she bursts out:

CAROL: NO, NO – I DON'T UNDERSTAND. DO YOU SEE??? I DON'T UNDERSTAND...
JOHN: What?
CAROL: Any of it. Any of it. I'm smiling in class, I'm smiling the whole time. What are you talking about? What is everyone talking about? I don't understand. I don't know what it means. I don't know what it means to be here ... you tell me I'm intelligent, and then you tell me I should not be here, what do you want with me? What does it mean? Who should I listen to...

(Mamet 1993: 36)

Thus John finds himself in a contradictory position. On the one hand, his educational theories are about empowerment of the individual student. On the other hand, he is confronted by a student who feels anything but empowered – who, on the contrary, is being made to feel stupid for valuing and wanting to succeed within the education system which John himself despises. 'What can that mean?' he asks about a poorly-written sentence in the student's term paper – insulting and demeaning her in the process. Yet his intentions in his dealings with her are generous in their intent: he wants her to succeed.

At one point, employing one of the radical tactics characteristic of the 'de-schoolers', he offers to give her an A-grade for the term's work – provided she comes back to see him frequently. He offers to become her mentor, seeing in her precisely the kind of failing and disempowered student with whom he himself identifies.

JOHN:	What's important is that I awake your interest if I can, and that I answer your questions. Let's start over ...
CAROL:	But we can't start over.
JOHN:	I say we can. (*Pause*) I say we can ...
CAROL:	There are rules.
JOHN:	Well. We'll break them.
CAROL:	How can we?
JOHN:	We won't tell anybody.
CAROL:	Is that all right?
JOHN:	I say that it's fine.
CAROL:	Why would you do this for me?
JOHN:	I like you. Is that so difficult for you to...
CAROL:	Um

(Mamet 1993: 26–7)

Despite the way in which this exchange ends, there is nothing even subliminally erotic about the encounter between John and Carol. Moreover throughout the first two acts of the play, John's status as a committed (if not entirely comfortable) family man is established by references to his wife and son, and by a sub-plot which involves his negotiations to buy a new house. In fact, a series of phone calls about the house purchase punctuates his pastoral conversation with Carol, culminating in one which interrupts a moment of confidence which she appears to be about to share with him. 'I always ... all my life ... I have never told anyone this,' she says – but at that moment the telephone rings and we never hear what she had been about to confide in him. In these 'business' calls John comes across as aggressive, bullying and self-centred. His attempts to balance the roles of hard-nosed property negotiator and concerned pastoral tutor are clumsy, and in the two discourses between which he continually switches, we see some of the contradictions of his own situation. His confirmation of tenure within the system he despises will enable him to continue the upward social progress, and the benefits which that system has brought him. He is not unaware of this, and is even self-mocking about the contradictions of an educational radicalism which also involves a social conformity: 'The new house ... To go with the tenure. That's right. Nice house, close to the private school ... We were talking about economic betterment' (Mamet 1993: 33).

The first act of the play is about many kinds of power: the power of the bosses, which John identified in his own educational experiences; the radical educational theories which he espoused in order to fight those power relationships; his own resulting position of professional power within the university system; the extent to which Carol feels demeaned and degraded not only by her inability to comprehend John's academic arguments, but also by his attitude towards her and her aspirations. Even in his attempts to counter one form of educational oppression, John acts oppressively. Yet Mamet does not portray him as a hypocrite or a predator: merely as someone enmeshed in the contradictions of power relationships within a particular social, educational and economic system. There is a delicate balance struck between a liberal audience's potential sympathy for John's original principles, and its more critical awareness of the ways in which these principles are being undermined by John's words and deeds.

In an article published elsewhere (Mangan 2002) I have suggested that a significant context of *Oleanna* was the British play (and film) *Educating Rita*, by Willy Russell. While I do not want to rehearse that argument in detail again here, a brief summary of some of the main points provides a useful way of focusing in on some of the specifics of Mamet's play. There are many obvious structural and thematic similarities between the two plays. Both are two-handers set in a university, and both dramatize a crisis of authority. Both deal centrally with an encounter between a male academic and a younger female student; both plays structure this encounter through a sequence of 'tutorial' scenes, in which the primary subject is teaching, but the secondary subject is the power relationships between a man and a woman from different backgrounds. Both narratives are set entirely in the claustrophobic and highly charged environment of the academic study. Both start with a telephone conversation, and subsequent phone calls become a key structural device which charts the academics' deteriorating relationships with the world beyond the classroom. In both plays there is an off-stage feminist presence which contributes to the development of the female protagonist. And both of the male university teachers see their personal and professional lives collapse about them during the course of the narratives – although the respective tones in which the two plays stage this collapse differ radically from each other.

In fact it is generally true that the similarities which exist between the plays serve also to highlight the significant differences between them, differences which stem from and reflect the times and places which produced them. I have no proof that Mamet deliberately wrote his play as a 1990s response to Russell's benevolent parable of fulfilment. Nonetheless, a response is what it becomes. *Educating Rita* is rooted in the English debates of the 1970s and 1980s about class, culture, education and (to a lesser extent) gender. It articulates a broadly optimistic, left-wing liberal-humanist attitude towards these issues. The education of Rita to some extent redeems the teacher Frank: he offers her new ways of making sense of her life and by doing so he finds meaning in his own life. The play leaves both the liberal assumptions about culture, and the gender structures of the institutions whereby that culture is mediated, more or less where it found them, and on the whole, in Willy Russell's play, issues of gender take second place to those of class and cultural politics. While the cultural authority of the teacher is gendered as masculine, while the teacher/pupil relationship exists in counterpoint to a male/female erotic dynamic, and while the genders of these two main characters could not be reversed without seriously disrupting the meanings of the play, Russell is not primarily intent on analysing gender roles in education. In *Oleanna*, however, this gendering of authority, and its implications, is at the heart of the play. *Oleanna* takes this as its starting-point, and turns the teacher/student encounter into a play about gender politics in the university.

If *Educating Rita*'s essential structure is reassuringly comic, that of *Oleanna* is clearly tragic: John starts out on the brink of success. He is about to be granted tenure and things are generally going well for him. His encounter with Carol precipitates a total collapse of all this. It is not, however, until the second act that the conflict between Carol and John turns into confrontation, and the debate about power and education is refocused as one about gender power. Between Acts 1 and 2 a month has passed, and Carol has – to John's amazement –

brought a series of complaints against him, including that of sexual harassment. These complaints threaten his tenure, his house-buying and family life.

> I find that I am sexist. That I am elitist. I'm not sure I know what that means, other than it's a derogatory word, meaning 'bad.' That I ... That I insist on wasting time in non-prescribed, in self-aggrandising and theatrical diversions from the prescribed text ... that these have taken both sexist and porno-graphic forms ... here we find listed... (*Pause*) Here we find listed ... instances '... closeted with a student'.... 'Told a rambling, sexually explicit story... moved to embrace said student'.
>
> (Mamet 1993: 47)

The meeting between them in the first act is re-presented in terms which the audience can recognize as accurate in letter but not in spirit. John's clumsy, and often arrogant, attempts to respond to Carol on a pastoral level are figured in the complaint as deliberate abuse. For a brief period at the start of the second act, as John states his case and mounts his defence, an audience might maintain some of the generally forgiving ambivalence towards John which the first act had established: 'Well, yes, it is possible to see how his paternalistic gestures might be interpreted as sexual advances, although we can also see that that is not, surely, how they were intended. We saw that his "move to embrace said student" had been meant as a comforting gesture, not as the sexual overture which the complaint implies. On the other hand, John's radical/liberal stance is more oppressive than he believes, perhaps he does need to be taught a lesson ...' The play, however, does not allow the audience to rest in that attitude for long.

The character of Carol is presented in a completely different light from Act 2 onwards. Whereas in the first act she was rarely able to express herself with coherence, now she is articulate and aggressive. More precisely, the dramatic and cultural stereotype which she inhab-its has undergone a radical shift: from that of the Inadequate Student to that of the Aggressive Feminist. This is explained by references to the fact that Carol is now part of an unspecified 'Group' – presumably a radical feminist group – who are encouraging her in her complaint against John. Her language is now identified as being the language of that Group, and the new accents in which she speaks become more marked as the play continues. She picks John up on the unconscious and casual sexism of his language when he refers to the Tenure Committee as 'Good Men and True':

Professor, I came here as a favor. At your personal request. Perhaps I should
not have done so. But I did. On my behalf, and on my behalf of my group.
And you speak of the tenure committee, one of whose members is a woman,
as you know. And though you might call it Good Fun, or An Historical
Phrase, or An Oversight, or, All of the Above, to refer to the committee as
Good Men and True, it is a demeaning remark. It is a sexist remark, and to
overlook it is to countenance continuation of that method of thought.

(Mamet 1993: 51)

Mamet has always been recognized as a playwright with an intense
interest in language, and in particular with language and power, and
the way in which language structures reality. By Act 3 of *Oleanna*, the
linguistic stakes have been raised. Firstly, there is no language with
which John is able to respond to the charges which Carol is making
against him.

CAROL: My charges are not trivial. You see that in the haste, I think,
          with which they were accepted. A joke you have told, with a
          sexist tinge. The language you use, a verbal or physical caress,
          yes, yes, I know, you say that it is meaningless. I understand. I
          differ from you. To lay a hand on someone's shoulder.
JOHN: It was devoid of sexual content.
CAROL: I say it was not. I SAY IT WAS NOT. Don't you begin to see
          ...? Don't you begin to understand? IT'S NOT FOR YOU TO
          SAY.

(Mamet 1993: 70)

This is one of the key moments of the play. In it, Carol asserts her
claim, and is backed up by institutional procedures in doing so, to
determine what the truth of John's gesture was. It does not matter how
John intended his words or deeds; Carol claims the moral right to
represent them in her own terms, as an act of abuse. This moment,
more than any other in recent playwriting, dramatizes a collapse of
hegemonic masculinity. Hegemony, after all, is precisely the ability to
impose one's own set of interpretations on other people, and to make
them seem natural. When Carol challenges John's right to do this –
and when it turns out that her challenge is supported by the institution
– it signals that a shift has taken place in the deeper structures which
underlie John and Carol's teacher/pupil relationship.

Dramatically, the stages in this relationship between John and Carol
are structured in terms of three 'acts': the word is meant both in the
sense of dramatic division and of physical action. Each of the play's
three acts contains a single significant moment of physical contact

between the two protagonists. These moments of physicality are all the more powerful because the play is otherwise so language-based, and its physical action so constrained by the office environment in which it is set. And, as in *Masterpieces*, much hinges on the way in which an audience interprets (or is encouraged to interpret) these moments of physical contact. In Act 1 there had been John's attempt to put his arm round Carol's shoulder, which she has represented as 'a move to embrace'. At the end of Act 2, as he endeavours to talk her out of continuing with her complaint, John also attempts to prevent Carol from walking out of the room:

> CAROL   You must excuse me... (*She starts to leave the room*)
> JOHN: Sit down, it seems we have a ... Wait one moment. Wait one moment ... just do me the courtesy to... (*He restrains her from leaving*)
> CAROL: LET ME GO.
> JOHN: I have no desire to hold you. I just want to talk to you...
> CAROL: LET ME GO. LET ME GO. WOULD SOMEBODY HELP ME? WOULD SOMEBODY HELP ME PLEASE?
>
> (Mamet 1993: 56)

This action, more aggressive than the first, leads to the stakes being raised once again. The charges against John are now being made, not merely to the university authorities, but to the police. It is only at the end of play that John realizes that, as a result of this gesture, he is about to be arrested for battery and attempted rape.

Yet in the end it is not this which precipitates the final and genuinely violent confrontation between the two of them, but, once more, language: as John speaks once more into the phone, replying to his wife, Carol tells him, as a parting shot '... and don't call your wife "baby" '. It is this which finally sends John over the edge:

> (*CAROL starts to leave the room. JOHN grabs her and begins to beat her*)
> JOHN: You vicious little bitch. You think you can come in here with your political correctness and destroy my life?
> (*He knocks her to the floor*)
> After how I treated you...? You should be... Rape you...? Are you kidding me...?
> (*He picks up a chair, raises it above his head, and advances on her.*)
> I wouldn't touch you with a ten-foot pole. You little cunt ...
> (*She cowers on the floor below him. Pause. He looks down at her. He lowers the chair. He moves to his desk, and arranges the papers on it. Pause. He looks over at her*)
> ... well...
> (*Pause. She looks at him*)

CAROL: Yes. That's right.

(Mamet 1993: 79–80)

The action, of course, is devastating. But so is the language – not only in John's use of the explosive word 'cunt', which signals his final collapse into unmitigated misogyny, but also in the previous line about 'political correctness'. This is a phrase which the play has studiously avoided up to this point. Its use at this point states the obvious, perhaps, but when it is finally articulated, the dichotomy which John has resisted for so long is finally established. It has taken a long time but war has finally been declared – with John as brutal misogynist finally face to face with the powers of political correctness. Carol's 'Yes, that's right' is a bleak vindication. The oppression, the brutality with which she charged him, has finally emerged. What she sees in his act of violence is the fulfilment of the prophecy which her charges against him constituted.

The play has been seen as a direct comment on Mamet's part on a high-profile academic legal case which had just happened in America – the Clarence Thomas confirmation hearings – and which bore certain similarities to the plot of *Oleanna* (Klaus et al. 1995: 1308). More generally, it is read as Mamet's response to the climate of 'political correctness' in the US academy, and the ensuing paranoia which was engendered among male academics at the time. Mamet's own claim is that the play is not really about sexual politics or political correctness at all.

> I never really saw it as a play about sexual harassment. I think the issue was, to a large extent, a flag of convenience for a play that's structured as a tragedy. Just like the issues of race relations and xenophobia are flags of convenience for *Othello* … [*Oleanna*] is a tragedy about power … The points Carol makes about power and privilege – I believe them all. If I didn't believe them, the play wouldn't work as well. It is a play about two people, and each person's view is correct. Yet they end up destroying each other.
>
> (Mamet 1995: 52–3)

That the forum in which Mamet expressed this defence of his play was the men's magazine *Playboy* should not itself, perhaps, impugn it. The context, however, is not irrelevant. Mamet seeks, in a publication which is anything but feminist, to distance himself from the implication that he is simply acting as a spokesperson for the threatened male in the sex wars. He also insists that the play's relationship to the Clarence Thomas case is purely coincidental, that indeed he began work on it before the Thomas hearings, and then laid it aside because he was having trouble with the last act (Walker 1997: 150).

But Mamet's reading of his own play is not entirely convincing. Certainly the play is 'a tragedy about power', but then sexual harassment *is* about power. Mamet also oversimplifies the issue by presenting the play as being far more balanced than it actually is. In *Oleanna* John and Carol do not 'destroy each other': John is destroyed and Carol is not. It is not just about two correct views: it is about what people *do* with those views.

Responses to the play tended to hinge upon how critics and audiences felt about the character of Carol. Peter Lewis, for example, writing in the *Guardian* soon after the play's UK premiere, supported her stand against John:

> I agree [with Carol]; the meaning of a message isn't totally controlled by its sender – the receiver's interpretation is equally valid. We are not just 'ourselves', we cannot escape being also members of a social or ethnic group, perhaps a profession, certainly men or women. In that sense, it wasn't just John browbeating and touching Carol, it was an expression of patriarchal and institutional power.
>
> (Lewis in Anthony et al. 1993: 2)

Lewis, however, was in the minority. Audiences rarely found much to sympathize with in what they saw as Carol's relentless and vindictive pursuit of John's destruction. A more representative response was that of Louise Chunn: '[Carol] is initially insecure and frustrated. But by the end she's a doctrinaire, cold-blooded bitch. A monster of Mamet's making' (Anthony et al. 1993: 2). In presenting Carol in the way he does, Mamet destroys any subtlety which he claims for the play's analysis of power. Ann Karpf, responding to Pinter's UK production, pinpointed the problem:

> Mamet's view is that feminists are deforming personal relationships. But personal relationships have always been inflected by social norms: it's just that most men never noticed it before.
>
> I went to see the play thinking Mamet had dramatised a debate between two viewpoints. What I found was the trouncing of one ideology by another. Mamet is anything but even-handed in his treatment of the characters and issues. He utterly discredits the student who accuses her professor of sexual harassment ...
>
> (Karpf in Anthony et al. 1993: 2)

Thus Carol becomes an outright villain, and to that extent the play turns into an anti-feminist polemic. Mamet – in whose work questions of gender and in particular questions about masculinity have always been a central theme – would probably not accept Karpf's general attribution to him of the naïve belief that 'feminists are deforming personal relationships'. Indeed, in many of his essays he has dealt quite subtly with gender relationships in a post-feminist world (see, for example, Mamet 1989: 22). Certainly, the play was not intended simply as a backlash diatribe against feminism. But like John, Mamet is subject to the fact that the meaning of the message is not simply determined by the sender. And in this case the message became understood as a decidedly anti-feminist one. It was read (by both men and women) as a *cri de coeur* of the embattled, beleaguered and disempowered male. In several of the performances at the Royal Court, the moment at the end of the play when John strikes Carol was greeted with applause from an audience (or a section of the audience) who interpreted it as an act of heroic male resistance to Carol's tyranny (Anthony et al. 1993: 2). Geoffrey Wheatcroft, writing in the *Guardian*, reported that at performances of the play in New York, 'there was said to have been fighting between men and women in the aisles', adding, disturbingly, that 'I don't think any man can yet have watched *Oleanna* without a silent cheer at the denouement when John turns on his tormentor' (Wheatcroft 1993: 22). Thus, whatever Mamet's intentions, the effect of his play, or perhaps of Pinter's production, was to provoke, in some audiences, an act of symbolic, suppressed or actual violence against women.

Oleanna addresses a fear, which was frequently articulated in American universities in the 1990s, concerning the potentially totalitarian effects of political correctness: in Act 3 Carol offers to withdraw charges against John in exchange for his rewriting the course book-list in order to exclude any texts – including his own – of which her Group disapproves. It also portrays a world in which the traditional structures of masculine authority from which John has benefited no longer work. To this extent the profession of the university teacher is being used as an Everyman figure in an allegory of the late twentieth-century crisis in masculinity, struggling (and failing) to come to terms with the implications of the feminist intellectual revolutions of the 1970s and 1980s. These implications do not involve a major shift towards actual material and professional equality: the Tenure Committee which is about to judge John contains only one woman, and it seems that the most senior academic positions are still largely a masculine prerogative. But power can operate in many different ways, and the way which most directly affects John is the realization that he does not even own his own intentions. For the scholar, the academic, used to seeing himself as an independent intellect, in control and in charge of his own thoughts, motives and world-view, this amounts to a particularly intense crisis: Mamet's instinct to set his confrontation of the sexes in the professional world of academia was a good one.

The play is, as Mamet says, a tragedy about power. It is also a tragedy of subjectivity: John starts with one understanding of himself and is then faced with another. The world of academia is a world of competing interpretations, and in this context power is defined by the extent to which one interpretation prevails over another. *Oleanna* shows the irony of this in action. John is interpreted as an oppressive misogynist, and so that eventually is what he becomes.

7.3.2   Cavemen and other defendants

David Thomas's backlash book *Not Guilty,* which was mentioned above, has not one subtitle but two. They are, respectively, *In Defence of the Modern Man* and *Men: the Case for the Defence*; between them they give a clear indication of the ideological framework within which the author operates.. Compare the rhetoric of Thomas's titles with that of Rob Becker and Mark Little's *Defending the Caveman,* which, as I wrote the first draft of this chapter in 1999, was in the middle of a successful West End run at the Apollo Theatre, and which is currently (2001–2) in the middle of a popular post-London provincial tour. Actor Mark Little puts on a one-man show in order to celebrate the man behaving – not badly so much as blokeishly. The explicit aim is to defend the modern male from the opprobrium of masculinity with the weapon of humour. Its premise, with which the audience is invited to agree, is that it is men, in the late twentieth century, who are oppressed and disempowered. It starts by charting the speaker's own attempts to construct a masculinity in response to 1970s feminism, desperately attempting to become 'sensitive' in the way demanded of him by the women in his life:

> So men would have these conversations with each other, you know 'I'm really sensitive.' 'Yeah? Well, I'm more sensitive than you.' 'Yeah? Well, I'm a lot less competitive than you!'
>
> (Becker/Little: transcript from live show)

The crisis point is the realization in the 1990s by Becker and Little that, according to his women friends, 'there are two genders: women and arseholes'. The rest of the evening is a humorous explanation of why men are not really 'arseholes' – or, as the Apollo's publicity material explains rather more grandly, an exploration of the question,

> Why do men and women misunderstand each other? The truth of course, can be traced back to THE CAVEMAN. This hilariously funny, but horribly truthful show brings the basic differences between men and women brilliantly up to date. Mark Little – much loved top comedian and TV star (Joe Mangel in *Neighbours* and co-presenter of the *Big Breakfast*) stars in the UK premiere of this witty and wise new comedy.
> If you're married see this show! If you're dating see this show! If you're single you need to see this show!
>
> (Publicity material, Apollo Theatre, London 1999;
> quoted on *Defending the Caveman* website)

The customary quotations from the critics are appended, including the following:

> 'Absolutely brilliant! should be seen by anyone who wants to understand the opposite sex' – John Gray, author of *Men are from Mars, Women are from Venus*
>
> (Publicity material, Apollo Theatre, London 1999;
> quoted on *Defending the Caveman* website)

John Gray's imprimatur is important: a best-selling author, his *Men are from Mars, Women are from Venus* (1992) is probably the best-known popular response of recent years to the gender problematizing of the late twentieth century, a response which interprets the failure to communicate between the sexes as being caused by essential biological as well as cultural differences between men and women. The programme for the Apollo production of *Defending the Caveman* makes the link between the show and the book even more explicit by quoting a large extract of *Men are from Mars,* and the show itself virtually amounts to a comic variation and fugue on the basic theme by Gray. The basic thesis is that the differences between men and women can be traced back to the earliest roots of human development.

> It goes back to the beginning of time. The image of the caveman is that of a guy bopping a woman on the head and dragging her back to his cave. But no serious anthropologist believes that ... The caveman, to me, became a symbol of man being misunderstood ... Men were hunters; women were gatherers. The hunter locks in on one thing, which is why guys have a narrow focus, whether it's watching TV, reading the newspaper or driving. They block everything else out because, as hunters, they had to focus on the

rear end of an animal. On the other hand, women, as gatherers, had to take
in the whole landscape. Their field of vision is wider.

(Becker 1994, on Cavemania website)

Defending the Caveman is an important theatrical text not because
it has new insights but because, on the contrary, it repeats old com-
monplaces. It links the old anthropological cliché of the hunter/gath-
erer with some slightly more recent popular evolutionary psychology,
and frames it within the discourse theories of *Men are from Mars*. The
show has only the most minimal of narrative structures. Becker
claims to have based it upon Joseph Campbell's classic of popular
anthropology, *The Hero with a Thousand Faces* (1949), a comparative
study of the hero- and quest-myths of cultures worldwide, which has
become essential reading for psychotherapists engaged in questions
of masculinity, and for screenwriters trying to sell a script to George
Lucas. It is true that there are the occasional gestures towards some
of the mythic patterns of rituals, journeys, trials, and shamanistic
encounters with sages. Essentially, however, this is little more than
the framework upon which to build an extended stand-up routine,
allowing the modern-day speaker a chance to pass judgements and
make observations on a variety of topics, such as why men hog the
TV remote control, why women want to talk about feelings, the difference between the ways in which men and women express themselves ('Women can say, "You're my oldest and dearest friend". A
guy will say, "Still driving that piece of s—?" It means the same
thing') and a range of other stereotypical conflicts between the sexes.
All of this is presented, largely by means of one-liners such as the
above, in the service of the thesis which Becker shares with Gray: that
there are essential genetic and evolutionary reasons for the differences between men and women, and that communication between
the sexes can be improved once both 'sides' accept these differences
rather than judging each other according to each one's own,
inevitably gender-based and gender-biased, criteria.

Mark Little was a canny casting choice for this play as far as audiences in the UK are concerned. As the publicity material indicates, the
actor and comedian was first introduced to British audiences as Joe
Mangel, in the redoubtable Australian TV soap opera *Neighbours* – a
character which already encoded some gender messages relevant to
Defending the Caveman, since Joe had a good deal of the Neanderthal
male about him already. Little went on to consolidate this 'blokeish'
persona when, briefly, he presented *The Big Breakfast* for Channel 4 in
the early 1990s, and now, in the 'legitimate' theatrical cultural milieu of

the West End and large-scale provincial touring bases, he is able to draw on the gender capital established earlier in his career. And of course, as an Australian actor in Britain, his nationality becomes an important part of this gender identity, since it plays into the common British cultural cliché, perpetuated by that most contemporary of art forms, the lager advert. According to this stereotype, the Australian male is one of the last bastions of old-fashioned unreconstructed 'masculinity': that is to say, he is primarily interested in beer, sport and being with his mates, he sees women as existing only for the purposes of sexual gratification and domestic chores, and 'sensitivity' as something for 'poofters'.

But the British/Australian axis is only secondary to *Defending the Caveman*, the authorship of which is a complex issue. In the Apollo programme Mark Little records his thanks to 'Rob Becker the writer and Erin Becker for giving him licence to make the play his own' (p. 13). In fact, the show began as a comedic vehicle for Becker, a Californian comedian who developed it out of his own stand-up act. Since neither the American nor the British script has been published, it is not possible to tell exactly where Becker's original material begins and ends, apart from obvious moments such as Little's occasional references to his own career in *Neighbours* and *The Big Breakfast*. The show started life in San Francisco in 1991, toured nationally in the USA, and then, having opened on 26 March 1995 at the Helen Hayes Theater on Broadway, went on to break box-office records by running for more than 400 performances and becoming the longest-running solo play in Broadway history. The day of its record-breaking achievement, 18 July 1996, was proclaimed 'Caveman Day' by the then Mayor of New York City, Rudolph Giuliani, who also renamed New York's West 44th Street 'Caveman Way'. The play's Broadway run finally ended almost a year later, in June 1997, when it began a national tour; parallel productions were mounted not only in London's West End but also, simultaneously, in South Africa. In the London production, Mark Little incorporated, with Becker's approval, material to make the show his own.

While making allowances for the nature of theatrical hype, Becker's own words state his sense of the play's importance:

> We've had grandparents, parents and their married children come to the show together, people in work boots sitting next to college professors, and many many marriage counselors. What blows me away is how touched people say they are. Many women have told me that, thanks to the show, they've fallen in love with their husbands all over again. Men have told me

that the show explains them to their spouses in ways they've never quite
been able to articulate before.

> (Becker, quoted by Simi Horowitz in *Theater Week*
> and reproduced on *Cavemania* website)

I think the show gives people a way to understand themselves and their
partners while they're laughing and I think some healing takes place when a
couple sits in a darkened theater, laughing with hundreds of other couples,
realizing they're not alone.

> (Becker, quoted by John Wolfe in *Playbill*
> and reproduced on *Cavemania* website)

The play, it seems, acts as a love potion, a philosopher and healer. And
whatever we may think about the writer's claims regarding his show, it
does seem – as the actions of the Mayor of New York City attest – that
the play has indeed attained a cultural importance independent of any
judgements of its artistic merit. Giving one's name to a day *and* a New
York street are no mean achievements for a play. But just in case it
seems *too* solemn, too sensitive, too worthy, one critic adds:

> Don't let the high-falutin' thoughts fool you. It's all jolly and lighthearted.
> (Simi Horowitz, review in *Theater Week*
> and reproduced on *Cavemania* website)

Defending the Caveman succesfully locates itself simultaneously within
two discourses. On the one hand it draws on the discourse of late twentieth-century gender theory, in which it claims to make an intervention. This intervention, as Becker insists, is not merely on the level of
ideas: he claims that the play can intervene in peoples' lives and con-
tribute positively to their relationships, making them happier, better
adjusted, more in love with each other. Nor do we have to take his
word alone for it; we have already seen that John Gray's commenda-
tion was used in the British (and American) publicity for the play.
Equally important is that of Anna Beth Benningfield, President of the
American Association of Marriage and Family Therapists, quoted in
the play's publicity as saying 'When I saw *Defending the Caveman*, I
knew I had a new homework assignment for my couples in therapy'
(cited on *Cavemania* website).

On the other hand, *Defending the Caveman* also relates to the discourse of 'showbiz', and in particular that of stand-up comedy. But
stand-up comedy is itself an aggressively masculine form of
performance. By this I mean not that there are no female stand-up
comics – although their emergence in Western culture is a compara-

tively recent thing. But it is a form for which women have had to work particularly hard to find a place – and, in many cases, managing to do so only at the cost of adopting a masculine style of performance (see Gray 1994: 117–19 and 133–42). Paradoxically, the stand-up comedian addressing an audience effectively offers that audience a form which is akin to a sermon, and the access of women to the pulpit, to the privileged public place from which it is possible to speak with authority, has always been limited. On a more pragmatic level, stand-up is a form which derives initially from music-halls, vaudeville theatres and working-men's clubs which catered to an overwhelmingly male audiences: consequently it was traditionally able to rely on a misogynist staple of routines about fat, lazy or unattractive wives, mothers-in-law and sex-objects. And on yet another level the man with the microphone has a particularly phallic potency: as the much-used gag on the alternative comedy circuit of the 1980s put it: 'Why do you think they call it "stand-up"?'

Thus the theatrical discourse interacts with the theoretical discourse in a very specific way – establishing a relationship between the speaker and the audience which is itself effectively gendered. Masculine in its orientation, and sanctioned by generations of masculine humour, the caveman's stand-up routine can speak the language of essentialist gender theory in the accents of showbiz, taking itself seriously, but always with the potential get-out clause that it's all 'jolly and light-hearted'.

The show's publicity machine continually describes its effect on the audience in terms of overcoming the misunderstandings which exist between the sexes. As well as Becker's own remarks quoted above, reviewers continually stress the show's *lack* of aggression.

> Becker sends you out of the theater with a smile on your face. You feel less alone. Couples who were arguing before the performance stroll out into the night afterward holding hands. You know there's going to be some serious snuggling going on when they get home. Seems to me that's well worth the price of admission.
>
> (Leslie Bennetts, review in *Variety*,
> and reproduced on *Cavemania* website)

Here a further theatrical commonplace is being mobilized – the notion that comedy is essentially about reconciliation, about bringing people together. This benevolent, non-threatening tone of *Caveman* is integral to its ideological position. Its rhetorical aim is to reassure people of the 'naturalness' of the old traditional gender order, to celebrate that order in so far as the opposition between masculine and feminine behaviour patterns is concerned, to demonstrate the depth of the roots of these patterns by reference to prehistoric hunter/gatherer societies, and to reconcile both the men and the women in the audience not only to each other but also to the inevitability of these differences, and to do so in a spirit of good humour rather than antagonism and judgement.

Within its own terms *Defending the Caveman* has been hugely successful, with British audiences and critics as well as with American. 'There is more good sense here than you would get from hours of counselling from Relate ... it is often uproariously funny ... a show of real humanity', approved the *Daily Telegraph*. 'I succumbed to the show's good nature, as did those around me. We all recognised something of ourselves in its observant humour', agreed *The Times* (cited in Albemarle website 2001). The play's whole aim is not to challenge the traditional, prefeminist gender order) but to enable people to accommodate themselves to it. It says, 'Men are like this, Women are like that – and that's how it should be.' For the majority of heterosexual couples this may well be a reassuring message.

But if couples do indeed emerge from *Caveman* holding hands and heading home for some 'serious snuggling', it is not because society in the 1990s as a whole has satisfactorily answered the questions about gender identity posed by the 1960s, 1970s and 1980s, but because a particular play has had a successful rhetorical effect on its audiences. The rhetoric of *Defending the Caveman* is a rhetoric of absolution, and seen from the right angle, it suggests, the gender differences which cause so much misunderstanding turn out to be just a matter of perspective. Nobody is to blame, neither men nor women. It is an optimistic message, and, clearly, to many of its audiences it is a very reassuring one. It also – conveniently enough – contrives to ignore an entire history of male oppression. Moreover there is an underlying problem with *Caveman*'s insistence on reconciliation through the recognition of essential differences: it slips all too easily from a reassuring message about what *is*, to a prescription about what *should be*. There is something, in the end, totalizing about the gender ideology, however affably presented, of the show. There is no room here for any alternative constructions of gender – no suggestion, even, that there are adequate constructions of masculinity other than the taciturn 'Still-driving-that-heap-of-shit?' variety. The gruffly heterosexual paradigm is paramount and inflexible, and its languages are set in stone. Even the most mainstream gay or lesbian identities are made invisible by the Becker/Little paradigm, and – as the otherwise approving review in the *Daily Telegraph* noted with some concern –

'homosexual men ... don't even merit a mention' in the play (cited in Albemarle website 2001).

As *Defending the Caveman* demonstrates, the theatrical text does not stand by itself. It engages with and relates to a variety of other texts, contexts and/or discourses, and it depends for its meaning upon the gender debates which surround it in the late twentieth century, from the radical feminist critiques of the previous decade through to the protests of David Thomas and the reassurances of John Gray. These texts and contexts are, now more than ever, international and intercultural in their scope, and are heavily dependent upon the media of television and film, whose images now set the agenda for the way in which theatre stages masculinity. Thus the West End production of *Caveman* mobilizes a British reading of Australian male identity as part of its overt message: Mark Little's well-established 'Ocker' TV persona is as important a part of the meaning of *Caveman* – to a British audience at least – as are the lines he delivers. At the same time, the show's meaning is to be found not only in the words spoken, but in the whole range of semiotic codes both theatrical and non-theatrical; consequently the experience of the show is framed by elements which have by now been incorporated into its mythology: its Broadway success, its 'adoption' by New York ('Caveman Way'), and the seal of approval given to it by several prominent members of the counselling profession. Moreover, the theatrical text does not merely 'reflect' the conflicts and ideological positions to be found in these other texts and discourses, but of necessity negotiates a new relationship with them, one which draws on the strengths, and is constrained by the limitations, of the performance conventions of its time and genre: *Caveman* mobilizes the 'masculine' codes of stand-up comedy in order to position itself in a particular way in terms of its explanation of gender relationships. It is a way which leaves little room for alternatives.

7.4 Crises? What crises?

It seems to have become more or less accepted in recent theatre criticism that the 1990s was the decade of plays by men and about masculinity:

> While in the eighties it was plays by women that headed new writing, and often made cutting-edge experiments in form, by the nineties the fad was for boys' plays ... [T]he advent of boys' plays was partly a reaction – by both media and theatre managements – to the women's plays of the eighties. ...

As Ian Rickson, Stephen Daldry's successor at the Court, says: 'One of the most important issues of the late twentieth century has been the crisis in masculinity – in the workplace and the family – and that's why there's been a lot of boys' plays.'

(Sierz: 2000: 153–4)

Both *Oleanna* and *Defending the Caveman* address directly that sense of crisis in contemporary masculinity to which Rickson points. They are, in their own ways, very different responses to what in recent years has become a sociological commonplace:

Masculinity in Western society is in deep crisis. The masculine gender has all kinds of benefits, but it also acts as a mask, a disguise, and what in psychotherapy is called a 'false self'. But who are we behind the false self? ... [M]any men are haunted by feelings of emptiness, impotence and rage. They feel abused, unrecognized by modern society. While manhood offers compensations and prizes, it can also bring with it emotional autism, emptiness and despair.

(Horrocks 1994: 1)

Educational achievement, crime figures, health figures and suicide rates have been the most commonly used statistical indicators of the crisis. Figures and conclusions like the following have been widely quoted:

In 1991, 886 women committed suicide in Great Britain. In the same year, 3,007 men committed suicide in Great Britain. Seventy-seven per cent of all suicides were male ... Since the early 1980s the rate of female suicide has nearly halved. Since the early 1980s the rate of male suicide has gone up by approximately 5 per cent. Similar patterns apply to America and Australia.

(Thomas 1993: 1)

and

Males are less likely than their female counterparts to achieve the independence, responsibility and maturity associated with adulthood by the age of 25. They tend ... to be dependent rather than independent, to have an absence of responsibility for themselves and others, and to remain with their family of origin rather than forming a family of their own.

(Audit Commission 1996: 23)

The causes of the crisis have been debated from a variety of ideological positions. Some of the emerging explanations, on their own or in combination with already existing social or political configurations, gathered popularity and support to the extent that they led to the formation of socially active groups whose aim was specifically to address issues of importance to men. The men's movement was never a mono-lithic organization speaking with a single voice. Rather, it comprised from the start a wide range of viewpoints and ideologies. Its main trends – and divisions – have been surveyed and analysed by Kenneth Clatterbaugh in his admirably comprehensive overview of contempo-rary theories of masculinity, in which he outlines eight major perspec-tives: the conservative perspective, the profeminist perspective, the 'men's rights' perspective, the mythopoetic perspective, the socialist perspective, the gay male perspective, the African-American men's perspective, and the evangelical Christian perspective (Clatterbaugh 1997). These perspectives offer a range of conflicting interpretations of the current crisis in masculinities, and of conflicting strategies for change. Its agenda was set by the women's movement of the 1960s and 1970s, but the men's movement was always divided in the responses which it offered to the questions posed by feminism; they range from a complete endorsement of feminist gender critiques through to back-lash misogyny, from the anguish of *Oleanna* to the bonhomie of *Defending the Caveman*.

One of the by-products of the men's movement(s) was an increased interest in the history of men and the issues which most concern them. Whereas the initial impulse had been to identify and respond to the current crisis of masculinity in late-capitalist society, a second wave of studies began to introduce a historical dimension and to see similar patterns in the past. This book comes out of that interest in history, which problematized the contemporary notion of crisis by introducing the possibility that each generation may be subject to its own crisis in masculinity. As I have attempted to show throughout this book, the theatre has always been responding to the recurring crises which constitute the very notion(s) of masculinity. Since gender identity is largely socially constructed, then as societies themselves evolve and develop, gender identities will undergo corresponding continual redefinition. We may indeed be experiencing a current crisis in masculinities, but there is no single stable anterior position against which this contemporary crisis is to be measured, no Edenic state from which modern masculinity has fallen. On the contrary, it now seems, crisis and anxiety are rather the conditions of masculinity itself (Breitenberg 1996).

Yet that, too, suggests a form of essentialism which I would want to resist. Certain themes and tropes, of course, may reappear with regu-larity. However, any search for a 'deep masculine' – a transhistorical and transcultural masculine gender identity which is universally true –

is self-defeating, whatever terms it is couched in. Gender identity is never truly stable, not even in the crises and anxieties which it experiences about its own instability. Its terms are continually being redefined and renegotiated, the gender performance continually being restaged. As to the more specific question of how central a place the live theatre will have in this staging in the future: that remains to be seen.

Bibliography

Primary sources: dramatic texts

Barrie, J. M., *The Definitive Edition of the Plays*, ed. A. E. Wilson, revised edn (London: Hodder and Stoughton, 1948).

Bevington, David (ed.), *Medieval Drama* (Boston, MA: Houghton Mifflin, 1975).

Daniels, Sarah, *Masterpieces* (London: Methuen, 1984).

Etherege, George, *The Man of Mode*, ed. John Barnard (London and New York, 1984; A. & C. Black and W. W. Norton, 1997).

Euripides, *The Bacchae and Other Plays*, trans. Philip Vellacott (Harmondsworth: Penguin, 1972).

Fletcher, John, *The Woman's Prize, or The Tamer Tamed*, in Daniel Fischlin and Mark Fortier (eds), *Adaptations of Shakespeare: A Critical Anthology of Plays from the Seventeenth Century to the Present* (London and New York: Routledge, 2000).

Gay, John, *The Beggar's Opera*, ed. Edgar V. Roberts (London: Edward Arnold, 1969).

Godber, John, *Five Plays: Bouncers, Teechers, Up 'n' Under, September in the Rain, and Happy Jack* (Harmondsworth: Penguin, 1989).

Happé, Peter (ed.), *English Mystery Plays* (Harmondsworth: Penguin, 1975).

Ibsen, Henrik, *An Enemy of the The People, The Wild Duck and Rosmersholm*, trans. James McFarlane (Oxford and New York: Oxford University Press, 1988).

Ibsen, Henrik, *Four Major Plays: A Doll's House, Hedda Gabler, and The Master Builder*, trans. James McFarlane (Oxford and New York: Oxford University Press, 1991).

Jones, Henry Arthur and Herman, Henry, *Breaking a Butterfly* (London: private printing, 1884).

Lillo, George, *The London Merchant*, ed. William H. McBurney (London: Edward Arnold, 1965).

Lillo, George, *The Dramatic Works of George Lillo*, ed. James L. Steffensen (Oxford: Clarendon Press, 1993).

Mamet, David, *Oleanna* (London: Methuen, 1993).

Osborne, John, *Look Back in Anger* (London: Faber, 1957, 1973).

Russell, Willy, *Educating Rita, Stags and Hens, and Blood Brothers: Two Plays and a Musical* (London: Methuen, 1986).

Shakespeare, William, *The Complete Works*, ed. Stanley Wells and Gary Taylor (Oxford: Clarendon Press, 1986).

Shaw, George Bernard, *Plays: Mrs Warren's Profession, Arms and the Man, Candida, Man and Superman*, with a Foreword by Eric Bentley (New York: Signet Classic, 1960).

Storey, David, *The Changing Room* (London: Cape, 1972).

Strindberg, August, *Plays One*, trans. and ed. Michael Meyer (London: Methuen, 1976).

Wilmot, John, Earl of Rochester, *Sodom*, ed. L. S. A. M. von Romer (Paris: H. Welter, 1904).

Wilmot, John, Earl of Rochester, *Complete Poems and Plays*, ed. Paddy Lyons (London: Dent, 1993).

Wycherley, William, *The Country Wife and Other Plays*, ed. Peter Dixon (Oxford: Oxford University Press, 1996).

Secondary sources: general

Aristotle, *Poetics*, trans. S. H. Butcher, ed. Francis Fergusson (New York: Hill and Wang, 1961).

Atkinson, Rita L., Atkinson, Richard, Smith, Edward E., and Bem, Daryl J., *Introduction to Psychology*, 11th edn (Fort Worth: Harcourt Brace, 1993).

Auerbach, Eric, *Mimesis*, trans. Willard R. Trask (Princeton, NJ: Princeton University Press, 1953).

Austin, Gayle, *Feminist Theories for Dramatic Criticism* (Ann Arbor, MI: University of Michigan Press, 1990).

Barthelemy, Anthony G., *Black Face, Maligned Race: The Representation of Blacks in English Drama from Shakespeare to Southerne* (Baton Rouge, LA and London: Louisiana State University Press, 1987).

Berger, Maurice, with Brian Wallis and Simon Watson, *Constructing Masculinity* (New York and London: Routledge, 1995).

Bly, Robert, *Iron John* (New York: Addison-Wesley, 1990).

Boone, Joseph, and Cadden, Michael (eds), *Engendering Men* (New York and London: Routledge, 1990).

Bornstein, Kate, *Gender Outlaw* (New York: Routledge, 1993).

Bristow, Joseph, *Sexuality* (London and New York: Routledge, 1997).

Brockett, Oscar G., *History of the Theatre* (Boston and London: Allyn and Bacon, 1991).

Brown, Ann, *Apology to Women: Christian Images of the Female Sex* (Leicester: Inter-Varsity Press, 1991).

Butler, Judith, *Gender Trouble: Feminism and the Subversion of Identity* (New York and London: Routledge, 1990).

Case, Sue-Ellen, *Feminism and Theatre* (Basingstoke: Palgrave Macmillan, 1988).

Chase, Cynthia, 'Oedipal Textuality: Reading Freud's Reading of *Oedipus*', *diacritics* IX, 1 (March 1979) 54–68.

Child, Francis J., *English and Scottish Popular Ballad* (New York: Dover, 1965).

Clark, Keith (ed.), *Contemporary Black Men's Fiction and Drama* (Urbana, IL: University of Illinois Press, 2001).

Clatterbaugh, Kenneth, *Contemporary Perspectives on Masculinity: Men, Women and Politics in Modern Society* (Boulder, CO: Westview Press, 1997).

Connell, Bob, *Masculinities* (Cambridge: Polity Press, 1995).

Craig, Steve (ed.), *Men, Masculinity and the Media* (California and London: Sage Press, 1992).

David, D. and Brannon, R., 'The Male Sex Role: Our Culture's Blueprint of Manhood and What it's Done for us Lately', in D. David and R. Brannon (eds), *The Forty-nine Percent Majority* (Reading, MA: Addison-Wesley, 1976).

de Jongh, Nicholas, *Not in Front of the Audience: Homosexuality on Stage* (New York and London: Routledge, 1992).

Dolan, Jill, *The Feminist Spectator as Critic* (Ann Arbor, MI: University of Michigan Press, 1988).

Easthope, Antony, *What a Man's Gotta Do*: *The Masculine Myth in Popular Culture* (London: Paladin 1986).

Finney, Gail, *Women in Modern Drama* (Ithaca, NY and London: Cornell University Press, 1989).

Foucault, Michel, *Discipline and Punish: The Birth of the Prison,* trans. Alan Sheridan (New York: Vintage Books, 1979).

Foucault, Michel, *The History of Sexuality,* 3 vols, trans. Robert Hurley (Harmondsworth: Penguin, 1981).

Freud, Sigmund, *The Essentials of Psychoanalysis,* trans. James Strachey, selected, with an Introduction and Commentaries by Anna Freud (Harmondsworth: Penguin, 1986).

Gilmore, David, *Manhood in the Making: Cultural Concepts of Masculinity* (New Haven, CT: Yale University Press, 1990).

Goodman, Lizbeth and de Gay, Jane, *The Routledge Reader in Gender and Performance* (London and New York: Routledge, 1998).

Goux, Jean-Joseph, 'The Phallus: Masculine Identity and the "Exchange of Women" ', *differences: a Journal of Feminist Cultural Studies* IV, 1 (Spring 1992) 40–75.

Gray, Frances, *Women and Laughter* (Basingstoke: Palgrave Macmillan, 1994).

Gray, John, *Men are from Mars, Women are from Venus: A Practical Guide for Improving Communication and Getting What You Want in your Relationships* (New York: HarperCollins 1992).

Green, J. R., *Theatre in Ancient Greek Society* (London and New York: Routledge, 1994).

Halberstam, Judith, *Female Masculinity* (Durham, NC, and London: Duke University Press, 1998).

Haraway, Donna, *Modest Witness @ Second Millennium: FemaleMan meets OncoMouse. Feminism and Technoscience* (New York and London: Routledge, 1997).

Harris, Ian M., *Messages Men Hear: Constructing Masculinities* (London: Taylor and Francis, 1995).

Hartnoll, Phyllis, *The Theatre,* 3rd edn (London: Thames and Hudson, 1998).

Harvey, Sir Paul (ed.), *The Oxford Companion to English Literature*, 4th edn, rev. Dorothy Eagle (Oxford: Clarendon Press, 1969).

Hearn, Jeff and Morgan, David (eds), *Men, Masculinities and Social Theory* (London: Unwin Hyman, 1990).

Horrocks, Roger, *Masculinity in Crisis: Myths, Fantasies and Realities* (Basingstoke: Palgrave Macmillan 1994).

Horrocks, Roger, *Male Myths and Icons: Masculinity in Popular Culture* (Basingstoke: Palgrave Macmillan 1995).

Jewett, Paul H., *Man as Male and Female* (Grand Rapids, MI: Eerdmans, 1975).

Kimmel, Michael S. and Messner, Michael A., *Men's Lives*, 3rd edn (Boston, MA: Allyn and Bacon, 1995).

Kipling, Rudyard, *Gunga Din and Other Favourite Poems* (New York: Dover, 1990).

Kirkham, Pat and Thumin, Janet (eds), *You Tarzan: Masculinity, Movies and Men* (London: Lawrence andWishart, 1993).

Klaus, C. H. with Gilbert, Miriam and Field, Bradford S. Jr, (eds), *Stages of Drama: Classical to Contemporary Theatre*, 3rd edn (New York: St Martin's, 1995).

Krutnik, Frank, *In a Lonely Street: Film Noir, Genre, Masculinity* (London and New York: Routledge, 1991).

Lacan, Jacques, *The Four Fundamental Concepts of Psycho-analysis*, trans. Alan Sheridan, ed. Jacques-Alain Miller (Harmondsworth: Penguin, 1979).

Lacan, Jacques, *Écrits: A Selection*, trans. Alan Sheridan, 2nd edn (London: Routledge, 1979).

Mac An Ghaill, Máirtín (ed.), *Understanding Masculinities: Social Relations and Cultural Arenas* (Buckingham: Open University Press, 1996).

MacInnes, James, *The End of Masculinity* (Buckingham and Philadelphia: Open University Press, 1998).

Moore, Robert and Gillette, D., *King Warrior, Magician Lover: Rediscovering the Archetypes of the Mature Masculine* (San Francisco, CA: HarperCollins, 1990).

Mulvey, Laura, *Visual and Other Pleasures* (Basingstoke: Palgrave Macmillan, 1989).

Neale, Steve, 'Masculinity as Spectacle: Reflections on Men and Mainstream Media', in Steven Cohan and Ina Rae Hark (eds), *Screening the Male: Exploring Masculinities in Hollywood Cinema* (London and New York: Routledge, 1993).

Neibaur, James L., *Tough Guy: the American Movie Macho* (Jefferson, NC: McFarland, 1989).

Padel, Ruth, *I'm a Man: Sex, Gods and Rock and Roll* (London: Faber and Faber, 2000).

Paglia, Camille, *Sexual Personae* (Harmondsworth: Penguin, 1990)

Pease, Allan and Pease, Barbara, *Why Men Don't Listen and Women Can't Read Maps: How We're Different and What to Do about It* (London: Orion-PTI, 1999).

Penley, Constance and Willis, Sharon (eds), *Male Trouble* (Minneapolis: University of Minnesota Press, 1993).

Restack, Richard, *The Brain* (New York: Warner Books/Doubleday, 1980).

Rowan, John, *The Horned God* (London and New York: Routledge and Kegan Paul, 1987).

Rudnytsky, Peter L., *Freud and Oedipus* (New York: Columbia University Press, 1987).

Schechner, Richard, *Performance Theory*, rev. edn (London and New York: Routledge, 1988).

Scher, Lawrence, *Parts of an Andrology: On Representations of Men's Bodies* (Stanford, CA: Stanford University Press, 1997).

Sedgwick, Eve Kosofsky, *Between Men: English Literature and Male Homosocial Desire* (New York: Columbia University Press, 1985).

Sedgwick, Eve Kosofsky, 'Gosh, Boy George, You Must Be Awfully Secure in Your Masculinity', in Maurice Berger, Brian Wallis and Simon Watson (eds), *Constructing Masculinity* (New York and London: Routledge, 1995).

Seidler, Victor, *Rediscovering Masculinity: Reason, Language and Sexuality* (London and New York: Routledge 1989).

Shepherd, Simon and Womack, Peter, *English Drama: A Cultural History* (Oxford: Blackwell, 1996).

Silverman, Kaja, *Male Subjectivity at the Margins* (London and New York: Routledge, Chapman and Hall, 1992).

Simpson, Mark, *Male Impersonators: Men Performing Masculinity* (London and New York: Cassell, 1994)

Stone, Lawrence, *The Family, Sex and Marriage in England, 1500–1800* (London: Weidenfeld and Nicolson, 1977).

Tannen, Deborah, *You Just Don't Understand Me* (New York: Ballantine Books, 1990).

Taplin, Oliver, 'Greek Theatre', in John Russell Brown (ed.), *The Oxford Illustrated History of the Theatre* (Oxford and New York: Oxford University Press, 1997).

Theweleit, Klaus, *Male Fantasies*, trans. Stephen Conway (Cambridge: Polity Press, 1987).

Thomas, David, *Not Guilty: In Defence of the Modern Man* (London: Weidenfeld and Nicolson, 1993).

Tokson, Elliot M., *The Popular Image of the Black Man in English Drama, 1550–1688* (Boston, MA: G. K. Hall, 1982).

Walby, Sylvia, *Theorizing Patriarchy* (Oxford and Cambridge, MA: Blackwell, 1990).

Williams, Mance, *Black Theatre in the 1960s and 1970s: A Historical Critical Analysis of the Movement* (Westport, CT: Greenwood Press, 1985).

Williams, Raymond, *Drama in a Dramatised Society* (Cambridge: Cambridge University Press, 1975).

Winkler, John J., *The Constraints of Desire* (New York and London: Routledge, 1990).

Secondary sources: medieval

Aers, David, *Community, Gender and Social Identity: English Writing, 1360–1450* (London and New York: Routledge, 1988).
Anderson, William, *The Green Man: The Archetype of Our Oneness with the Earth* (London: HarperCollins, 1990).
Aquinas, Thomas, *Summa Theologica,* 22 vols (London: Fathers of the English Dominican Province, 1921–32).
Axton, Marie and Williams, Raymond, (eds), *English Drama: Forms and Development* (Cambridge: Cambridge University Press, 1977).
Axton, Richard, *European Drama of the Early Middle Ages* (London: Hutchinson, 1974).
Beidler, Peter G. (ed.), *Masculinities in Chaucer: Approaches to Maleness in the 'Canterbury Tales' and 'Troilus and Criseyde'* (Cambridge: D. S. Brewer, 1998).
Bullough, Vern, 'On Being a Male in the Middle Ages', in Clare A. Lees (ed.), *Medieval Masculinities: Regarding Men in the Middle Ages* (Minneapolis: University of Minnesota Press, 1994).
Copland, William, *The Gest of Robin Hood* (London, *c.*1560).
Dobson, R. B. and Taylor, John, *The Rhymes of Robin Hood* (London: Heinemann, 1976).
The Good News Bible (Glasgow: Collins/Fontana, 1976).
Hadley, D. M. (ed.), *Masculinity in Medieval Europe* (London and New York: Longman, 1999).
Hayes, Tom, *The Birth of Popular Culture: Ben Jonson, Maid Marian and Robin Hood* (Pittsburgh, PA: Duquesne University Press, 1992).
Holt, J. C., *Robin Hood* (London: Thames and Hudson, 1982).
Knight, Stephen, *Robin Hood: A Complete Study of the English Outlaw* (Oxford: Blackwell, 1994).
Langland, William, *Piers Plowman*, ed. with notes and glossary by J. A. W. Bennett (Oxford: Clarendon Press, 1972).
Laqueur, Thomas, *Making Sex: Body and Gender from the Greeks to Freud* (Cambridge, MA and London: Harvard University Press, 1990).
Latimer, Hugh, *Seven Sermons before Edward VI,* ed. Edward Arber (London: Murray, 1869).
Lees, Clare A. (ed.), *Medieval Masculinities: Regarding Men in the Middle Ages* (Minneapolis: University of Minnesota Press, 1994).
McNamara, Jo Ann, 'The *Herrenfrage*: The Restructuring of the Gender System, 1050–1150', in Clare A. Lees (ed.), *Medieval Masculinities: Regarding Men in the Middle Ages* (Minneapolis: University of Minnesota Press, 1994), 3–29.
Medieval Masculinities: Heroism, Sanctity and Gender, dir. Jeffrey Jeremy Cohen 1995; Interscripta, 11 December 1997, <www.georgetown.edu.labyrinth/e-center/interscripta/mm.html>

Meredith, Peter (ed.), *Mankind: An Acting Edition* (Leeds: Alumnus Playtexts in Performance, 1997).

Rastall, Richard, 'Female Roles in All-Male Casts', *Medieval English Theatre*, 7:1 (1985) 25–50.

Spivack, Charlotte, 'Feminine vs. Masculine in English Morality Drama', in *Fifteenth-Century Studies* 13 (1988) 137–144.

Sponsler, Claire, *Drama and Resistance: Bodies, Goods and Theatricality in Late Medieval England* (Minneapolis and London: University of Minnesota Press, 1997).

Stokes, James D., 'Robin Hood and the Churchwardens in Yeovil', *Medieval and Renaissance Drama in England* 3 (1986) 1–25.

Stubbes, Philip, *The Anatomy of Abuses in England in Shakespeare's Youth*, ed. F. J. Furnivall (London: New Shakespeare Society, 1877–9).

Swanson, R. N., 'Angels Incarnate: Clergy and Masculinity from Gregorian Reform to Reformation', in D. M. Hadley (ed.), *Masculinity in Medieval Europe* (London and New York: Longman, 1999), 160–177.

Walters, Jonathan, ' "No More than a Boy": the Shifting Construction of Masculinity from Ancient Greece to the Middle Ages', *Gender and History* 5.1 (Spring 1993) 20–33.

Whitta, James, ' "Adest sponsus, qui est Christus": Performing the Male Monastic Body in *Sponsus* (1)', *Didaskalia* 4.1 (Spring 1997), ed. Sallie Goetsch and C. W. Marshall, University of Warwick online journal:<http://didaskalia.berkeley.edu/issues/vol4no1/whitta.html>.

Wickham, Glynne, *Early English Stages, 1300–1600,* vol. 3 (London: Routledge, 1981).

Wickham, Glynne, *The Medieval Theatre,* 3rd edn (Cambridge: Cambridge University Press, 1987).

Wiles, David, *The Early Plays of Robin Hood* (Cambridge and Ipswich: D. S. Brewer, 1981).

Secondary sources: Shakespeare and the Renaissance

Agnew, Jean-Christophe, *Worlds Apart: The Market and the Theatre in Anglo-American Thought, 1550–1750* (Cambridge: Cambridge University Press, 1986).

Appelbaum, Robert, ' "Standing to the wall": the Pressures of Masculinity in *Romeo and Juliet'*, *Shakespeare Quarterly* 48.3 (1997) 251–272.

Aughterson, Kate (ed.), *Renaissance Women: A Sourcebook. Constructions of Femininity in England* (London and New York: Routledge, 1995).

Backscheider, Paula R., *Spectacular Politics: Theatrical Power and Mass Culture in Early Modern England* (Baltimore, MD and London: Johns Hopkins University Press, 1993).

Bacon, Francis, *Essays* (London, 1625).

Baldwin, T. W., *The Organization and Personnel of the Shakespearean Company* (Princeton: Princeton University Press, 1997).

Barish, Jonas, *The Antitheatrical Prejudice* (Berkeley and Los Angeles: University of California Press, 1981).

Barker, Deborah E., and Kamps, Ivo (eds), *Shakespeare and Gender: A History* (London and New York: Verso, 1995).

Bray, Alan, *Homosexuality in Renaissance England* (London: Gay Men's Press, 1982).

Breitenberg, Mark, *Anxious Masculinity in Early Modern England* (Cambridge: Cambridge University Press, 1996).

Brooks, Cleanth, 'The Naked Babe and the Cloak of Manliness', in Norman Rabkin (ed.), *Approaches to Shakespeare* (New York: McGraw-Hill, 1964), 66–89.

Bryson, Anna, 'The Rhetoric of Status: Gesture, Demeanour and the Image of the Gentleman in Sixteenth- and Seventeenth-Century England', in L. Gent and N. Llewellyn (eds), *Renaissance Bodies: The Human Figure in English Culture c.1540–1660* (London: Reaktion, 1990), 136–153.

Chedgzoy, Kate, *Shakespeare's Queer Children: Appropriation in Contemporary Culture* (Manchester: Manchester University Press, 1995).

Dod, John, and Cleaver, Robert, *A Godly Form of Household Government: For the Ordering of Private Families According to the Direction of God's Word* (London, 1621).

Dolan, Frances E. (ed.), *'The Taming of the Shrew: Texts and Contexts* (Boston, MA and New York: St Martin's Press, 1996).

Edelman, Charles, *Brawl Ridiculous: Swordfighting in Shakespeare's Plays* (Manchester and New York: Manchester University Press, 1992).

Elyot, Sir Thomas, *The Book Named the Governor* (London, 1531).

Fletcher, Anthony, *Gender, Sex and Subordination in England, 1500–1800* (New Haven, CT and London: Yale University Press, 1995).

Foyster, Elizabeth A., *Manhood in Early Modern England: Honour, Sex and Marriage* (London and New York: Longman, 1999).

Fraser, Antonia, *The Weaker Vessel*, 2nd edn (London: Mandarin, 1989).

Frye, Susan, 'The Myth of Elizabeth at Tilbury', *Sixteenth Century Journal* XXIII: 1 (1992) 95–114.

Gosson, Stephen, *The School of Abuse* (London, 1579).

Gosson, Stephen, *Plays Confuted in Five Actions* (London, 1582).

Greenblatt, Stephen, *Renaissance Self-Fashioning: From More to Shakespeare* (Chicago, IL and London: University of Chicago Press, 1980).

Haring-Smith, Tori, *From Farce to Metadrama: A Stage History of 'The Taming of the Shrew', 1594–1983* (Westport, CT and London: Greenwood Press, 1985).

Howard, Jean, 'Cross-Dressing, the Theatre and Gender Struggle in Early Modern England', *Shakespeare Quarterly* 39:4 (1988) 418–40.

Jackson, Gabriele Bernhard, 'Topical Ideology: Witches, Amazons and Shakespeare's Joan of Arc', in Deborah E. Barker, and Ivo Kamps (eds), *Shakespeare and Gender: A History* (London and New York: Verso, 1995) 142–167.

James, M., *English Politics and the Concept of Honour, 1485–1642,* Past and Present Supplement 3 (The Past and Present Society, 1978).

Jorgens, Jack J., *Shakespeare on Film* (Bloomington: Indiana University Press, 1977).

Kahn, Coppelia, *Man's Estate: Masculine Identity in Shakespeare* (Berkeley, CA: University of California Press, 1981).

Keeble, N. H., *The Cultural Identity of Seventeenth-Century Woman: A Reader* (London and New York: Routledge 1994).

Kelso, Ruth, *Doctrine for the Lady of the Renaissance* (Urbana, IL: University of Illinois Press, 1956).

Langland, John, *Piers Plowman*, ed. J. A. W. Bennett (Oxford: Clarendon Press, 1972).

Levine, Laura, 'Men in Women's Clothing: Antitheatricality and Effeminization from 1579 to 1642', in *Criticism* 28:2 (Spring 1986) 121–143.

McCandless, David, *Gender and Performance in Shakespeare's Problem Comedies* (Bloomington, IN: Indiana University Press, 1997).

Markham, Gervase, *Honour in his Perfection* (London, 1624).

Montrose, Louis, '*A Midsummer Night's Dream* and the Shaping Fantasies of Elizabethan Culture: Gender Power, Form', in Margaret W. Ferguson, Maureen Quilligan and Nancy J. Vickers (eds), *Rewriting the Renaissance: The Discourses of Sexual Difference in Early Modern Europe* (Chicago, IL: University of Chicago Press, 1986).

Moulton, Ian, ' "A Monster Great Deformed": the Unruly Masculinity of Richard III', *Shakespeare Quarterly* 47:3 (1996) 251–268.

Orgel, Stephen, 'Nobody's Perfect: Or Why Did the English Stage Take Boys for Women?', *South Atlantic Quarterly* 88:1 (Winter 1989) 7–29.

Orgel, Stephen, *Impersonations: The Performance of Gender in Shakespeare's England* (Cambridge: Cambridge University Press, 1996).

Pierce, William, *The Marprelate Tracts, 1588–9* (London: James Clarke, 1911).

Plutarch, 'The Life of Marcus Antonius', trans. Sir Thomas North, in T. J. B. Spencer (ed.), *Shakespeare's Plutarch* (Harmondsworth: Penguin, 1964).

Prynne, William, *Histriomastix* (London, 1633).

Rabkin, Norman (ed.) *Approaches to Shakespeare* (New York: McGraw-Hill, 1964).

Rainolds, John, *Th' Overthrow of Stage-Plays* (Middleburg: 1599).

Shakespeare, William, *The Taming of the Shrew*, ed. Brian Morris (London: Methuen, 1981).

Shepherd, Simon, *Amazons and Warrior Women: Varieties of Feminism in Seventeenth-Century Drama* (Brighton: Harvester, 1981).

Simmons, J. L., 'Masculine Negotiations in Shakespeare's History Plays: Hal, Hotspur and "the foolish Mortimer"' , *Shakespeare Quarterly* 44:3 (1993) 440–463.

Stubbes, Philip, *The Anatomy of Abuses* (London, 1583).

Taunton, Nina, 'The Turn of the Shrew', in *Skin Two* 15 (1994) 90–94.

Underdown, David, 'The Taming of the Scold: the Enforcement of Patriarchal Authority in Early Modern England', in Anthony Fletcher and John Stevenson (eds), *Order and Disorder in Early Modern England* (Cambridge: Cambridge University Press, 1985) 116–136.

Warner, William, *Albion's England* (London,1589).

Wells, Robin Headlam, *Shakespeare on Masculinity* (Cambridge: Cambridge University Press, 2000).

Secondary sources: Restoration

Aldington, Richard, *A Book of Characters* (London: Routledge, 1924).

Allestree, Richard, *The Gentleman's Calling* (London, 1660).

Avery, Emmett L., 'The Restoration Audience', *Philological Quarterly* 45 (January 1966) 54–61.

Birdsall, Virginia Ogden, *Wild Civility: The English Comic Spirit on the Restoration Stage* (Bloomington, IN: Indiana University Press, 1970).

Boyer, Abel, *Letters of Wit, Politicks and Morality* (London, 1701).

Braverman, Richard, *'The Rake's Progress* Revisited: Politics and Comedy in the Restoration', in J. Douglas Canfield and Deborah C. Payne (eds), *Cultural Readings of Restoration and Eighteenth-century English Theatre* (Athens, GA: University of Georgia Press, 1995) 141–168 .

Brennan, T. and Pateman, C., ' "Mere auxiliaries to the Commonwealth": Women and the Origins of Liberalism', *Political Studies* 27:2 (1979) 183–200.

Canfield, J. Douglas and Payne, Deborah C. (eds), *Cultural Readings of Restoration and Eighteenth-Century English Theatre* (Athens, GA: University of Georgia Press, 1995).

Gailhard, J., *The Compleat Gentleman: or Directions for the Education of Youth as to their Breeding at Home and Travelling Abroad* (London, 1678).

Gould, Robert, 'The Play House: A Satyr', in *Poems* (London, 1689).

Greene, Graham, *Lord Rochester's Monkey* (London: Bodley Head, 1974).

Hitchcock, Tim and Cohen, Michèle (eds), *English Masculinities, 1660–1800* (Harlow: Longman, 1999).

Holland, Peter, *The Ornament of Action: Text and Performance in Restoration Comedy* (Cambridge: Cambridge University Press, 1979).

Holmes, Jeremy, *Narcissism* (Cambridge: Icon Books, 2001).

Howe, Elizabeth, *The First English Actresses: Women and Drama, 1660–1700* (Cambridge: Cambridge University Press, 1992).

Hume, Robert D., *The Rakish Stage: Studies in English Drama, 1660–1800* (Carbondale and Edwardsville: Southern Illinois University Press, 1983).

Love, Harold, 'Who were the Restoration Audience?', *The Yearbook of English Studies* 10 (1980) 21–44.

McCarthy, B. Eugene, *William Wycherley: A Biography* (Athens, OH: Ohio University Press, 1979).

Maguire, Nancy Klein, *Regicide and Restoration: English Tragicomedy, 1660–1671* (Cambridge: Cambridge University Press, 1992).

Milhouse, Judith and Hume, Robert D., *Producible Interpretation: Eight English Plays 1675–1707* (Carbondale and Edwardsville: Southern Illinois University Press, 1985).

Munns, Jessica, 'Change, Skepticism and Uncertainty', in Deborah Payne Fisk (ed.), *Cambridge Companion to English Restoration Theatre* (Cambridge: Cambridge University Press, 2000) 142–157.

Pepys, Samuel, *The Diary of Samuel Pepys*, ed. Robert Latham and William Matthews, 11 vols (London: G. Bell and Sons, 1970–83).

Picard, Liza, *Restoration London* (London: Weidenfeld and Nicolson, 1997).

Ray, John, *A Collection of English Proverbs* (London, 1670).

Roberts, David, *The Ladies: Female Patronage of Restoration Drama, 1660–1700* (Oxford: Clarendon Press, 1989).

Scouten, Arthur H., and Hume, Robert D., ' "Restoration Comedy" and its Audiences 1660–1776', *The Yearbook of English Studies* 10 (1980) 45–69.

Shepherd, Simon, ' "The body", Performance Studies, Horner and a Dinner Party', *Textual Practice* 14.2 (2000) 285–303.

Weber, Harold, 'Carolinean Sexuality and the Restoration Stage: Reconstructing the Royal Phallus in *Sodom*', in J. Douglas Canfield and Deborah C. Payne (eds), *Cultural Readings of Restoration and Eighteenth-century English Theatre* (Athens, GA: University of Georgia Press, 1995), 67–88.

Wilmot, John, Earl of Rochester, *Letters*, ed. Jeremy Treglown (Oxford: Basil Blackwell, 1980).

Wilson, John Harold, *Mr Goodman the Player* (Pittsburgh, PA: University of Pittsburgh Press, 1964).

Secondary sources: the eighteenth century

Anonymous, *A Narrative of All the Robberies, Escapes &c of John Sheppard* (London, 1724).

Barker, Hannah and Chalus, Elaine, *Gender in Eighteenth-Century England: Roles, Representations and Responsibilities* (London and New York: Longman, 1997).

Brady, Frank and Pottle, Frederick (eds), *Boswell in Search of a Wife, 1766–69* (London: Heinemann, 1957).

Brewer, John, *The Pleasures of the Imagination: English Culture in the Eighteenth Century* (London: HarperCollins, 1997).

Burgess, C. F., 'Lillo sans Barnwell, or the Playwright Revisited', *Modern Philology* LXVI:1 (August 1968) 5–29.

Carter, Philip, 'An "Effeminate" or "Efficient" Nation? Masculinity and Eighteenth-century Social Documentary', *Textual Practice* 11:3 (1997), 429–443.

Carter, Philip, 'James Boswell's Manliness', in Tim Hitchcock and Michèle Cohen (eds), *English Masculinities, 1660–1800* (Harlow: Longman, 1999), 111–130.

Carter, Philip, *Men and the Emergence of the Polite Society, Britain 1660–1800* (Harlow: Longman, 2001).

Cibber, Theophilus, *Lives of the Poets of Great Britain and Ireland*, 5 vols (London, 1753).

Cohen, Michèle, *Fashioning Masculinity: National Identity and Language in the Eighteenth Century* (London and New York: Routledge, 1996).

Davies, T., 'The Life of Mr. George Lillo', in *The Works of Mr George Lillo; With Some Account of his Life* (London, 1775).

Defoe, Daniel, *Novels and Selected Writings*, 14 vols (Oxford: Shakespeare Head, 1927–8).

Friedman, Michael D., ' "He was just a Macheath": Boswell and *The Beggar's Opera*', in Paul J. Korshin (ed.), *The Age of Johnson*, vol. 4 (New York: AMS Press 1991), 92–108.

Gatrell, V. A. C., *The Hanging Tree: Execution and the English People, 1770–1868* (Oxford: Oxford University Press, 1994).

Guerinot, J. V. and Jilg, Rodney D., *Contexts 1: The Beggar's Opera* (Hamden, CT: Archon Books, 1976).

Hitchcock, Tim and Cohen, Michèle (eds), *English Masculinities, 1660–1800* (Harlow: Longman, 1999).

Linebaugh, Peter, *The London Hanged: Crime and Civil Society in the Eighteenth Century* (London: Allen Lane, 1991).

Nokes, David, *John Gay: A Profession of Friendship* (Oxford: Oxford University Press, 1995).

Orgel, Stephen (ed.), *Satire and Sense: Important Texts, For the Most Part Dramatic, from the Restoration and Eighteenth Century* (New York: Garland Press, 1987)

Pottle, Frederick (ed.), *Boswell's London Journal, 1762–1763* (London: Heinemann, 1950).

Price, Cecil, *Theatre in the Age of Garrick* (Oxford: Basil Blackwell, 1973).

Ryskamp, Charles and Pottle, Frederick, *Boswell: The Ominous Years, 1774–1776* (London: Heinemann, 1963).

Scouten, Arthur H., *The London Stage, 1660–1800*, vol. 3: *1729–1747* (Carbondale and Edwardsville: Southern Illinois University Press, 1968).

Shoemaker, Robert B., *Gender in English Society, 1650–1850: The Emergence of Separate Spheres?* (London and New York: Longman, 1998).

Smith, Alexander, *A Complete History of the Lives of the Most Notorious Highwaymen* (London, 1713).

Spierenburg, Peter, *The Spectacle of Suffering. Executions and the Evolution of Repression: From a Preindustrial Metropolis to the European Experience* (Cambridge: Cambridge University Press, 1984).

Steele, Richard, *The Guardian*, ed. John Calhoun Stephens (Lexington, KY: University Press of Kentucky, 1982).

Steele, Richard, *The Tatler*, ed. Donald F. Bond (Oxford: Clarendon Press, 1987).

Stone, G. W. (ed.), *The London Stage, 1660–1800*, vol. 4: *1747–1776* (Carbondale and Edwardsville: Southern Illinois University Press, 1960).

Straub, Kristina, *Sexual Suspects: Eighteenth-Century Players and Sexual Ideology* (Princeton, NJ: Princeton University Press, 1992).

Straub, Kristina, 'Actors and Homophobia', in J. Douglas Canfield and Deborah C. Payne (eds), *Cultural Readings of Restoration and Eighteenth-Century English Theater* (Athens, GA: University of Georgia Press, 1995).

Thomas, David (ed.), *Theatre in Europe: A Documentary History. Restoration and Georgian England, 1660–1778* (Cambridge: Cambridge University Press, 1989).

Trumbach, Randolph, 'London's Sodomites: Homosexual Behaviour and Western culture in the Eighteenth Century', *Journal of Social History* XI:1 (1977) 1–13.

Trumbach, Randolph, 'Sex, Gender and Sexual Identity in Modern Culture: Male Sodomy and Female Prostitution in Enlightenment London', *Journal of the History of Sexuality* II:2 (1991) 186–203.

West, Shearer, *The Image of the Actor: Verbal and Visual Representation in the Age of Garrick and Kemble* (London: Pinter 1991).

Secondary sources: the nineteenth and early twentieth centuries

Ackerman, Gretchen, *Ibsen and the English Stage, 1889–1903* (New York and London: Garland, 1987).

Adams, James Eli, *Dandies and Desert Saints: Styles of Victorian Masculinity* (Ithaca, NY and London: Cornell University Press, 1995).

Adler, Jacob H., 'Ibsen, Shaw and Candida', *Journal of English and Germanic Philology* LIX (1960) 50–58.

Barrie, J. M., *Courage: The Rectorial Address to St. Andrew's University, 3 May 1922* (London: Hodder and Stoughton, 1922).

Beer, Gillian, *Darwin's Plots: Evolutionary Narrative in Darwin, George Eliot and Nineteenth-Century Fiction* (London: Routledge and Kegan Paul, 1983).

Behrendt, Patricia Flanagan, *Oscar Wilde, Eros and Aesthetics* (Basingstoke: Palgrave Macmillan, 1991).

Birkin, Andrew, *J. M. Barrie and the Lost Boys* (London: Constable, 1979).

Booth, Michael, *Prefaces to English Nineteenth-Century Theatre* (Manchester: Manchester University Press, 1980).

Bristow, Joseph, *Effeminate England: Homoerotic Writing after 1885* (Buckingham: Open University Press, 1995).

Carnes, Mark C., *Secret Ritual and Manhood in Victorian America* (New Haven, CT: Yale University Press, 1989).

Clarke, Norma, 'Strenuous Idleness: Thomas Carlyle and the Man of Letters as Hero', in Michael Roper and John Tosh (eds), *Manful Assertions: Masculinities in Britain since 1800* (London and New York: Routledge, 1991), 25–43.

Corr, H. and Jamieson, L. (eds), *The Politics of Everyday Life: Continuity and Change in Work, Labour and the Family* (Basingstoke: Palgrave Macmillan, 1990).

Crompton, Louis, *Shaw the Dramatist* (Lincoln: University of Nebraska Press, 1969).

Danahay, Martin A., *A Community of One: Masculine Autobiography and Autonomy in Nineteenth-century Britain* (Albany: State University of New York Press, 1993).

Davin, Anna, 'Historical Masculinities: Regulation, Fantasy and Empire', *Gender and History*, 9:1 (1997) 135–138.

Dawson, Graham, *Soldier Heroes: British Adventure, Empire and the Imagining of Masculinity* (London and New York: Routledge, 1994).

Dervin, Daniel, *Bernard Shaw: A Psychological Study* (Lewisburg, PA: Bucknell University Press, 1975).

Dowling, Linda, 'The Decadent and the New Woman in the 1890s', *Nineteenth-Century Fiction*, XXXIII (1978–9) 434–453.

Dunbar, Janet, *J. M. Barrie: The Man Behind the Image* (London: Collins, 1970).

Evans, T. F., *Shaw, the Critical Heritage* (London: Routledge and Kegan Paul, 1976).

Fitzsimmons, Linda and Gardner, Viv (eds), *New Woman Plays* (London: Methuen, 1991).

Fromm, Harold, *Bernard Shaw and the Theater in the Nineties* (Lawrence, KS: The University of Kansas Press, 1967).

Gardner, Viv and Rutherford, Susan (eds), *The New Woman and her Sisters* (New York and London: Harvester Wheatsheaf, 1992).

Geduld, Harry M., *James Barrie* (New York: Twayne, 1971).

Gordon, David, *Shaw and the Comic Sublime* (New York: St Martin's Press, 1990).

Grene, Nicholas, *Bernard Shaw: A Critical View* (Basingstoke: Palgrave Macmillan, 1984).

Haakonsen, Daniel, *Contemporary Approaches to Ibsen*, vol. V: *Reports from the Fifth International Ibsen Seminar, Munich 1983* (Oslo, Bergen, Stavanger and Tromsø: Universitetsforlaget AS, 1985).

Hall, Donald E. (ed.), *Muscular Christianity: Embodying the Victorian Age* (Cambridge: Cambridge University Press, 1995).

Hobsbawm, E. J., *The Age of Capital, 1848–1875* (London: Weidenfeld & Nicolson, 1975).

Holbrook, David, *Images of Women in Literature* (New York and London: New York University Press, 1989).

Jones, Henry Arthur and Herman, Henry, *Breaking a Butterfly* (London: privately printed, 1884).

Kelley-Lainé, Kathleen, *Peter Pan: The Story of Lost Childhood* (Shaftesbury, Dorset and Rockport MA: Element Books, 1997).

Kestner, John, *Masculinities in Victorian Painting* (Aldershot: Scolar Press, 1995).

Kiley, Dan, *The Peter Pan Syndrome: Men Who Have Never Grown Up* (London: Corgi, 1984).

Mander, Raymond and Mitchenson, Joe, *Theatrical Companion to Shaw* (London: Rockliff, 1955.)

Mangan, J. A., *Athleticism in the Victorian and Edwardian Public School: The Emergence and Consolidation of an Educational Ideology* (Cambridge: Cambridge University Press, 1981).

Mangan, J. A. and Walvin, James (eds), *Manliness and Morality: Middle-Class Masculinity in Britain and America, 1800–1940* (Manchester: Manchester University Press, 1987).

Meyer, Michael, *Ibsen* (London and Sydney: Sphere Books, 1992).

Meyer, Michael (ed.), *Ibsen on File* (London: Methuen, 1985).

Meyer, Michael (ed.), *File on Strindberg* (London: Methuen, 1986).

Meynell, Viola (ed.), *The Letters of J. M. Barrie* (London: Peter Davies, 1942).

Powell, Kerry, *Oscar Wilde and the Theatre of the 1890s* (Cambridge: Cambridge University Press, 1990).

Powell, Kerry, *Women and Victorian Theatre* (Cambridge: Cambridge University Press, 1997).

Roper, Michael and Tosh, John (eds), *Manful Assertions: Masculinities in Britain since 1800* (London and New York: Routledge, 1991).

Rose, Jacqueline, *The Case of Peter Pan, or the Impossibility of Children's Fiction*, rev. edn (Basingstoke: Palgrave Macmillan, 1992).

Rutherford, Jonathan, *Forever England: Reflections on Masculinity and Empire* (London: Lawrence and Wishart, 1997).

Shaw, George Bernard, *Our Theatres in the Nineties* (London: Constable, 1948).

Shaw, George Bernard, *Collected Letters*, ed. Dan H. Laurence (New York: Dodd, Mead, 1972).

Shaw, George Bernard and Ellen Terry, *Ellen Terry and Bernard Shaw: A Correspondence*, ed. Christopher St. John (New York: Putnam's, 1932).

Shearman, Montague, *Athletics and Football* (London: The Badminton Library, 1888).

Silver, Arnold, *Bernard Shaw: The Darker Side* (Stanford, CA: Stanford University Press, 1982).

Sinfield, Alan, *The Wilde Century: Effeminacy, Oscar Wilde and the Queer Moment* (London and New York: Cassell, 1994).

Sinha, Mrinalini, *Colonial Masculinity: The 'Manly Englishman' and the 'Effeminate Bengali' in the Late Nineteenth Century* (Manchester and New York: Manchester University Press, 1995).

Sussman, Herbert, *Victorian Masculinities: Manhood and Masculine Poetics in Early Victorian Literature and Art* (Cambridge: Cambridge University Press, 1995).

Templeton, Joan, *Ibsen's Women* (Cambridge: Cambridge University Press, 1997).

Tosh, John, 'Domesticity and Manliness in the Victorian Middle Class: the Family of Edward White Benson', in Michael Roper and John Tosh (eds), *Manful Assertions: Masculinities in Britain since 1800* (London and New York: Routledge, 1991), 44–73.

Weeks, Jeffrey, *Sex, Politics and Society: The Regulation of Sexuality since 1880* (London: Longman, 1981).

Weintraub, Rodelle, *Fabian Feminist: Bernard Shaw and Women* (University Park and London: Pennsylvania State University Press, 1977).

Wisenthal, J. L., *Shaw and Ibsen* (Toronto: University of Toronto Press, 1979).

Secondary sources: contemporary

Albemarle of London's West End Theatre Guide, ed. Paul Dixon, 6 July 2001, <http://www.albemarle-london.com>

Anthony, Andrew et al., 'Acts in a Sex War', *Guardian*, 7 July 1993, G2 2.

Audit Commission, *Young People and Crime* (Audit Commission for Local Authorities and the National Health Service in England and Wales, 1996).

Becker, Rob, interviewed by Cheryl Lavin (1994). *Cavemania* 6 July 2001, <http://www.cavemania.com/reviews/index.html>

Bennett, John, 'John Godber', in John Bull (ed.), *Dictionary of Literary Biography*, vol. 233: *British and Irish Dramatists since World War II* (Second Series) (Detroit: Bruccoli Clark, 2001).

Bull, John, *New British Political Dramatists* (Basingstoke: Palgrave Macmillan, 1984).

Bull, John (ed.), *Dictionary of Literary Biography*, vol. 233: *British and Irish Dramatists since World War II* (Second Series) (Detroit: Bruccoli Clark, 2001).

Cahn, Victor L., *Gender and Power in the Plays of Harold Pinter* (Basingstoke: Palgrave Macmillan, 1994).

Campbell, Joseph, *The Hero with a Thousand Faces* (New York: Pantheon. 1949).

Canadine, David, *Class in Britain* (Harmondsworth: Penguin, 2000).

Cavemania, 6 July 2001, <http://www.cavemania.com/reviews/index.html>

Clatterbaugh, Kenneth, *Contemporary Perspectives on Masculinity*, 2nd edn (Boulder, CO: Westview Press, 1997).

Cohan, Steven, *Masked Men: Masculinity and Movies in the Fifties* (Bloomington, IN: Indiana University Press, 1997).

Cohan, Steven and Hark, Ina Rae, *Screening the Male: Exploring Masculinities in Hollywood Cinema* (London and New York: Routledge, 1993).

Defending the Caveman (website) 20 September 1999, < http://www.stoll-moss.com/caveman.htm>

Elsom, John, *Post-war British Theatre* (London: Routledge and Kegan Paul, 1976).

Eyre, Richard and Wright, Nicholas, *Changing Stages: A View of British Theatre in the Twentieth Century* (London: Bloomsbury, 2000).

Godber, John, 'Backchat: Interview at Derby Playhouse, 24 October 1996', reported and transcribed by John Bennett, *The John Godber Website*, ed. John Bennett, 1 July 2001, <http://www.johngodber.co.uk/interview.htm>

Godber, John, 'Three by Three: Alan Ayckbourn, Tim Firth and John Godber in Conversation at the Stephen Joseph Theatre on 4 July 1998', reported and transcribed by John Bennett, *The John Godber Website*, ed. John Bennett, 1 July 2001. <http://www.johngodber.co.uk/interview.htm>

Holt, John, *How Children Fail*, 2nd edn (Harmondsworth: Penguin, 1969).

Illich, Ivan, *Deschooling Society*, 2nd edn (Harmondsworth: Penguin, 1973).

Kempley, Rita, 'Oleanna' review. *Washingtonpost.com* (11 November 1994) 12 July 2001, <http://www.washingtonpost.com/wp-srv/style/longterm/movies/videos/oleannanrkempley_a0a499.htm>

McDonough, Carla J., 'Every Fear Hides a Wish: Unstable Masculinity in Mamet's Drama', *Theatre Journal* 44 (1992) 195–205.

McDonough, Carla J., *Staging Masculinity: Male Identity in Contemporary American Drama* (Jefferson, NC and London: McFarland, 1997).

Mamet, D., *Some Freaks* (New York: Viking, 1989).

Mamet, D., 'A Candid Conversation with America's Foremost Dramatist about Tough Talk, TV Violence, Women, and Why Government Shouldn't Fund the Arts: interview by Geoffrey Norman and John Rezek', *Playboy* 42. 2 (1995) 52–3.

Mangan, Michael, 'Appalling Teachers: Gender and Professionalism in David Mamet's *Oleanna* and Willy Russell's *Educating Rita*', in Daniel Meyer-Dinkgräfe (ed.), *The Professions in Contemporary Drama* (Bristol: Intellect Books 2002).

Mikkelson, Barbara, 'A Pinch of Snuff'. *Urban Legends Reference Pages*, ed. Barbara and David P. Mikkelson (February 1999), 25 June 2001, <http://www.snopes.com/movies/other/snuff.htm>.

Osborne, John, *Almost a Gentleman: An Autobiography*, vol. 2: *1955–1966* (London: Faber and Faber, 1991).

Rebellato, Dan, *1956 and All That: The Making of Modern British Drama* (London: Routledge, 1999).

Roberts, Philip, *The Royal Court Theatre, 1965–1972* (London: Routledge and Kegan Paul, 1986).

Schacht, Steven P., 'Misogyny on and off the "Pitch": the Gendered World of Male Rugby Players', *Gender and Society* 10.5 (1996) 550–565.

Sierz, Aleks, *In-Yer-Face Theatre: British Drama Today* (London: Faber and Faber, 2000).

Thornber, Robin, '*Masterpieces*' Review, *Guardian* 30 October 1984, 21.

Vorlicky, Robert, *Act Like a Man: Challenging Masculinities in American Drama* (Ann Arbor, MI: University of Michigan Press, 1995).

Wainwright, Hilary, *Labour: A Tale of Two Parties* (London: Hogarth, 1987).

Walker, Craig, 'Three Tutorial Plays: *The Lesson, The Prince of Naples* and *Oleanna*', *Modern Drama*, XL:1 (1997) 149–162.

Wandor, Michelene, *Look Back in Gender: Sexuality and the Family in Post-War British Drama* (London: Methuen, 1987).

Wheatcroft, Geoffrey, 'Campus Followers', *Guardian* 16 September 1993, 22.

Index